The book of Enoch

George Henry Schodde 1854-1917

BOOK OF ENOCH:

TRANSLATED FROM THE ETHIOPIC,

WITH

INTRODUCTION AND NOTES.

BY

REV. GEORGE H. SCHODDE, PH.D.

PROFESSOR IN CAPITAL UNIVERSITY, COLUMBUS, OHIO.

Andover:

WARREN F. DRAPER.

1911

To my honored Teacher,

PROF. FRANZ DELITZSCH, D.D.,
Leipzig, Germany,

and to my kind Friend,

PROF. EZRA ABBOT, D.D.,
Cambridge, Mass.

PREFACE.

SCARCELY any department of theological science has, in the last few decades, received such marked attention and cultivation as that branch for which the Germans have adopted the felicitous appellation *Neutestament-liche Zeitgeschichte*, — the study of the age of Christ in its political, social, and religious aspects. Observant readers will not have failed to detect that the tendency of modern evangelical theology is to transfer the centre of interest from the work of Christ to the person of Christ. Hand in hand, and in close connection with this general tendency, certain auxiliary branches have assumed an importance hitherto not attributed to them. When the person of Christ forms the cynosure of all eyes, his surroundings proportionally grow in interest and importance; and hence it is not surprising that so much acumen and learning have been employed in the truly fascinating study of the Palestine of Christ's day in all its relations. The central sun casts its rays of resplendent light on every-day objects, and these become prominent in proportion as they reflect this light.

In more than one respect the Book of Enoch is an

important factor in these investigations.   Being one of
the oldest specimens of apocalyptic literature; reflecting
in its different parts the convictions, feelings, and longings of the people of God at different stages of their
development; written in imitation of the spirit of the
prophets, with religious purposes and spiritual objects;
it can safely be said to be an invaluable aid to the
understanding of the religious and moral atmosphere in
which the Saviour lived.   It does not belong merely to
the curiosities of literature, but is a book of positive
worth, and the source of much information to the patient
investigator.

   This will suffice as an apology for a new translation of
Enoch.   In the translation the object has been to render
as literally as possible, even if thereby the English should
become a little harsh.   Of course the notes do not pretend to unravel all the mysteries in this most mysterious
of books; but it is hoped they will be of some assistance
in understanding these intricacies.   Naturally, these
and the Introduction are, in part, a compilation; but
the thoughts of others have been used with judgment
and discrimination, and the sources are indicated.   In
all questions the writer has been independent, as will be
seen by the fact that he has frequently departed from
beaten paths.

   Much remains yet to be done before this book will be
entirely understood.   Both its connection in sentiment
and expression with the Old Testament, as well as its

influence on Talmudic and Rabbinical lore, especially the latter, must, to a great extent, be the work of future investigations. But even with the limited means at hand this book, which an inspired writer thought worthy of citation, will not be read by the Christian theologian and minister without deep interest.

In conclusion the translator desires to express his thanks to his friend Prof. Dr. Adolf Harnack, of Giessen, Germany, for kind words and deeds in connection with this work; and to Prof. Dr. Ezra Abbot for his interest and aid in its publication.

GEORGE H. SCHODDE.

Columbus, Ohio, Nov. 21, 1881.

GENERAL INTRODUCTION.

ENOCH (חֲנוֹךְ, LXX Ἐνώχ) is the name of four biblical persons. The first is the oldest son of Cain (Gen. iv. 17); the second, the son of Jared (Gen. v. 18); the third, the son of Midian (Gen. xxv. 4); the fourth, the oldest son of Reuben (Gen. xlvi. 9; Ex. vi. 14).[1] Of these the second alone is of importance and interest for us, not only on account of the mysterious prominence given him in Gen. v., but especially from the fact that an inspired writer of the New Testament, Jude, in his letter ver. 14, mentions him as a prophet, and produces a quotation from a book attributed to the patriarch. The existence of such a book does not, however, rest on the authority of this statement alone; but in the early literature of the church there is a whole chain of evidences to this effect. Nearly all of the church Fathers knew of an apocryphal Book of Enoch, and their description of the work and citations from it prove satisfactorily that it was virtually the same as that which now lies before us. Among the Apostolic Fathers, the Epistle of Barnabas refers to such a work. In chap. iv. 3 of that letter, Enoch is cited, and the character of the quotation points to chap. 80 of our book as its probable source, while in the statement of the same Epistle xvi. 5, although in-

[1] The last two are transcribed in the authorized version *Hanoch*, the others *Enoch*.

1

troduced with the important words: λέγει γὰρ ἡ γραφή,
we find almost the very words of En. 89 : 56. From
that time on to about the seventh century Christian literature, to which alone we owe the preservation of the
important work, produces ample proof of the constant
use and high standing of this book. Beside the Jewish-
Christian *Testament. XII Patriarch.*,[1] a production of the
second century, the church Fathers [2] Justin Martyr,[3]
Clemens of Alexandria,[4] Origen,[5] Irenaeus,[6] Tertullian,[7]
Eusebius, Jerome, Hilary,[8] Epiphanius,[9] Augustine, and
others refer to and use it.[10] The majority of these statements are indeed simply allusions and general references ; but they are of such a character that their source
in the present Book of Enoch can generally be found to a
certainty, the writers in this respect following the example of Jude, whose citation is taken from En. 1: 9,
and is not a literal reproduction. The Fathers all,
with possibly the one dissenting voice of Tertullian (*De
Cult. Fem.* i. 3), deny the canonicity of this book, and
properly regard it as apocryphal ; some going even so
far as to deny the canonicity of Jude because he had
dared to quote an apocryphal work.[11] The precedent
for this step was given in the Apostolic Constitutions,
vi. 16, in strong words. When, after the time of Au-

---

[1] Cf. on 2 : 1 ; 15 : 5 ; 19 : 2 ; 25 : 5 ; 61 : 10 ; 89 : 50.

[2] Their references have been collected and discussed in Fabricius, *Codex
Pseudepigraphus Vet. Test.* vol. i. 1722, pp. 160–224, and in Philippi, *Das
Buch Henoch*, 1868, p. 102–118.

[3] Cf. on 15 : 8, 9 ; 16 : 2.   [4] Cf. on 8 : 3 ; 16 : 2 ; 19 : 3.

[5] Cf. on 6 : 5, 6 ; 19 : 1, 3 ; 21 : 1.   [6] Cf. on 10 : 3 ; 14 : 7.

[7] Cf. on 8 : 2 ; 16 : 2 ; 19 : 1 ; 82 : 3 ; 99 : 6, 7.   [8] Cf. on 6 : 6.

[9] Cf. on 6 : 6 ; 16 : 2.

[10] Cf. the discussion of these in Hoffmann, *Das Buch Henoch*, 1830–38,
pp. 887–916.

[11] Cf. Jerome, *Catal. Script. Eccles.* 4.

gustine, the period of literary death robbed the church
of many of her noblest monuments of literature, the
Book of Enoch, too, was lost, and later investigators had
to be content with the references in the Fathers, and a
few extracts made by the learned monk of the eighth
century, Georgius Syncellus, in his Chronography.[1] A
short time after him, in the ninth century, the book is
mentioned as an apocryphon of the *New* Testament by
the Patriarch Nicephorus.[2] The fragments preserved
by Syncellus, varying indeed in minor points of expression, are still virtually an extract from the book as we
have it now. They are divided into two parts; the
first containing chap. 6 : 1 to chap. 9 : 4, the second
chap. 8 : 4 to chap. 10 : 14, and chap. 15 : 8 to chap.
16 : 1 ; in addition to which there is a small part not
found in the Ethiopic. Here comes into consideration
also a small fragment of the Greek Enoch found after
the discovery and publication of the Ethiopic version.
We refer to the Greek text of chap. 89 : 42–49, written with tachygraphical notes, and published from a
Codex Vaticanus (*Cod. Gr.*1809) in facsimile, by Angelo
Mai in *Patrum Nova Bibliotheca*, vol. ii. These verses
were deciphered by Prof. Gildemeister, who published
his results in the *Zeitschrift d. Deutsch. Morgenländ.
Gesellschaft*, 1855, pp. 621–624. In Jewish literature,
the Book of Enoch did not stand in such high regard as
it did among Christian writers, and consequently was
not so extensively used. It was, however, neither unknown nor ignored altogether. Already in the work
so frequently cited in early Christian literature as *Tà
'Ιωβηλαῖα* or *ἡ λεπτὴ γένεσις*, a production of the first

---

[1] Published in Dillmann's translation, pp. 82–86.
[2] Cf. Niceph. (ed. Dindorf), i. 787.

Christian century, the references are frequent and un-
mistakable.[1]   A comparison of the statements of this
book of the Jubilees, especially p. 17 sq. of the Ethiopic
text (ed. Dillmann), with those of Enoch forces us to
the conclusion that the author of the former book could
not have written as he did without an exact knowledge of the contents of the latter.   Of the use made of
the book by later Jewish writers, we have a brief account by A. Jellinek in the *Zeitschrift d. D. M. G.*
1853, p. 249.   The clearest example in this respect is
found in *Sohar*, vol. ii. *Parasha* בשלח p. 55 *a* (ed. Mant.
et Amsterd.) : " Comperimus in libro Hanochi, Deum
illi, postquam, sustulisset eum in sublime, et ostendisset
ei omnes thesauros superiores et inferiores, monstrasse
etiam arborem vitae et arborem illam, quam inter-
dixerat Adamo, et vidit locum Adami in Paradiso, in
quo si Adamus observasset praeceptum illud, vixisset
perpetuo et in aeternum mansisset."   In vol. i. *Parasha Bereshit*, p. 37 *b* there is a remark that covers
about the same ground, with the additional statement
that the Book of Enoch was "handed down" to him
from the time when he began to associate with super-
terrestrial beings.[2]

The existence of such a Book of Enoch, made certain
from these numerous quotations, was the source of
considerable perplexity and anxiety to Christian theologians, and numerous and curious were the conjectures
concerning its authorship and character.   In the be-

[1] Rönsch finds nineteen such references in the book of the Jubilees.
Cf. Drummond, *The Jewish Messiah*, p. 71.

[2] The Hebrew text of this quotation is found in Philippi, l. c. p. 121.
According to Philippi's statements there are also references to Enoch in
the *Assumptio Mosis*, a fragmentary production of the first or second century, A.D., and in 4 Ezra and in the Sibylline Books.   Cf. l.c. p. 105 sq.

ginning of the seventeenth century it was confidently asserted that the book, mourned as lost, was to be found in an Ethiopic translation in Abyssinia, and the learned Capuchin monk Peirescius bought an Ethiopic book which was claimed to be the identical one quoted by Jude and the Fathers. Ludolf, the great Ethiopic scholar of the seventeenth and eighteenth centuries, however, soon proved it to be a miserable production of a certain Abba Bahaila Michael.[1] Better success attended the efforts of the famous English traveller James Bruce, who discovered three copies of the book, and brought them, in 1773, with him to Europe.[2] One of these found its way into the Bodleian Library, the other was presented to the Royal Library of France, the third was kept by Bruce. Since that time other copies have been brought from Abyssinia. Strange to say, no use was made of these important documents until the year 1800, when Silvestre de Sacy, in his *Notice sur le livre d'Enoch*, in the *Magazin Encyclopédique, an* vi., tome I. p. 382, gave as specimens of the book the extracts and Latin translation of chap. 1 and 2, chap. 5–16, and chap. 22 and 32, from which then, in 1801, a German translation was made by Rink. There again the matter rested until 1821, when Prof. Laurence, afterwards Archbishop of Cashel, published an English translation from the MS. in the Bodleian, with the title: " The Book of Enoch, the Prophet: an apocryphal production, supposed to have been lost for ages; but discovered at the close of the last century in Abyssinia; now first translated from an Ethiopic MS. in the Bodleian Library. Oxford, 1821." The second edition of this work ap-

---

[1] Cf. Ludolf, *Commentarius in Hist. Aethiop.*, p. 347.
[2] Cf. Bruce, *Travels*, vol. ii. p. 422 sq.

peared in 1833, the third in 1838. In the same year in which the third edition appeared, Laurence edited the Ethiopic text as: " Libri Enoch Prophetae Versio Aethiopica." Both text and translation are unreliable, and must now be regarded as entirely antiquated.[1] Laurence's text is divided into one hundred and five chapters, which division was accepted by investigators down to Dillmann. He very properly made the division into one hundred and eight chapters. Prof. A. G. Hoffmann, of Jena, issued a full translation of Enoch with copious notes, in two parts, as: *Das Buch Henoch in vollständiger Uebersetzung, mit fortlaufendem Commentar, ausführlicher Einleitung und erläuternden Excursen.* For Part I., chap. 1–57, issued 1833, Hoffmann could use only Laurence's text and translation, but for Part II., chap. 58–108, he, in addition to these aids, consulted a MS. copy brought by Dr. Rüppell from Abyssinia and deposited in Frankfurt am Main. In the second part many of Laurence's mistakes are corrected, but not all by any means. With these aids at his disposal, Gfrörer made his Latin translation of the book in 1840, as: " Prophetae veteres Pseudepigraphi, partim ex Abyssinico vel Hebraico sermonibus Latine versi "; but this was again unsatisfactory. The book of Rev. Edward Murray, " Enoch Restitutus, or an Attempt," etc., London, 1836, must be regarded as a total failure.[2] All these sins were atoned for when the master-hand of A. Dillmann issued the Ethiopic text in 1851, as: " Liber Henoch, Aethiopice, ad quinque codicum fidem editus, cum variis lectionibus."[3] Two years later the same

---

[1] Cf. the severe judgment on Laurence by Dillmann, *Das Buch Henoch*, p. lvii.

[2] Cf. Hoffmann, *Zweiter Excurs*, pp. 917–965.

[3] From this edition our translation has been made.

author published his accurate translation of the book, with reliable notes, as : *Das Buch Henoch, übersetzt und erklärt*, a work of singular acumen and vast learning, which is the standard translation of Enoch to this day. The publication of these two works inaugurated a series of happy studies by Lücke, Ewald, Köstlin, Hilgenfeld, Volkmar, Langen, Gebhardt, Tideman, and others, who have all sought to give solutions of the many difficulties presented by this most mysterious book, but with very different results.[1]

Before proceeding to the special examination and analysis of the book before us, it is highly important that the question of the trustworthy or untrustworthy character of the Ethiopic translation be discussed. Is the Ethiopic translation a reliable version of the Greek Enoch ? For it is evident that the translation belongs to the early period of Ethiopic literature, when the literature in the Greek language was copied and translated by the Abyssinian theologians, before the introduction of Arabic influence and models. Enoch is, then, like all of the best specimens of literature in Abyssinia, — the Bible, the Book of the Jubilees, the fourth Book of Ezra, Ascensio Isaiae, and Pastor Hermae, — translated from the Greek. Whether the Greek is the original language of the book, or the Hebrew or Aramaic, will be discussed later ; here we have to decide on the relation existing between the Ethiopic and the Greek, from which our Enoch is a translation. As the Greek text, with the exception of some fragments, has been lost, this question cannot be apodictically decided, but there are means of reaching a probable result, sufficient to

---

[1] The results of these investigations will be mentioned and used in the Special Introduction and in the Notes.

permit us to trust the text as we find it in the Ethiopic translation. This result can be reached in two ways, first by analogy, by seeing whether those translations of which the original Greek has been preserved are faithful representatives of these originals, and thus learning the general manner in which translations were made in Ethiopia, and secondly by comparing the fragments of Enoch that still remain with the translation. Following the first method, we naturally begin with the comparison of the version of the Bible, translated in the early days of Christianity among the Ethiopians, not from the Hebrew, but from the Septuagint. Here only one authority has a right to speak, the editor of the *Octateuchus Aethiopicus*, Prof. Dillmann. As late as 1877, after years of diligent research on this subject, his judgment of this translation and its relation to the Greek is as follows:[1] " With regard to the translation, it must be said that it is a very faithful one, generally giving the Greek text *verbatim*, often even the relative position of the words; it abbreviates only now and then whatever seemed superfluous, and must, on the whole, be called a successful and happy version. Notwithstanding its entire fidelity to the Greek text it is very readable and, especially in the historical books, smooth, and frequently coincides with the meaning and words of the Old Testament in a surprising manner. Of course there is a difference in this respect between the different books. The Ethiopic translators were by no means very learned men, and had not an absolute command of the Greek language; especially when they had to translate rare words and technical terms this clearly appears, and consequently

[1] Cf. Herzog, *Real-Encyklopädie* (2d edition), vol. i. p. 204.

some misunderstandings and mistakes have crept into the text through the fault of the translators." This version of the Old Testament is, then, on the whole, a faithful copy of the Septuagint.

The same must be said of the translation of Pastor Hermae, although here " the sins of omission " are much more frequent, especially in *Similitudines* iv., v., and vi., which are rather an epitome of the Greek than a translation. Positive mistakes do, indeed, now and then occur,[1] but the main deviations from the Greek are found in the omissions. These are by no means of much importance as to contents, except possibly in Sim. v. 2, and it would be difficult to decide who made these omissions, whether they were already found in the original of the translator, or introduced by him, or are to be ascribed to a copyist.[2] A close comparison between the Ethiopic and the Greek text proves conclusively that the former is what can be called a good translation.

As the Greek text of the Physiologus has never been issued in a critical edition, a reliable examination of the fidelity of the old Ethiopic translation can scarcely be made, yet the evidences seem sufficient to justify an opinion equally as favorable as that passed on the version of the Bible and on Pastor Hermae.[3]

The Greek text of the Ascensio Isaiae recently discovered, and published by Gebhardt in Hilgenfeld's *Zeitschrift für wissenschaft. Theologie*, 1878, pp. 330–353, is evidently a different recension from the one

[1] Cf. Dillmann, in *Zeitschrift d. D. M. G.* xv. p. 121 sqq.

[2] Cf. *Patres Apostol.* ed. Gebhardt, Harnack et Zahn, Prolegomena to Hermas, p. xxx.

[3] Cf. Hommel, *Die Aethiop. Uebersetzung des Physiologus, etc.*, 1877, p. xliii, sq.

from which the Ethiopian made his translation, hence a comparison could produce but few positive results.

From the evidences, then, that can be regarded as valid we are, from analogy, allowed to expect that the Ethiopic translation of Enoch will, on the whole, be a faithful one, although occasional mistakes and omissions may occur. This opinion is confirmed by an examination of the remaining fragments of the Greek text. Comparing our text with that of Syncellus it is at once apparent that they do not always agree. But this does not impeach the veracity of the Ethiopic, for Syncellus furnishes his own evidence that he did not quote literally, but in a free manner. Chap. 8 : 4 to chap. 9 : 4 he gives twice, and the two quotations are far from being alike, thus showing that Syncellus, in his extracts from Enoch, as he was accustomed to do when citing other works, does not pretend to quote literally, but simply to give the sense. Certainly Syncellus has occasionally, as in 6 : 6, the better text, but in other places the Ethiopic wording, as the notes show, is decidedly to be preferred. This comparison, then, in no manner injures the claim of the trustworthy character of the version before us.

Gebhardt[1] has attempted to draw capital from the Greek fragment of 89 : 42–49, and on the basis of these few verses has reached a very pessimistic conclusion on the Ethiopic text of Enoch, especially chap. 89 and 90. But here there is really but one verse where the Greek presents a better reading,[2] and this verse is of little importance, and can in no wise affect the con-

---

[1] Cf. Merx, *Archiv für wissenschaftl. Erforschung des A. T.*, ii. 2, p. 242 sq.

[2] Cf. Notes. Tideman, l.c. p. 282 sqq., reaches the same conclusion.

clusion that we have in Enoch, as translated by the early Ethiopic church, a faithful copy of the Greek. Consequently we can proceed to the examination of the book itself with but little hesitancy.

SPECIAL INTRODUCTION.

§ 1. The book of Enoch is an apocryphal work. Etymologically the word *apocrypha* does not, and originally did not, possess the *sensus in malam partem* in which it is now generally used. Ἀπόκρυφον was, in contradistinction from ἀναγιγνωσκόμενον, i.e. read openly in a congregation, employed either to designate a book that was hidden, used only in private circles, or it signified a book of which not only the origin was hidden or unknown, but whose contents were also, i.e. veiled in the language of allegory, symbolism, and other figurative speech.[1] Canonical and apocryphal are then not in themselves contradictory terms, and a book could be both at the same time. Hence, too, we can easily understand how Epiphanius can call the Revelation an ἀπόκρυφον without thereby casting the least reflection on its apostolic origin and canonical authority.[2] Although the Old Testament books now called *apocrypha* were received with some suspicion by the early Fathers, practically they were regarded as of equal authority with the canonical writings. Only Jerome, in his *Prologus Galeatus* to Samuel, assumes an opposing position, and calls them apocrypha; but the merit of making this

[1] Cf. Schürer in Herzog, *R. E.* (2d ed.), vol. i. p. 484.
[2] Cf. Volkmar, *Das vierte Buch Esra und apokal. Geheimnisse überhaupt.* p. 2.

word synonymous with non-canonical remained for Carlstadt, who seized on Jerome's idea and developed it in his tract, *De canonicis scripturis libellus*, 1520. Since that time the Protestant church has used this word in this latter sense.[1] In the English Bible the word Apocrypha was not used for these books until the second edition of Cranmer's Bible in 1549, while in the first edition, in 1539, and Matthew's translation, 1537, they are still called Hagiographa.[2]

Of these apocryphal works one species is embraced under the term apocalyptic. This latter class is of a prophetic character, and under the assumption of a superhuman source of information seeks to unravel the mysteries of the present and the future. The contents are generally of a strictly religious character, and contain revelations concerning the kingdom of God and its development, but also discussions of theological questions, such as the relation existing between man's sin and God's justice, and explanations of the wonderful workings of God in nature and its laws. The incitement to the composition of such pseudo-prophecies must not be sought for so much in a morbid curiosity and a fanciful imagination as in an anxious desire to understand the workings of Providence, or even in a doubt concerning the promises given of old. They frequently owe their existence to the birth-throes of the persecuted and despairing children of God. Consequently the object is generally an apologetic and exhortative one. Both in contents and form they differ from the prophetic books of the old covenant. While these latter form a

---

[1] Cf. Schürer, l.c., and the different Introductions to the Old and New Testament.

[2] Cf. Kitto, *Cyclopaedia of Bibl Lit.* (3d ed.), i. 168.

2

collection of prophecies, or anthology of different prophecies uttered at different times, and are often unchronologically arranged, the apocalyptic writings generally contain a chain of such prophecies closely connected with each other. In form the enigmatical method of presentation is followed. Symbolical representations and figurative speech in general are employed, names and dates that could disclose the true author and his time are studiously avoided, and to give the whole the impress of antiquity and authority the most notable and pious [1] in the history of Israel are made the bearers of these revelations. All these works, to a greater or less extent, connect with the book of Daniel as the first and typical apocalyptical writing, and, like it, direct the suffering faithful from the afflictions of their own times to the speedy inauguration of the Messianic times, as the period when their hopes shall be realized and the promises of God redeemed.

That one specimen of this peculiar literature is ascribed to Enoch can certainly be no surprise, as the enigmatical words in which his history is recorded Gen. v. 21–24 was a valuable possession in the hands of an apocalyptic writer. The statements there left ample room for a vivid imagination to supply unwritten history, while antiquity and piety made Enoch a welcome name to give force and authority to a book, and the " walking with God" of Enoch and his translation to heaven, which correct exegesis has always read in this passage,[2] founded his claim of having enjoyed close

---

[1] Thus we have the Apocalypse of Baruch, the Assumptio Mosis, the Ascensio Isaiae, Fourth Ezra, and here the book of Enoch.

[2] Enoch is not again mentioned in the canonical books of the Old Testament, but twice in the Son of Sirach, xliv. 16 and xlix. 4, and in both passages the " and he was not" is regarded as synonymous with trans-

communion with God and having possessed superhuman knowledge. That the ויתחלך את־האלהים is conceived by our author as a retirement from the earth to the region of higher angelic beings, and the acquisition of superhuman knowledge there, is clear from En. 12 : 2,[1] and the method of receiving revelation is shaped accordingly, Enoch receiving his information not so much by dreams and visions as the prophets of old, but rather on a tour in company with the angels made to the ends of the earth and the heavens. In the Parables, 37–71, however, this does not so much exert an influence on the manner of acquiring heavenly wisdom, although the close communication with the angels is there too a prominent characteristic. The number of years in Enoch's life being three hundred and sixty-five, corresponding to the number of days in a solar year, this fact suggested the idea of making him the bearer of all kinds of secrets concerning nature and its operations and laws. Whether our author thereby gave expression to an ancient tradition among the people or originated the idea must, in the nature of the case, remain doubtful, although the former might seem probable, as a writer of the first century B.C., Alexander Polyhistor, as quoted by Eusebius, *Praeparatio Evangelica*, ix. 17, 5 (ed. Heinichen, vol. ii. p. 21), contends that Enoch first discovered (εὑρηκέναι πρῶτον) astrology (astronomy),

---

lation into heaven, proceeding from the correct assumption that the word ויארנכי, Gen. v. 24, forms a contrast to the well-known וילמת, used when speaking of the death of the other patriarchs. The same view is expressed by the LXX on Gen. v. 24, by Josephus *Antiq.* ix. 2, 2, by the author of the Epistle to the Hebrews xi. 5, the Targum of Jonathan, 1 Clem. *ad Cor.* ix. 3, and early writers in general. For the view of the other Targumim, and the Oriental versions, see Pichard, *Le Livre d'Hénoch sur l'amitié*, p. 23 sq.

[1] Cf. also *Liber Cosri* (ed. Buxtorf), p. 153.

over against the claims of the Egyptians. In harmony with this claim is the tradition recorded by Josephus, *Antiq.* i. 8, that Abraham first brought the knowledge of astronomy and arithmetic from Chaldea to Egypt, and from there they were then transplanted to Greece. Accordingly later Jewish tradition has made Enoch not only the father of arithmetic and astrology, but also the inventor of the alphabet and the first author, to whom many books were ascribed.[1] Thus we read of the " books " of Enoch in the Book of the Jubilees, *Test.* xii. *Patriarch.;* Origen, *c. Celsum* v. p. 267, and *Homil.* 28 *in Num.* 34 ; Augustine, *Civ. Dei,* xv. 23 ; Jerome, *Script. Eccles.* 4 ; and Georgius Syncellus quotes from the *first* book of Enoch concerning the watchmen. With his literary fame walked hand in hand his renown for piety, so that the translated Enoch is even made the Metatron i.e. μετὰ θρόνον or chief of those angels that stand before the throne of God.[2]

Among Mohammedan writers Enoch stood high as an inventor and literary character. In addition to the discoveries attributed to him by Jewish tradition, Moslem fame honors him with the invention of sewing.[3] He is mentioned but once in the Koran, in Sura xix. 57, under the name of *Edris,* i.e. the learned, and is called a prophet. Beidawi, the best Arabic commentator on the Koran, remarks on this passage that no less than thirty divinely revealed books were ascribed to his authorship.[4] Of the writings attributed to this

---

[1] Cf. Winer, *Bibl. Realwörterbuch,* Art. " Henoch."

[2] Cf. *Targ. Jonath.* to Gen. v. 24, and Pichard, l.c. p. 29 sq. Buxtorf, *Lex.* under מֵטַטְרוֹן, and Jellinek, *Bet-ha-Midrasch,* ii. p. xxx, and 114–117 ; iii. p. 155–160.

[3] Cf. Pichard, l.c. p. 37.

[4] Cf. Beidawi, *Commentarius in Coranum* (ed. H. O. Fleischer), p. 583.

ancient and pious favorite of God one of a prophetic character is made especially famous and important by being quoted by a canonical writer, Jude, Epist. 14, 15, of which work Tertullian [1] asserts that it still existed in his times. This is, as we have seen, the work before us.

§ 2. CONTENTS. — Chap. 1:1, Superscription. Chap. 1–5, Introduction. The source and divinely inspired character of this revelation given to Enoch during his intercourse with the angels, as well as its object: to announce the overthrow and destruction of the sinners when God shall come to judge, and the Messianic blessings in store for the righteous in the world now to come. Chap. 6–16, The historical basis of the book, containing an account of the fall of the angels through their carnal connection with the daughters of men, as the author's exegesis of Gen. vi. 1 sqq. The determination of God to inflict a temporal punishment upon them, which is to last until their condemnation in the final judgment, and the record of how this determination was carried out; the prediction of the flood as the means of cleansing the earth. Enoch, as a man privileged to communicate with higher beings, is requested by the fallen angels to write for them a petition for mercy. This he does; but is sent back by God himself to renew the previous announcement of the certain punishment of these angels. The object of this narrative is to prove historically that God will certainly punish sinners, and is thus to add force to the prediction of the true author in announcing the destruction of the sinners in his days. Chap. 17–36, Description of what Enoch saw during his trip around and above the earth. He describes the divine

[1] Cf. *De Idol.* 4 and *De Cultu Feminar.* ii. 10.

2*

origin of nature and its laws, sees the place of departed spirits both good and bad, the place of final punishment, the tree of life in the south, and the tree of knowledge in the garden of the just, and many of the secrets of nature. Chap. 37–71 form a rounded whole, and are entitled: The second vision of wisdom. It is divided into three parables by the writer himself; 38–44, being the first, contain a prophetic account of the congregation of the holy as it will be after the removal of the sinners. Enoch views the mysteries of heaven, sees the myriads of the angels, and notes four, Michael, Rafael, Gabriel, and Fanuel, as the archangels. He speaks also of some of the secrets of nature, and lauds wisdom, which he personifies. 45–57, introduced as the second parable, treat chiefly of the Messiah, his nature and work, especially his judgment, and glorify the period of blessing and peace that his coming shall inaugurate. 58–69 : 25 (with the exception of 60 : 65–69 : 25, which are from another hand), as the third parable, contain an account of the blessed condition of the righteous and of the judgment and condemnation in store for the wicked. Chap. 70 and 71 contain a suitable close to all the parables. Chap. 72–82, with the special title, The book of the courses of the luminaries, the astronomical book proper, contain a long and tedious account of the course and movements of the sun, moon, and stars, respecting which the angel Uriel, "who is over them," instructed the seer. Chap. 83–91 contain two visions in dreams, the first, 83 and 84, predicting the flood and the first judgment, the second, 85–90, giving an allegorical account of the development of the world-history from the creation to the time of completion in the Messianic future, the whole from a purely theocratic stand-point. Under the symbolism of wild and tame animals the relation of Israel to the neighboring nations is recorded, the whole, as far as historical, from a biblical view. Chap. 91 gives a fitting admonition of Enoch to his children. Chap. 92–93 (and 91 : 12–17) pass over the same ground that the second dream does, only more briefly, as ten " world-weeks." Chap. 94–105, the paraenetic part proper and the practical application of the instruction given to the times of the author, the cry of woe over the sinners, and the exhortation to hope and fidelity to the righteous. Chap. 106–107 have an account of the birth of Noah and his wonderful appearance, and prediction of the flood. Chap. 108, introduced as " another book of Enoch," contains a renewed brief prediction of the sure destruction awaiting the sinners and of the certain blessing in store for the righteous. The revelation is received from an angel.

§ 3. ANALYSIS. — The varied contents of the book, its many apparently incongruous elements, its obscure language and symbolical figures, together with the total lack of all outer evidences respecting author or authors, time of composition, and object of writing, have occasioned much perplexity to investigators, and given rise to a vast number of different opinions on the questions suggested by a perusal of Enoch. Neither combination or integrity, nor author or time or language, has been settled to the satisfaction of all, as scarcely two of those that have examined the book agree on all these points. This is not surprising in a book that seeks by all means to hide its authorship and period of composition, and in the nature of the case a full agreement on these topics can scarcely ever be expected, especially as preconceived notions concerning the New Testament canon, principally concerning the Epistle of Jude, have unfortunately influenced the interpretation in both orthodox and liberal investigators. The results of an analysis will, then, in every case bear only the stamp of a possibility, or at best, a probability; absolute and convincing certainty will only be realized if some new outer aids, e.g. a new reliable Greek text, or earnest investigation in ancient Rabbinical and Talmudic lore, should throw light on the subject. Before proceeding to a further examination of the composition and compilation of the book, it will be well to survey the opinions of those who have devoted learning and critical acumen to this topic.[1]

Both Laurence and Hofmann, in their translations and notes, had complained of a want of unity and connection in the book. They therefore resorted to a transposition of different parts to more harmonizing places, but not to the satisfaction of later critics, as the necessary inner harmony and connection was not thereby restored. That plan was then dropped, and the idea that the book consisted of several independent parts, written by different authors at different times, became an almost universal conviction.

LÜCKE[2] analyzes the book as follows: The present book of Enoch consists *first* of an older portion, embracing chap. 1–36 and 72–108, and *secondly* of a younger portion, contained in chap. 37–71, in which, however, are some later interpolations. The former

---

[1] These opinions have been mostly collected from the original sources themselves, and where this source failed the deficiency was supplied by Schürer, *Neutestamentliche Zeitgeschichte*, Leipzig, 1874, p. 521 sqq.

[2] *Elnleit. in die Offenb. Johannes*, 1852, pp. 89–144.

was written in the beginning of the Maccabaean contest, 166–160 B.C., as the "great horn," 90:9, is Judas Maccabi, the later during the first years of the reign of Herod the Great. No date can be assigned to the interpolations. In his "Nachträge," however, p. 1072, he holds that the older portion was written during the reign of John Hyrcanus, 135–105 B.C., adopting Ewald's view.

J. CHR. K. VON HOFMANN [1] claims that the main body of the work was written by one and the same Christian author in the second century after Christ. For him the small lambs in 89–90 are not the heroes of the Maccabaean struggle, but the early Christians. The quotation in Jude is, then, not from Enoch, but was the occasion of the production of this apocryphal writing. Later interpolations are found in 59–71; 82:4–20; 92; 106–108. Hofmann has the honor of being the first to discover the correct interpretation of the seventy shepherds in 89 and 90.

DILLMANN [2] also claimed one author for the main body of the work, but did not deny later additions and interpolations. These are: (1) the historical 6–16, 93 and 91:12–17; 106–107. (2) the Noachic 54:7–55:2; 60; 65–69:25. (3) then chap. 20, 70, 75:5; 82:9–20; 108. The book was written about 110 B.C., as the "great horn" in 90:9 is John Hyrcanus. The additions, however, were made in the first century before the Christian era. Later [3] he admits that, irrespective of the interpolations, the book must be regarded as a compilation of two, or even three, different works. He, with

---

[1] *Zeitschrift der Deutschen Morgenländ. Gesellschaft*, vol. vi. 1852, p. 87–91, and *Schriftbeweis* (2d ed.), vol. i. pp. 420–423.

[2] *Das Buch Henoch*, 1853, p. v sqq.

[3] Herzog, *R. E.* (1st ed.), vol. xii. pp. 308–310, and Schenkel's *Bibel-Lexikon*, vol. iii. pp. 10–13.

Ewald, regards 37–71 as the older portion, and places it in the first years of the Asmoneans, while the union of the different parts was probably effected about the middle of the first century B.C.

EWALD [1] discovers the following parts in the book: (1) The groundwork, 37–71, written about 144 B.C. (2) The second Henókh book, 1–5; 91–105, and other fragments, in the beginning of the reign of John Hyrcanus. (3) The third Henókh, book of which remnants have been preserved in 8; 20–36; 72–90; 106–108, written about 128 B.C. (4) The Noah book, found in 6: 3–8; 17–19; 54:7–55:2; 65–69:1, somewhat younger than the preceding. (5) The present complete Henókh, whose editor added considerable in 6–16, and wrote about the middle of the first pre-Christian century.

KÖSTLIN [2] divides thus: (1) The groundwork, embracing 1–16; 21–36; 72–105, and written about 110 B.C. (2) The Parables, 37–71 (with the exception of the Noachic fragments), written between 100 and 64 B.C. The same author wrote 17–19. (3) The Noachic fragments 54:7–55:2; 60; 65–69:25, possibly 20 and 82:9–20, and probably 106–107, and also some things in 6–8. (4) Chap. 108, an Essenic addition about the time of Herod the Great or his successors.

HILGENFELD [3] considers 1–16; 20–36; 72–105 the groundwork, written in the first years of Alexander Jannai. Later additions are found in 17–19; 37–71; 106–108, and these later portions are all the work of a Christian adherent of Gnosticism about the time

[1] *Abhandlung über des Aethiop. Buches Henókh Entstehung, Sinn und Zusammensetzung,* 1855.

[2] *Theol. Jahrbücher,* 1856, pp. 240–279; 370, 386.

[3] *Die jüd. Apokalyptik,* 1857, pp. 91–184, and *Zeitschr. f. wissensch. Theol.* iii. pp. 319–334; iv. pp. 212–222; v pp. 216–221; xv. pp. 584–587.

between Saturninus and Marcion. Hilgenfeld lays special stress on a pretended Christian character of the Messiah in 37–71. He declines to separate Noachic fragments. Later he modified his idea concerning the first part by claiming that it was written about 98 B.C. This result is reached by interpreting the periods of the seventy shepherds as each of seven years, so that 7×70 or 490 years from 588 B.C., as the acknowledged commencement of the reign of these shepherds, would establish the period of writing.

VOLKMAR [1] claims that the periods of the shepherds each embrace terms of ten years, so that the whole period of this rule would be 70, or rather 72, according to his idea, times 10, i.e. 720 years, and counting from 588 B.C. this would indicate 132 A.D. as the year in which the book was written. It is claimed to be the first connected account of the commencement of the insurrection of Bar-cochebas, and was written by a disciple of Akiba. He rejoices in this conclusion exceedingly, and later [2] characterizes the book of Enoch as " a warlike zelotic announcement of the final victory of Bar-cochebas after the defeat of Hadrian 132 A.D. " !

LANGEN [3] admits that in its present shape the book is the work of different authors, but claims that the internal harmony is such that a great difference of time cannot exist. As he interprets the " great horn " as Judas Maccabi, he places the composition of the groundwork at about 160 B.C.

[1] *Zeitschrift d. Deutschen Morgenländ. Gesellschaft*, xiv. pp. 87–134, 296 ; *Zeitschrift f. wissensch. Theol.* iv. pp. 111–136, 422 sqq. ; v. p. 46 sqq., and *Eine neutest. Entdeckung*, etc. Zürich, 1862.

[2] *Das vierte Buch Esra ... als ältester Commentar zum N.T.* Tübingen, 1863, p. 408.

[3] *Das Judenthum in Palästina*, 1866, pp. 35–64.

SIEFFERT[1] considers 1–16 ; 20–36 ; 72–81 ; 91–105 as the oldest portion, written about the time of Jonathan, 165–160 B.C., and interprets the seventy shepherds in 82–90, which he regards as a separate addition, in Hilgenfeld's style, but begins the rule of these shepherds already 598 B.C., and thus makes the book ten years older than Hilgenfeld, i.e. it was written about 108 A.D. Chap. 17–19 ; 37–71 ; 106–108 were written by an Essene, and before the invasions of the Parthians in 64 B.C.

PHILIPPI[2] defends the absolute integrity of the book. With Hofmann he regards the small lambs as Christians, and interprets the period of the shepherds like Volkmar, but assumes only seventy shepherds and, counting either from 606 or 588 B.C., considers the book as one of a Christian origin, and written about 100 A.D.

WITTICHEN[3] revives to a great extent Dillmann's old opinions, considering the main body of the book as the work of one author, but written by him at different times. The oldest portion, 83–91, was produced about 166–161 B.C. Later interpolations are 6–16 ; 93 and 91 : 12–17 ; 106–107. A second interpolator, in the first pre-Christian century, added 20 ; 54 : 7–55 : 2 ; 60 ; 65–69 : 25 ; 70 ; 82 : 9–20 ; and 108 is a later independent addition, also written before Christ.

GEBHARDT[4] does not analyze the book, but gives a minute and telling criticism on the different views expressed on the seventy shepherds in chap. 89 and 90. His conclusions are of a negative character, claiming that unless

---

[1] *De apocryphi libri Henochi origine et argumento*, 1867.

[2] *Das Buch Henoch, sein Zeitalter und sein Verhältniss zum Judasbrief*, 1868.

[3] *Die Idee des Menschen*, 1868, and *Die Idee des Reiches Gottes*, 1872.

[4] Merx, *Archiv f. wissensch. Erforschung des Alt. Test.*, 1872, **Vol. ii** Heft 2, pp. 163–246.

a better text is discovered it will be impossible to find the true interpretation of the author's idea.

SCHÜRER (p. 529 sqq.) considers as settled that there are, at least, three distinct parts in the book: (1) The groundwork, 1–37 and 72–105; (2) The Parables, 37–71, with the exception of (3) the Noachic portions 54 : 7–55 : 2; 60; 65–69 : 25, and probably 106–107. The last chap. 108 is an independent and late addition. The groundwork was written in the last third of the second century before Christ, as the " great horn " is John Hyrcanus; the Parables, during the reign of Herod the Great, as the invasion of the Parthians is presupposed as an historical event in chap. 56, while the Noachic additions are of uncertain date. Schürer adopts Hofmann's interpretation of shepherds as angels.[1]

VERNES[2] regards the Messiah of the Parables as a Christian one, and hence (pp. 264 and 269) claims the end of the first Christian century as the time when they were written. As 90 : 9 refers to John Hyrcanus, the groundwork was written in his days. He does not settle the time of the Noachic additions.

TIDEMAN[3] claims that 83–91 do not belong to the original book, but were inserted afterwards, probably a few years later by an Essenic writer. He claims that the dream-visions interrupt the connection. His conclusions are: The oldest book contains 1–16; 20–36; 72–82; 93; 91 : 12–19; 92; 94–105, and was written by a Pharisee between 153 and 135 B.C. The second book, 83–

---

[1] Castelli's work : *Il Messia secondo gli Ebrei*, Firenze, 1874, could not be consulted.

[2] *Histoire des Idées Messianiques depuis Alexandre jusqu'à l'empereur Hadrien*, Paris, 1874, pp. 69–117 and 264–270.

[3] *De Apokalypse van Henoch en het Essenisme*, in the *Theologisch Tijdschrift*, Mei, 1875, pp. 261–296.

91, is by an Essene between 134 and 106 B.C., and thirdly the Apocalypse of Noah, 17–19; 41:3–9; 43:1, 2; 44; 54:7–55:2; 59; 60; 65–69:25; 70; 106; 107, written after 80 A.D. by a person versed in Jewish Gnosticism and the Cabala. The Parables are by a Christian of the days of Domitian or Trajan, 90–100 A.D. The final redactor, the author too of 108, was a Christian Gnostic of the tendency of Saturninus, after 125 A.D.

DRUMMOND'S[1] chief contribution to the understanding of Enoch is his peculiar view of the Messiah in the Parables. He thinks the Messiah must be a Christian one, but at the same time will not give up the Jewish source of the Parables, and therefore regards the Messianic passages in the second part as Christian interpolations, and explains the absence of the then expected references to the historical Christ by saying, rather unsatisfactorily (p. 61), that " an interpolator would be careful not to depart too widely from the character of the book in which he made his insertions." As the great horn is John Hyrcanus, the time in which the original book was written is " the latter half of the second century before Christ" (p. 43). The original book embraces the chapters that are ascribed to it by Tideman (p. 37). In the Noachic fragments he seems to admit a post-Christian influence in 67:4 sq. (pp. 57, 58). He adopts Hofmann's and Schürer's view of the shepherds (p. 40).

The majority of critics deny that the book, as we have it now, is the work of one author, and Philippi stands absolutely alone in his refusal to acknowledge later additions or interpolations to a more ancient groundwork. In fact, this point can be regarded as settled, and the

[1] *The Jewish Messiah, from the rise of the Maccabees to the closing of the Talmud.* London, 1877, pp. 17–73.

question that remains to be discussed is the number of
component parts and the chapters that belong to each
part. As we are in this examination restricted to inner
evidences alone, to the harmony or disharmony in style
and sentiment, it will be necessary to inquire what evidences the book itself furnishes for the solution of this
problem. It is important to notice that certain portions
claim to be revelations not of Enoch, but of Noah, and
this fact alone is sufficient to force the acceptance of a
different author. The book pretends to be a revelation
given to Enoch, and as it contains revelations given to
Noah after the death of Enoch, we must conclude that
these latter are parts foreign to the original work.
Here we have first the whole of chap. 60 given " in the
year five hundred of the life of Noah," [1] concerning the
flood, as the most important event in the life of that
patriarch. The difference in style and sentiment, such
as the masculine and feminine water, the Behemoth
and Leviathan, and others,[2] are so characteristic that it
would be impossible for the same mind to have conceived
this chapter and the groundwork of the book. With
these indices, authorship, time, and sentiment on hand,
it will be seen that 54 : 7–55 : 2, which verses there form
an unexpected interruption of the connection, and the
whole connected account in 65–69 : 25 form with 60 a
separate element, that has very properly been called,
The Noachic additions or fragments. In addition, to
make certainty more certain, the Parables, i.e. 37–71,
are expressly quoted in 68 : 1. To these additions undoubtedly must be reckoned also 106–107, as the sim-

---

[1] That it must be Noah, and not Enoch, as the Ethiopic text reads, is
proved in the notes on this chapter.
[2] Cf. notes.

ilarity of subject-matter and of style point to this fact. They are intended to give an account of the bearer of revelation in these additions, and describe his worthiness for this office.

Not to these additions belongs chap. 108.   It is introduced with the words: "This is another writing of Enoch," as an independent tract. It is a later, undoubtedly the last, portion of the book. The object is clear; it is a renewed exhortation to fidelity and hope to those disappointed ones who might lose confidence in the prophecies of the old book.   We are, then, justified in separating at least 54 : 7–55 : 2 ; 60 ; 65-69 : 25 ; 106–108 from the original book.

With equal, yes with greater, certainty can this same thing be done with 37–71, which are not only distinguished in a marked manner from the Noachic fragments, but from 1–36 and 72–105 also.   A mere perusal of this certainly most beautiful part of the whole work shows that it forms by itself a complete whole, is introduced as a separate tract, divides itself into three Parables, treats of a different subject-matter, and this not simply as a complement to the other part. It is directed against peculiar enemies, and has the distinguishing feature of peculiar standard names for God, and differs in its angelology and demonology, in its eschatology and Messianic idea. We will here speak only of the different names of God and of angelology, as therein both parts can more easily be considered together, and at the same time sufficiently justify a separate examination of the Parables. The discussions of the other characteristics of the groundwork and of the Parables will be best given in the separate examinations of both.

The two appellations of God peculiar to 37–71 are " Lord of the spirits " and " the Ancient of days," the latter of these, of course, being taken from the book of Daniel (cf. note on 46 : 1). The classical name in the Parables, however, is " the Lord of the spirits " (cf. note on 37 : 1 sq.), and is an appellation that nicely harmonizes with the general spiritual and trans-mundane character of this part, although there may be some doubt as to the exact idea which the author intended to convey in it. Again, the Parables lack at least one name of God characteristic of 1–37 and 72–105, i.e. The Holy and Great one (cf. note on 1 : 3). Certainly this exclusive use of different names in different parts would, if it were the only reason, scarcely justify a separation of the book into two or more portions, but taken in connection with the other indices it has considerable weight.

A better reason for such a separation we find in the angelology and demonology of the Parables over against the statements in this respect in the other parts. In accordance with the more systematical character of the Parables in general, the classification of the angels is a stricter one than in the first part. In 71 : 7 those that guard the throne of God are classified as Cherubim, Seraphim, and Ophanim ; and 61 : 10, the whole host of heaven are divided as Cherubim, Seraphim, Ophanim, angels of power and of government. A certain class, of which Michael, 71 : 3, 8, 13, is one, are called archangels, and are probably the same as the four angels before the throne of God in chap. 40. The angel of peace (cf. note on 40 : 8) is peculiar to this part, and in general it will be observed that its angelology is of a higher, almost more philosophical, character than in the other

3*

portions. This is apparent from the fact that the functions assigned them are all of an ethical character (cf. notes on 39:13; 40:1 sqq., 47:4, etc.), regulated entirely by the relation they sustain to the development of the Messianic kingdom, and hence their connection with the physical world is not dwelt upon to any extent. Whether 1–37 and 72–105 have a distinct classification of angels is more than doubtful. Aside from chap. 20, which being of doubtful authenticity cannot be used as evidence, the author seems only to know a class called Cherubim, 14:11, and the number of a peculiar class given differently in 87:2; 90:21–31 do not admit of any conclusion. Yet the greatest difference exists on the subject of evil spirits. The first part claims, 15:8, that the spirits of the giants, the sons of the fallen angels and of the women, are demons, who work violent destruction, and afterwards become the objects of false worship, 99:7. A different account is given in the Parables. Here we meet with satans, 40:7, of whom one, *the* Satan, is chief, 53:3; 54:6. The fall of the angels consisted in becoming subjects of Satan, 54:6, in whose service, 53:3, are the angels of punishment so frequently mentioned (cf. note on 53:3), whose work it is to punish the kings and the powerful after the final judgment. The idea of placing over against the kingdom of God an opposing kingdom of Satan, with a retinue of servants such as God has in the angels, can be traced back to the general plan of the author. His polemics are directed against the kings of the earth, hence he not only emphasizes the royalty of the Messiah as the future conqueror of these kings, but sees even in their future tormentors the emissaries of a prince called Satan. As the archangels are the chosen instruments for the special punishment of the fallen beings of their own kind, on account of the terribleness of their crimes, chap. 54, thus the kings, as special sinners, shall have their special tormentors. The kingdom of Satan, although opposed to God, still seems in some way dependent upon his will. The idea has a great similarity with that of Satan presented in the book of Job. This is but one of the many differences existing between 1–36 and 72–105, but is sufficient to prove that the same man did not pen both, that consequently the Parables are from a different author. How this conclusion is strengthened and verified will be seen presently in the separate examination of each part.

But is the rest of the book, i.e. 1–37 and 72–105, from one hand? Here the following chapters are probably interpolations: 20; 70; 75:5; 82:9–20, for the reasons assigned in the notes. Whether the account of the world-weeks, 93 and 91:12–17, is altogether an interpolation, or only the account of the last three weeks, may be doubtful. That the account 91:12–17, at least, is such, is manifest from the fact that it makes no mention whatever of a Messiah, which we have a right to expect if it were written by the author of 90:9. But as the whole account is a connected one, it is best to regard it as an addition made by some admirer of Daniel, and in imitation of him. The question as to the authenticity of 105 is difficult, as it is simply impossible to decide what idea the author desired to express with the " my son." We have no right to see it in a ὁμοουσία nor to see in it the one who is κατ᾽ ἐξοχήν, the chief one of those who are the children of God, as Israel is frequently called, e.g. 2 Sam. vii. 14. If the latter is the case, it can easily be understood from the author's Messianic idea.

for here the Messiah grows out as a prominent one from among the faithful in Israel, and has nothing of the supernatural that characterizes him in the Parables.

We can see no reasons for making any more separations from the book. There can scarcely be a cause for doubting that 72–105 are from the author of 1–37, nor for considering the dream visions 83 sqq. (Tideman) out of connection (cf. notes).

The conclusions, then, on the probable division of the work are these: In addition to the Noachic fragments 54:7–55:2, 60; 65–69:25 (106–107) and the Parables 37–71 (with the exception of the interpolations), which are parts most certainly foreign to the original groundwork, 108 is clearly an independent addition, and 20; 70; 75:5; 82:9–20; 93 and 91:12–17 are, in all probability, later interpolations. In 105 not even a probability *pro* or *con* can be decided upon.

§ 4. THE GROUNDWORK 1–36 and 72–105. *a. Object.*— The author writes out of his time and for his time, and hence, before learning what his object is, we must discover the characteristics of his period, the grievances and wants of his people, and then what solutions he has for the problems that were suggested by the condition of affairs. In the pursuit of this effort the parenetic chapters 94–105 furnish us with the best material, and here again it is especially the address in 103:9–15 that gives us the clearest idea. The author is one of the faithful in Israel, one of the Chasidim, and his work is written principally for them. He finds them a disappointed and despondent party. God's promises given of old to those that would adhere to his law were clear and defined. Although these did not distinctly remove the veil from eternity and offer retribution and reward beyond the grave, they had opened up to the just all the glories and wealth that this world afforded. The retribution taught by the Old Testament (at least as it was conceived by the Jews) was a purely terrestrial one, and the degree of happiness on earth was made the index to moral worth and fidelity to God. External advantages, fruitful harvests, victory over enemies, quiet possession of the land, long life, numerous descendants, were what the faithful had a right to expect. For his faithfulness it " should be well with him in the land that the Lord his God had given him." But how different was his condition at the time the author writes! In 103 : 11 the faithful complain, " We hoped to be the head, and became the tail, and the unrighteous have made their yoke heavy for us." They are subjected to the will of their enemies, for ver. 12 laments that their haters had become their rulers, and they are the objects of the rapine, injustice, and persecution of the sinners. The Chasidim are a persecuted race ; yes, they are often killed, and must descend into Sheol in sorrow, 102 : 5. No charge is more frequently made than that of persecution and oppression of the righteous by the unrighteous 94 : 6 ; 95 : 7 ; 96 : 7, 8 ; 97 : 6 ; 99 : 13, etc., and the undercurrent of thought is this, that at the time of the author the just were as a minority under the tyranny of the sinners as the dominant party. It is important to notice this fact, not only because it explains why the period of the sword, the time of vengeance on the un- righteous, is so horribly pictured, but because it will give an important hint as to the time when the author wrote. In other respects the righteous do not possess what had been promised, for in addition to the political power all the honor and wealth of the earth belong to the unrighteous, so that they appear as the just, 96 : 4, i.e. they are in possession of that which God had promised to the righteous. To their crimes of sin against the faithful is added the great one against God, that of reviling him; in fact "sinners" and "revilers" are almost constantly spoken of in the same breath (cf. 5 : 4; 81 : 8; 91 : 7, 11; 94 : 9; 96 : 7; 97 : 6; 98 : 11 sq. (15); 99 : 1; 100 : 9, etc.), and they go so far as to betray the "inheritance of the fathers," 99 : 14, i.e. the God of Israel. With these data on hand it becomes clear what the writer wanted. Under the heavy yoke of the supremacy and persecution of the sinners, and seeing these "eat the marrow of the wheat and drink the root of the fountain," 96 : 5, they are beginning to doubt the promises of God, to question the truth of God's justice and his faithfulness in carrying out what had been prophesied by Moses and the prophets. That such doubt was beginning to grow in the hearts of the cruelly wronged band is only too certain from 103 : 9–15. To wipe this out, to defend the truth of the revealed promises, and to vindicate the justice of Jehovah, *that* is the chief aim of the author. His object is, then, primarily an apologetical biblical one, but this only as the groundwork of the practical, exhortative one of admonishing them faithfully and patiently to endure for the present. His answer to the questions of his suffering friends consists in directing them from the trials and tribulations of the עילם הזה to the triumphs of the עילם הבא, and therefore his admonitions centre in the words "hope" (96 : 1; 104 : 2, 4) and "believe" (97 : 1), for the day of Jehovah would surely come. It is inaugurated by "the period of the sword," of the destruction of the sinners by the righteous; and the vividness with which this period is pictured in 99 and 100, especially 100 : 3, shows how important it was for the author. He is a Jew, writes for Jews, and his standard of retribution is the Jewish one of " an eye for an eye and a tooth for a tooth." The character of the sin shall determine the character of the punishment, and this terrible scene of carnage inflicted by the righteous on the unrighteous in the day of vengeance, 95 : 3; 90 : 19; 91 : 11, 12; 94 : 7, 9; 95 : 3; 98 : 12, etc., can only be regarded as the development from the sufferings of the righteous in the time of the author. It should be noticed here that the Parables, which do not presuppose a condition of persecution for the faithful, say little or nothing concerning the period of the sword. But this feature of the author's eschatological hopes are like his Messianic idea, developments out of the immediate wants and longings of his times. Here he meets an objection. The sinners say that God does not regard their actions, 104 : 7. The author knows better than this, for these acts are known in heaven, 98 : 6, 7, 8; 104 : 7, written on the tablets of heaven (cf. note on 81 : 1), and are even remembered and related by the powers of nature, 100 : 10; 104 : 8. This peculiar method of polemics is prompted by the manner in which he received his revelations as recorded chap. 12 sqq., and his intimate knowledge of the divine course of nature. An objection, however, more subtile yet meets the author here that he must refute. The fulfilment of his prophecies rests on the assumption that there is a retribution after death, and this the sinners deny. They claim that death ends all, and no righting of the wrongs of life can be expected after death. It must be especially noticed that the author nowhere presupposes the objection that there

is no life after death, but only that there is no retribution then. Thus, 102 : 6–11, the sinners do not boast
that the souls die with the bodies, but only that the fate
of all is similar after death, and that the darkness of
Sheol will receive both good and bad. The same idea
lies in 103 : 5, 6. Therefore, too, in his exalted tone,
the author emphasizes the fact, 103 : 1 sqq., that after
death the good will receive their reward, and the evil
their punishment, 103 : 7, sqq. The simple existence of
the soul after death and the resurrection of the departed
are never mentioned in a polemical spirit, but always
as acknowledged facts ; but for the defence of a retribution after death the author brings in all his power of
persuasion. He seems to appreciate the fact that he
has the letter of the old covenant against him, that he
must take a step beyond the Old Testament, and therefore, with a powerful appeal to the greatness of God
103 : 1, he assures his readers of the truth of what he
says. In this way, then, he has removed the difficulties and cleared the way for the description of the
manner in which this future retribution shall take
place ; he can now proceed to what is his main intention — to a description of the world to come, to his peculiar eschatology. Historically, his object and its origin
can be easily understood. It is a well-known fact that
ever since the time when Alexander and his successors
attempted to establish Greek culture in the East, there
had been two parties in Palestine also, the Hellenistic,
or friends of progress, and the Chasidim, or those that
clung to the law and to all Jewish peculiarities, and
bore within their hearts all the hopes and promises of
Israel. It is equally well known that this class of
faithful ones were generally in the minority and sub-

ject to the persecution of the opposite party. Especially
was this the case in the ever memorable conflict between
the tyrannical and singular Antiochus (IV.) Epiphanes
and the Maccabean party. That in this long struggle
between the conservative and advanced elements the
defeat and sufferings of the former, who knew that
God had given them the promises, should excite doubts
in their hearts such as the author meets is natural. To
encourage them in their tortured condition, to defend
the promises given them, to predict the downfall of
their enemies and the enemies of God, *this* was the object and aim the author had in writing. It might be
called a proclamation or manifesto to the Chasidim,
exhorting them to steadfastness, announcing that the
long-delayed retribution would surely and speedily
come.

b. Contents. — As the author seeks to direct his
readers from the tribulations of their times to the
glories of the future, his description will naturally be
chiefly an eschatological one, embracing the topics of
the period of the sword, the judgment, the punishment
of the wicked, Sheol, hell, the reward of the righteous,
and the Messiah with his kingdom. These topics are,
in fact, the objects of his prophecies. During his trip
with the angel, Enoch, by a historical lapsus, sees Sheol
already inhabited. It is the place of departed spirits
both good and bad, for the righteous descend there also,
102 : 5. Although Sheol is but a temporary abode, to
serve till the time of the final judgment, the fate of its
inhabitants is already foreshadowed by their condition
while there. In chap. 22, which is devoted to its description, we learn that it has four apartments : one for those
righteous who died at the hands of sinners, the second

4

for the other saints, the third for the sinners who were not punished on earth, the fourth for those whose retribution was at least partially given them before death.[1] The last class, however, shall remain here, and not be subjected to a farther condemnation, ver. 13. This peculiar division well reflects the author's time. Only one that had seen with his own eyes the numerous persecutions of the righteous could think of making for them a special apartment in Sheol with the prototype of martyrs, Abel, where they have the special privilege of continuing their cry for vengeance. The inhabitants of three apartments shall rise again, the unrighteous for punishment, the righteous to take part in the glories of the Messianic kingdom. It should be noticed here that the author presupposes in this connection the resurrection of the wicked, although in other places he mentions only the rising of the saints, cf. 91 : 10; 92 : 3; 100 : 5; 103 : 4. Preceding the judgment of the living and dead, and also the period of the sword, there will come the signs of the last times, of which we have a graphic description in chap. 80. Before the judgment, as 90 : 19 compared with sqq. shows, there will be the terrible period of the sword of which we have already spoken. Then comes the judgment in which God himself judges, 1 : 9; 90 : 20; 91 : 7; 100 : 4. Although the judgment is stated to be universal, embracing the just also, 1 : 7, it is evident that it is restricted to those who took active part in the conflict between the faithful and the unrighteous, either as foes or friends, and is thus not universal in an absolute sense. Were it such, it would be impossible to conceive

---

[1] We simply give here and in the following the results reached in the notes.

how the author can speak of an increase of the Messianic kingdom after the judgment through the arrival of the hitherto neutral heathen nations. The place of judgment is Palestine, or rather Jerusalem, 90 : 20. The order is, first the fallen angels and the seventy shepherds 90 : 20 sqq., and then the renegades in Israel. The condemnation of the sinners is eternal, 5 : 5, 6; 10 : 12; 12 : 4, 5; 22 : 11, sqq., and consists of burning, 10 : 14, in a pool of fire, 10 : 6; 90 : 24, etc., or fiery abyss, 10 : 13; 90 : 25, etc., or in prison, 10 : 13, or in a fiery oven, 98 : 3, or in hell, 99 : 11. There are two places of punishment, one for the fallen angels, who are temporarily bound under the hills, 10 : 4 sqq., which is found " on the ends of the earth," 18 : 14 and chap. 21. It is the same place that is described in 90 : 24, 25, where again no geographical locality is assigned to it. The place of torture for the theocratic sinners is better outlined. Going out from the Old Testament idea he places it in the valley of Hinnom, chapters 26, 27, 90 : 26. After the removal, 1 : 1, and destruction, 1 : 9; 97 : 1; 94 : 10, of the sinners, the happy period of the rule of the righteous is inaugurated. His description is in accordance with his ethics and dogmatics. What the faithful lacked before they shall then abundantly possess. These are both physical and moral blessings. They shall enjoy the good of the land, 10 : 18, 19, the temple shall be built anew and the old one removed, 90 : 28, 29, and around it then will be gathered all the saints, 90 : 33, they shall eat of the tree of life, 24 : 4, 5, which has been transplanted to the north, i.e. to Jerusalem, 25 : 5, they will have wisdom, 5 : 8; 91 : 10, there will be absolute moral perfection without sin, 5 : 8; 92 : 5, and this state shall

be eternal, 91 : 17 ; 92 : 4 ; 105 : 2, and in these glories
the risen just shall take part, 103 : 4 ; 91 : 10 ; 92 : 3 ;
100 : 5. The centre of the kingdom is in Jerusalem.
But all this so far without a Messiah. He does not establish the kingdom, but grows out from among the
faithful after the establishment. We hear of him only
90 : 37, 38. For the author, this Messiah is one who is
especially prominent by his fidelity religiously, for he is
born a bullock while the others are sheep, and by his
strength, as he has large horns. The description does
not transcend the human, and thus forms a decided
contrast to the Messiah of the Parables. Both Messiah
and the Messianic kingdom are capable of development,
for he grows, and they grow with him. He becomes
strong, so that the nations who have hitherto been mere
lookers-on fear him, and all come and take part in his
kingdom. This chief characteristic of the Messiah, as
that of a military hero who will protect the just and
establish their rule over all the nations, was suggested
to the author as the fitting counterpart to the subjection of the righteous to the supremacy of the sinners
in his days.

Not a small portion of the author's work is devoted
to a tedious account of nature and its laws. Besides
notices here and there, he devotes the whole section
72–82 to this topic. The sun, moon, stars, the phenomena of nature, such as lightning, thunder, rain,
dew, etc., are the objects of his wisdom. For him
these all have a moral purpose ; they demonstrate the
power and wisdom of God, and in their relation to him
are an example of how men should conduct themselves,
5 : 3, 4 ; 101 : 1 sqq.[1]

[1] Cf. notes, and Dillmann, p. xv sqq.

c. Age. — The *terminus ad quem* is the Epistle of Jude, written in the first century after Christ, probably before the destruction of the second temple. This letter not only quotes the book of Enoch, 1 : 9, directly in ver. 14 and 15, but evidently uses it also in ver. 6. Hofmann and Philippi, indeed, claim that an inspired writer could not have cited an apocryphal work, and Jerome says that many regarded Jude as unauthentic, or placed it among the *Antilegomena*, for the same reason. Accordingly Hofmann and Philippi regard the words in Jude as the incitement that occasioned the writing of the apocryphal work. But if Paul could quote from the Gentile poets, it is certainly hard to understand why Jude could not cite a work that was evidently in high standing among the faithful. As, however, Jude quotes the book as a well-known work, its composition must fall quite a number of years before he wrote ; but just when it was composed can only be determined by internal evidences. In chap. 90 the author finishes his survey of the world's history, reaching his own time in 8–13, and passing over prophetically in 14 sqq. It has been shown in the notes that in all probability the " great horn " is not John Hyrcanus, but Judas Maccabi, and that according to the historical account there the book would be written before the death of Judas, in other words, in the midst of the Maccabean struggle. It remains now to be seen whether the other internal evidence, the spirit of the book, best harmonizes with the historical foundation furnished by the events of Judas's time or by those of the reign of John Hyrcanus. It has been shown that the struggle between the conservative and orthodox party of the faithful and the new friends of advanced ideas had reached a certain decided

point, in which the latter are masters and the former
are under their dominion. The Chasidim throughout
appear as a persecuted and abased band, while the sinners enjoy the political power and possess all the wealth
and blessings of the land. In seeking to fix this to the
history of the famous struggle Josephus (Antiqq. xii.
5 sqq.) gives a fitting and appropriate answer. It is the
time of the terrible persecutions under the reign of
Antiochus (IV.) Epiphanes and the uprising of the faithful under the Maccabees. And while the history presupposed in the book entirely suits this period, it does
not at all that of John Hyrcanus. Here the historical
facts were entirely the reverse of what is here demanded.
His reign, an eminently peaceful one, and not "full of
war and rumors of war," as 90 : 8–13 demands, was
one characterized by the rule of the Chasidim over the
sinners. It is a well-known fact that in no period in
the history of Israel, from the exile on, the party that
is represented here as the persecuted, enjoyed such absolute control and such perfect political and religious
freedom as just in this reign, and therefore the guess
at John Hyrcanus is the most unlucky that could be
made. Schürer (p. 117) closes his review of this reign
with the significant words that since the days of David
and Solomon no period had been so glorious and grand.
We can, then, have no hesitancy in saying that a book
prophesying to the faithful what they really then possessed would be without meaning and purpose, while
making it a product of the Maccabean struggle, a word
of encouragement to the little band of the faithful
amidst their trials, can alone explain its origin, object,
and peculiar contents. Just at what time in this period
it was written cannot be decided, but certainly, as chap.

90 shows, before the death of Judas, and after his first victories.

This statement cannot be overthrown with the remark that it would bring its composition too near that of Daniel. Even accepting, what is by no means an absolutely certain result of investigation, that the Book of Daniel was written during the struggle of the Maccabees, this itself does not exclude the composition of Enoch during the same period. This part of the book now under discussion does not, as the Parables so evidently do, show any positively certain dependence on Daniel, not even in the account of the seventy shepherds. There is not one passage of which we can say, as we can of many in 37–71, with a certainty, or even probability, that it has been taken from Daniel. In some respects indeed the general train of thought is the same, as might be expected from two authors writing about the same time and with almost the same object, but the discrepancies and differences are equally apparent.

We are, then, forced to the conclusion that this part of the book was written before the death of Judas in 160 B.C., as from the historical data of that period alone the original character of the work can be intelligently understood, while the pre-eminently peaceful reign of John Hyrcanus, and the prosperity of the faithful during that time, excludes the idea of putting its origin in his days.

d Language. — It is almost universally acknowledged that the book was originally written in a Semitic tongue, either in Hebrew or Aramaic; Volkmar and Philippi alone from their false stand-points maintaining a Greek original. That the generally accepted opinion is the correct one admits scarcely of any doubt. Time, object, and character speak emphatically for its correctness, while the names of the angels, that is of the nonbiblical ones, and the Semitic etymology of the names of the winds in 77 and of the names in 78:1, 2 put the Hebrew or Aramaic original beyond all rational doubt. The book must, then, be regarded as the Hebrew or Aramaic production of a Palestine Jew, written before the year 160 B.C.

§ 5. THE PARABLES, 37–71 (with the exception of the interpolations). *a. Object.* — The intimate connection between the Parables and the Book of Daniel is apparent at a glance, and admits of no rational doubt. The fundamental idea of the canonical writer, who sees in the rulers of his own times the radically opposites of the realized idea of theocratic kings, who must therefore give way to the God-pleasing and predicted Messianic kingdom, is copied throughout by his imitator in the Parables. The enemies this writer must oppose and the sins he must reprove are entirely different from those in the first part. Hence his aim is a different one, although his ultimate object, the prediction of the speedy arrival of the long-promised kingdom, is the same as that of apocryphal writers in general, and of the author of the first part also. His polemics are no longer directed against the class of sinners in general, but are particularly directed against the kings and the powerful, 38 : 4, 5 ; 46 : 4 ; 48 : 8 ; 53 : 5 ; 55 : 4 ; 62 : 1, 3, 6, 9 ; 63 : 1, 12, etc. Occasionally, indeed, they are accused of injustice and actual persecution, 46 : 7 ; 47 : 4 ; but this state of affairs has by no means the prominence that it occupies in the first part. This, too, will explain the fact that in the judgment to come over the sinners the period of the sword is not only not emphasized, as in the first part, but there is even some doubt whether the author teaches such a period at all. The passages that might be interpreted in this direction, 38 : 5 ; 39 : 2 ; 48 : 9 ; 46 : 4 sq.; 50 : 2, could all be well understood as referring in general to the overthrow and destruction of the sinners in the last judgment. The crimes of the author's enemies are of a bloodless character and centre in the great one of atheism ; not in a sin against the children of God, which is the basis of the first part, but rather in a sin against God himself. For they deny the Lord of the spirits, 38 : 2 ; 41 : 2 ; 45 : 1, 2 ; 46 : 7 ; 48 : 10 (cf. 43 : 4 ; 63 : 4–8), and a heavenly world, 45 : 1, and the Messiah, 48 : 10 (and the Spirit of God, 67 : 10, and the just judgment, 60 : 6). Hence, too, they rely on their wealth and are idolaters, 46 : 7 ; and in their confession, 63 : 1 sqq., they acknowledge that their cardinal sin and the ground of their condemnation was their failure to acknowledge God as their King and Lord, that they had placed their hope in their own power, and had not admitted that this power was from God. The author then directs his words against the doings of the aristocratic class among his people, who have deserted the God of the fathers and departed from the hope of Israel. The connection between the author's ideas and the Old Testament idea of royalty, especially as laid down in the books since the days of David and Solomon, is apparent. The kings of Israel were not to be merely political figure-heads but were, as theocratical rulers, the instruments and deputies of God, ruling the people in his name and in his spirit. They had, then, a religious as well as a political aim to follow, and they, conse-

quently, above all others, were called upon to aid in
the development of Israel to that ultimate aim, the realization of the promises given it in the glorious
kingdom of the Messiah.[1] In the fulfilment of this
theocratic object, the rulers, in the author's days, had
signally failed ; instead of being the leaders of the
faith and hope of Israel, the royalty and aristocracy
had become the home of rationalism and infidelity.
The perception of this fact, that there was " corruption
in high places," will explain the peculiar apology of
the writer, the judgment, the pre-eminently royal and
judicial character of the Messiah, and the final punishment of the sinners. Historically, the status here
presupposed is easily understood. The Asmoneans,
although originally faithful adherents of the religion of
Jehovah, soon after the assumption of royalty departed
from the path of the Maccabean heroes. With the
single exception of Alexandra (78–69 B.C.) all the rulers
from Aristobulus I. (105–104 B.C.) were wicked and
godless, by no means realizing what an earnest Jew
might expect from theocratic rulers. This, too, makes
clear the author's object. Over against the infidel
rulers and the unjust rule of his day he maintains the
speedy coming of the chosen ruler of God, $\kappa\alpha\tau$᾿ $\dot{\epsilon}\xi o\chi\acute{\eta}\nu$,
the Messiah and his rule of justice and peace. He pre-
dicts the downfall of false royalty and its unbelieving
adherents, and the establishment of the true God-
pleasing royalty through the Messiah as the head of
the congregation of saints.

   b. *The Messiah.*—The contents centre in the Messiah,
as the proper theocratic counterpart of a false royalty,

<hr />

[1] Cf. on this subject, on which we cannot enter more minutely here,
the article of Diestel, in *Jahrbücher f. Deutsche Theol.*, viii. 3, pp. 536–587.

and the Parables could well be called the book of the Messiah. The chief interest of the book lies in his person and object. It has been a constant dispute among investigators whether the Messiah here is a Christian or a Jewish one, the latter position being generally held by older investigators, the former by the later ones. The first glance may speak with some probability for a Christian origin, but a closer examination necessitates the acceptance of a Jewish source. This conclusion is already made probable by the general character of the Messiah as the embodiment of the true theocratic idea of the Old Testament royalty, and he is thus to be the realization of a pre-eminently Jewish hope. The positive statements of the book make this probability a certainty. The most important remark concerning the person of the Messiah is found 48 : 3, where it is stated that before the sun and the signs and the stars were made his name had been called before the Lord of the spirits; and, 48 : 6, it is said that he was chosen and hidden before the world was created, and was hidden, 62 : 6, 7, but preserved and revealed to the just, 48 : 7; 62 : 7. It is further stated that he "had arisen," 49 : 2; 51 : 5, or "appeared," 52 : 9; 38 : 2, and was "revealed," 69 : 26. The author here does not teach simply a predestination, but a pre-existence, or rather a pre-mundane existence, of the Messiah. For by his words "before the world" and "before the creation of the sun" the author shows that he does not teach a pre-existence from eternity in an absolute and metaphysical sense, without a beginning or origin, but only in the sense in which מֵעוֹלָם is used in Hebrew, from a time the limit of which is for the writer object-

ively beyond the horizon of his vision.[1] The **writer,**
who manifestly does not desire to give an exhaustive
treatise on the person of the Messiah, has a special object in emphasizing the pre-existence. By stating that
the author of the glorious times to come is now already
prepared, and has been so before the creation of the
world, he does not desire simply to vindicate the certainty of the fulfilment of his prophecy, but rather, by
ascribing this supernatural character to the Messiah,
lays stress on the fact that he will *be able* to judge and
condemn even the powerful kings. That the *ability* of
the Messiah to carry out what is here stated of him is a
thesis that the author must establish beyond all doubt,
is only too manifest from 55 : 4. In thus ascribing
pre-existence to the Messiah, the author does nothing
more than is done in other respects by apocryphal
writers in general. These frequently, in order to emphasize the religious importance of a person, or even of
a thing, ascribe to him or it a pre-existence or an arche-
type in heaven. Thus *Assumptio Mosis*, i. 14, Moses
speaks of himself *qui ab initio orbis terrarum prae-
paratus sum,* and Baruch, *Apoc.* iv. speaks of Jerusalem
as having been shown to Adam before he sinned, and
the book of the Jubilees remarks that the Sabbath was
kept by the angels before it was revealed to man, and
Assumptio Mosis, i. 17, speaks of the temple as a place
quem fecit ab initio creaturae orbis terrarum. A reflex
of this idea is found in early Christian literature, where
pre-existence is ascribed to the church in *Hermae Pastor,* Vis. ii. 4, 2 *Clem.* 14.[2] Yet it is not even necessary

---

[1] Cf. Orelli, *Heb. Synonyma der Zeit und Ewigkeit,* p. 69 sqq.

[2] On this whole matter cf. Harnack's notes on these two passages in the new edition of the *Patres Apostolici.*

to go to the post-biblical literature of the Jews for the development of the idea of pre-existence. The kernel, yes, the idea itself, we find already in one canonical book that has been extensively used by our author. In Prov. viii. 22–31, the personified wisdom speaks of itself as pre-existent and is thus conceived in En. 42. It is even probable that the different expressions with which the pre-existence of the Messiah is decribed are imitations of those in Prov. viii. The statement that the Messiah was before the sun and stars were made finds its parallel in Prov. viii. 27, where wisdom is said to have been there " when he prepared the heavens; " and the words that the Messiah was before the creation of the world find their parallel in Prov. viii. 22–26. The connection between the pre-existent Messiah of Enoch and the pre-existent Wisdom of Proverbs is strengthened by the fact that it is stated of him that he has the spirit of wisdom, 49 : 3, and in his days the fountains of wisdom shall flow and the just drink from them, 48 : 1 ; 49 : 1, as well as by the use of the word נִסַּכְתִּי, *unctus sum*,[1] in Prov. viii. 23, which corresponds to one of the classical appellations of this supernatural being, i.e. the name Messiah.[2] But if the occurrence of pre-existence can cause no surprise when found in a work like the Parables, which are based upon close exegetical study of the Old Testament, and if the author possibly received some of the embellishments of the idea from Prov. viii., the idea itself he did not get there. If it can be stated as a fact that the Parables in general are closely connected with the Book of

---

[1] Cf. Gesenius, *Thes.*, p. 890.

[2] The pre-existence of wisdom is also spoken of in a weakened sense in Sirach i 4 ; xxiv. 9. Cf. also Mal iii. 1 ; Isa. vi. 1 ; Bertholdt, *Christol.* p. 131.

Daniel, this can be said to be especially true concerning
the Messianic idea.   Whatever may be the final conviction of critics concerning the one " who was like a Son
of man," Dan. vii. 13, whether, on the basis of ver. 18,
22, 27, he is to be regarded as the embodiment of the
ideal Israel, or to be considered as the personal Messiah,
so much is absolutely certain that for our author, as
46 : 1 sqq. shows beyond all doubt, he was the personal
Messiah.   With this established, the source of the idea
of pre-existence is given ;   it is a development from
Dan. vii. 13.   The sudden appearance there indicated
an existence before that time, and the coming in the
clouds with the Ancient of days pointed to a supernatural being, and thus the author's exegesis on that passage finds expression in ascribing pre-existence to the
Messiah, and is a legitimate conclusion from the premises there given.   And then our author bases his description of the Messiah, to a great extent, on Isaiah
and Micah, the two prophets who, more than others,
emphasize the personality of the Messiah and allow their
descriptions to go beyond that which is terrestrial in
both his person and his work.   For that the עבד יהוה of
Isa. xl.–lxvi. is for the author of the Parables, probably,
no one else but the personal Messiah seems to be clear
from many passages.[1]   And as eternal existence in the
future is frequently ascribed to the Messiah and his
kingdom in the Old Testament, the step to eternity in
the past is easily made.   The eternity *a parte post*
easily suggests the pre-existence *a parte ante*, and is a
process actually gone through in En. 49 : 2, where his
glory from eternity is placed in juxtaposition with his
power to all generations, and the two are placed on a

[1] Cf e g. note on 48 : 4.

level. And should there still be any doubt that the author stands on Old Testament ground this will be dispelled by a reference to Micah v. 1 (Heb.), where it is said of the Messiah that his going forth is from of old, from everlasting. Certainly the word there used, קדם, is rather *priscus* (with which it corresponds etymologically) than *antiquus*,[1] but being placed parallel here, as in other passages, with מִימֵי עוֹלָם it is evident in what sense the author understood it. As to the supernatural character of the Messiah, it is, then, not only not necessary to go to the New Testament and Christianity for an explanation, but it is even unlawful to do so, as the idea was developed from Dan. vii. 13, and is justified by an exegesis of other passages in the Old Testament.

Although the nature of the Messiah is thus of a supernatural character, and transcends that which is purely human, he is far from being equal to God. The author is very particular to state that he holds his office and performs his functions under the command and authority of God and in his name. He has been chosen by God for this special work, and is his deputy; cf. 45 : 4 ; 46 : 3 ; 48 : 6 ; 49 : 4 ; 51 : 3 ; 55 : 4 ; 61 : 8 ; 69 : 27 ; 71 : 17, etc., and is thus in reality a "servant of God" (Isa. xl.–lxvi.) In him, then, the theocratic idea of royalty, that the true king of Israel is ambassador and vicegerent of God — an idea which the regents of the author's days, through their selfishness and impiety, had deserted — shall be realized. In no passage is divine honor bestowed on him. In 40 : 5 he is indeed praised by an angel, but as the chosen ones are there placed in the same category with the Chosen One, it is evident that nothing but the glorifica-

[1] Cf. Orelli, l.c., p. 76.

tion of the Messianic kingdom, in head and members, is there meant; and in one passage where the sinners are arraigned for not glorifying the Chosen One we must find a parallel to the passage where they deny the Anointed, 48 : 10, i.e. both passages indicate one phase in the general unbelief in the world to come.

The Messiah appears under different names, some of which are taken from the Old Testament, and the rest owe their origin to the special work assigned to him in the Parables. He is called the Just or Righteous One, 38 : 2; 53 : 6; the Chosen One, the title most frequently used (cf. note on 40 : 5); Son of man, 46 : 2, 3, etc.; the Anointed, 48 : 10; 52 : 4; and once the Son of the woman, 62 : 5. None of these, when considered as coming from a Jewish source, occasion any difficulty, with the exception of the last. It is claimed that the union of the divine and the human here presupposed could not have been made by any one before the coming of Christ into the flesh, that consequently this name proves a Christian origin.[1] The objection would be valid if we had a right to suppose the author understood a ὁμοουσία or a θεανθρωπία by this term. But the case is different; it is manifestly a name that is to be regarded as a parallel to the frequently-used appellation, Son of man, which the author, as 46 : 1–3 conclusively shows, has taken from Dan. vii. 13. If the expression "Son of the woman" proves a Christian origin, we have a right to claim the same thing of the expression "Son of man" in Daniel—a conclusion that would certainly be most uncritical. The case is very similar to Micah v. 1, where it is said of the Messiah that, although being from everlasting, he shall nevertheless

[1] The last to use this objection was Drummond, p. 60.

come forth, i.e. be born in Bethlehem. The pre-existent being is still to be earth-born. And if Daniel's and Micah's expressions can be regarded as within the bounds of the Old Testament, it is difficult to see why a post-canonical writer should not be able to use the same or similar expressions.

This supernatural Messiah shall appear and inaugurate the long-expected kingdom of glory. It had already been revealed, i.e. by the prophets to the righteous, 48: 7; 62: 6, 7, and was their hope, 48: 4, and they believed in him. They shall form the congregation of the holy, 38: 3; 39: 1; 53 : 6; 62 : 8. It is held by many that in the Old Testament Messianic prophecies the chief interest does not centre in the person of the Messiah, but in the Messianic kingdom, and this idea may be correct. That it should be so is easily understood from the character of the Israelites, who knew themselves to be the children of God and the bearers of his promises. In this respect our author is a true Jew; his main object is the same that apocryphal writers in general have — the announcement of the speedy realization of the promises given of old; and the Messiah's importance lies in the fact that he is to be the medium through which this realization shall take place, and after that shall be the prince and ruler of the established new kingdom. And as this establishment is in the first place of such prime importance, the person of its medium is dwelt so largely upon. But that the kingdom itself, the time when Israel shall rule in glory, is the chief object of the writer seems to be clear from the first Parable, which shows that the first and great news the author has to announce is the appearance of the congregation of the holy. This appearance is simultaneous with the

appearance of the Messiah, and is so intimately connected with him and his work that an account of these
is also virtually a record of the fate of the former.
The congregation of the holy is represented as already
existing in heaven, like its head, the Messiah, and
both shall appear in the proper time. The author
assures his readers that both the kingdom and its head
are already realities, and their appearance is only a
question of time. This spiritualistic view evinces a
mind of speculative tendencies, and is a product of the
continued disappointed hope of Israel, and a strong
apology for the promises of God. Just when this kingdom and king shall appear the author nowhere definitely states ; but it is evident from the fact that the
rulers against whom he speaks shall be surprised by
their coming, that the immediate future is the time.
This is also clear from the statements that the saints
contemporaneous with the author shall see them coming.
But when the prophecy is realized, the first work of the
Messiah shall be to exercise a just judgment. He is
κατ᾽ ἐξοχήν, judge. This fact has induced some, and
among them Holtzmann, to claim a Christian origin
for the Messiah here taught, as the Old Testament nowhere, while repeatedly attributing royal and even
priestly and prophetic attributes to the Messiah, ever
represents him as judge, whereas this is one of the chief
offices of Christ in the New Testament. The difficulty
is, however, more seeming than real. The Messiah is
the realized ideal of a theocratic king, and as the royal
and judicial power were united in the Old Testament,
and are to this day in the Semitic nations of the Orient,
the Messiah could easily be conceived as a judge. The
emphasis laid on this peculiar trait is explained by the

fact that it was a matter of importance to the author to show that, above all things, the wicked and godless kings, as the chief obstruction to the development of the Messianic kingdom, should be judged and condemned. The state of affairs in his days necessitated the attributing pre-eminently of the office of judge to the Messiah The hearts of the faithful longed for a punishment of the wicked rulers, and this longing finds expression in the judicial character of the Coming One. The judgment that shall come is to be held in a purely forensic spirit. It is universal, embracing both righteous and unrighteous, 62 : 3, and even the dead shall rise for this purpose, 51 : 1. That, however, this universality is not an absolute one, but restricted to those who took part, either as friends or foes, in the affairs of Israel, is not only clear from the general character of the book, whose horizon in this respect does not go beyond the pale of Israel on earth, but also from the fact that after the establishment of the kingdom it shall grow and increase by the addition of the hitherto neutral nationalities around, 52 : 4 sqq.; 57 : 1 sqq. The same idea underlies 50 : 2, where some of the sinners, on the basis of repentance, shall be received. The criterion according to which the Messiah will judge is the deeds done in the flesh, for the deeds of all are weighed, 41 : 1; 61 : 8. The first to be judged are the fallen angels, 55 : 3, 4, and then the sinners. Both shall be condemned to be destroyed by fire, 48 : 9. But, unlike the first part, the place of condemnation (for there is but one) is certainly not Gehenna. The sinners are to be destroyed, 53 : 5; 56 : 4, and expelled, 38 : 1, removed from the face of the earth, 45 : 6, and will be neither in heaven nor on earth, 45 : 2, 5; 53 : 2, and darkness and worms will be their dwelling-place, 46:6. Geographically, this place of torture, called a burning valley, 54:1, 2, or an oven of fire, 54:6, is not located, but seems to correspond to the place for the fallen angels in the first part. After the removal of the wicked rulers by the angels of punishment (cf. above p. 30), a period of peace shall be inaugurated, 53:7, and the new kingdom shall centre in Jerusalem, 56:6, 7, and it shall repel the last assault of the enemies, 56:1 sqq. The moral character of the kingdom is strictly such as could be expected from an Old Testament basis. The ruler is endowed with all the characteristics desirable in a theocratic king, whose rule is, if anything, a just one; and the ruled shall partake of great blessings, 39:4, 7; 51:5; 48:1; 58:1 sqq., etc., which shall be both physical, 45:4, 5, and ethical. The angels shall dwell with them, 39:1, also the Chosen One, 62:14, and the risen righteous shall take part, 51:2 sqq. The kingdom shall become powerful, 52:4, and all the nations shall take part in it, 57:3, and its members shall be clothed with the garments of (eternal) life, 62:16, and there shall be nothing perishable in it, 69:29, and hence the kingdom is eternal, 71:17, etc. That the above picture of the Messiah and his kingdom can be perfectly well understood from Old Testament premises, in fact, has been drawn from them exclusively, is our earnest conviction, and in this opinion we stand with Ewald, Dillmann, Anger, Langen, Schürer, and others, while Hilgenfeld, Kuenen, Tideman, Vernes, and Drummond claim a Christian origin. But this latter is encumbered with the greatest of difficulties. Schürer has very correctly drawn attention to the fact that a Christian would certainly not have passed over the person of the historical Christ without mentioning his death or resurrection. Drummond has felt the full weight of this difficulty, and therefore invents his curious theory of a Christian interpolation. He sees very well that the whole idea and contents of the Parables place it beyond doubt that they are a Jewish production, but he is unwilling to sacrifice his idea of a Christian Messiah. But here the same difficulties meet him; a Christian interpolater would certainly, as little as a Christian author, have avoided the references to Christ which we have a right, from the nature of the case and from the analogy of other interpolators, to expect. When he tries (p. 61) to excuse this by saying " that an interpolator would be careful not to depart too widely from the character of the book in which he made his insertions," this must be regarded as entirely too flat. His foundation of sand will not bear the superstructure of theory he has built on it. Interpolators are not so delicate concerning their insertions, as many interpolations, e.g. the Christian ones in the *Sibylla* and the *Ascensio Isaiae*, conclusively show

The idea, too, of the kingdom is so peculiarly Jewish that it excludes every notion of a Christian source. The Messiah comes but once, and then to judge, and before that time he was hidden. But a Christian, who knew of the historical Christ, could not ignore his first coming, and say that Christ was hidden until he should come to judge. Even had he been a Chiliast, knowing that Christ had once come, an event of prime importance to all Christians, whether orthodox or heterodox, he could not have passed over in silence the first coming. But our author, like all Jewish writers, knows only of one coming of the Messiah, and that in glory.

Everything before that time belongs to חצילם הוה, while his coming shall inaugurate the הציולם הבא, but for a Christian this latter period had already commenced with the first coming into the flesh. Then it must not be overlooked that the question concerning the relation between God and the Messiah, as to the nature of the latter, is treated in no place whatever in the Parables, while in the early church that was *the* question around which all interest centred. There is no phase of orthodoxy or heterodoxy in the early Christian church in which we could find a place for the Messiah of the Parables.

The conclusion, then, is that it is not only improbable but even impossible to give a rational explanation of the Messianic idea here developed by accepting a Christian source, while it is perfectly intelligible from a Jewish origin, and must be attributed to such.

c. Age.— In trying to determine when the Parables were written we are again restricted to internal evidences alone. The only place where an historical event could be regarded as having been before the eyes of the writer is the prophesied invasion of the Parthians and Medes in 56:5 sqq. It has been argued that the author here had in his mind the invasion of Parthians, 40–38 B.C., that consequently the book was not written until soon after that time, and that the time of composition would then fall somewhere in the reign of Herod the Great, 37–4 B.C. But the allusion here is so vague that it does not necessarily rest on an armed invasion into Palestine, but seems rather to be developed from a general idea that these nations were at that time formidable, and thus the author in seeking for the last enemies, who in apocryphal systems occupy a place of prominence, selects these. The possibility, however, that the author does refer to this historical fact cannot be denied, as other things point to the composition of the Parables about the time of Herod. The author's complaints of the untheocratic and impious character of the rulers and the aristocratic class of his day can best be explained from his period. It is a well-known fact that Herod, as an alien and not a true Jew, was a thorn in the eyes of the true Israelites, while his introduction and encouragement not only of Hellenistic culture, but even of strange gods, and his alliance with the free-thinking wealthy class of the Sadducees, made him perfectly detestable. His government, in the eyes of all the faithful, was justly considered one that was the exact opposite of what it should be according to the Old Testament idea of royalty, and consequently it was endured with murmurings that found expression in conspiracy.[1] From such a historical basis, the origin of the Parables as well as the peculiar eschatological prophecies in them, especially the character of the Messiah, finds a suitable explanation, and it would probably not be far from the truth to say that they were written some time during his or his immediate successor's reign. This conclusion must of course be regarded as a probable one only, since it is simply impossible to come to anything like a certainty as long as we have no better indices of the time of writing than are at our disposal at present.

d. Language. — The object, character, and readers of the Parables make it probable that they are a Hebrew or Aramaic production written in Palestine. Their Semitic original is also vouched for by the Noachic fragments. These, themselves written in He-

[1] Cf Joseph. *Antiqq.* xv. 8 3-4.

brew or Aramaic, have used the Parables extensively, something that would not have been done if 37–71 had been written in Greek.

§ 6. THE NOACHIC FRAGMENTS, 54 : 7–55 : 2 ; 60 ; 65–69 : 25 ; 106–107. The object which these additions have is clear from their contents. In the rest of the book the final judgment had been sufficiently dwelt upon ; but the first, that of the flood, had simply been prophesied, but not recorded. To supply this deficiency these fragments were added. And as Noah was the chief person in this judgment, he is made the medium of revelation, an office he holds by virtue of his piety, Gen. vi. 1 sqq. In addition to the account of the flood and matters related to it, the author dwells on the various secrets of nature, and by his cabalistic manner and fanciful explanations[1] forms a strange contrast to the rest of the book. He evidently seeks to imitate the author of the Parables, as the use of such expressions as " Ancient of Days," " Satans," " Angels of punishment," " Son of man " (used of Noah, 60 : 10), the special citation of the Parables, 68 : 1, and other things sufficiently show. As to the time of composition nothing definite can be said, only that it is a Jewish work, without the least indication of a post-Christian origin, not even in 67 : 7 sqq.[2] The language is, as the names of the angels, 69 : 2 sqq. and the different etymologies of the name Noah in 106–107 show, either Hebrew or Aramaic.

As to a precise determination of the time when these different parts were united into one book of Enoch, no one could come to a decision, as this would have only the merit of a conjecture.

[1] Cf. Notes.   [2] Cf. Notes.

THE BOOK OF ENOCH.

SECTION I.

CHAP. 1. — The words of the blessing of Enoch where-with he blessed the chosen and just, who will exist on the day of tribulation when all the wicked and impious shall be removed. 2. And *then* answered and spoke Enoch, a just man, whose eyes were opened by God so that he saw a holy vision in the heavens, which the angels showed to me, and from them I heard everything, and I knew what I saw, but not for this generation, but for the far-off generations which are to come. 3. Concerning the chosen I spoke and conversed concerning them with the Holy and Great One, who will come from his abode, the God of the world. 4. And from there he will step on to Mount Sinai, and appear with his hosts, and appear in the strength of his power from heaven. 5. And all will fear, and the watchers will tremble, and great fear and terror will seize them to the ends of the earth. 6. And the exalted mountains will be shaken, and the high hills will be lowered, and will melt like wax before the flame. 7. And the earth will be submerged, and everything that is on the earth will be destroyed, and there will be a judgment upon every thing, and upon all the just. 8. But to the just he will give peace, and will protect the chosen, and mercy will abide over them, and they will all be God's, and will be prosperous and blessed, and the light of God will shine for them. 9. And behold, he comes with myriads of the holy to pass judgment upon them, and will destroy the impious, and will call to account all flesh for everything the sinners and the impious have done and committed against him.

CHAP. 2. — I observed everything that took place in the heavens, how the luminaries, which are in the heavens, do not depart from their paths, that each one rises and sets in order, each in its time, and they do not depart from their laws. 2. See the earth and observe the things that are done on it, from the first to the last, how no work of God is irregular in appearing. 3. See the summer and the winter, how *then* the whole earth is full of water, and clouds and dew and rain rest over it.

CHAP. 3. — I observed and saw how *then* all the trees appeared as if withered, and all their leaves are shaken off, except fourteen trees, whose leaves are not shaken off, *but* which abide with the old from two to three years, till the new come.

CHAP. 4. — And again I observed the days of summer, how the sun is *then* above it [i.e. the earth], opposite to it, but ye seek cool and shady places on account of the heat of the sun, and the earth also burns with fervent heat, but ye cannot step on the earth or on a rock because of their heat.

CHAP. 5. — I observed how the trees cover themselves with the green of the leaves and bear fruit; but observe ye all this and learn how he who lives forever has made all these for you ; 2. how his works are before him in every year that comes, and all his works serve him and are not changed, but as God has ordained, so everything takes place. 3. And see how the seas and the rivers together accomplish their work. 4. But ye have not persevered and have not done the commandment of the Lord, but have transgressed, and have slandered his greatness with high and hard words from your unclean mouths. Ye hard-hearted, ye will have no peace. 5. And therefore ye will curse your days, and the years of your lives perish ; the everlasting curse will increase and ye will receive no mercy. 6. On that day ye will give away your peace for an everlasting curse to all the just, and they will ever curse you as sinners, you together with the sinners. 7. But for the chosen there will be light and joy and peace, and they will inherit the earth, but for you, the impious, there will be a curse. 8. And then also wisdom will be given to the chosen, and they will all live and not continue to sin ; neither through wickedness nor through pride ; *but* they in whom there is wisdom will be humble without continuing to sin. 9. And they will not be punished all the days of their lives, and will not die through plagues or *judgments of* wrath, but the number of the days of their lives will be completed, and their lives will become old in peace, and the years of their joy will be many in everlasting happiness and peace, for all the days of their lives.

Chapters 1 to 5 contain the author's introduction to his book, i.e. to 1–36 and 72–105.

CHAP. 1, 1 gives the superscription. *The blessing of Enoch is* here introduced like the blessing of Moses over Israel before his death (Deut. xxxiii. 1). The writer proposes a double object — to announce the blessed condition of the just on the day of the final judgment, and the destruction of the sinners. The former is the more important object; and therefore he announces it first, and adds the second in a subordinate manner. The *removal* of the sinners is not their annihilation, but, as will soon appear, their removal from the earth to the place of punishment.— 2. Cf. Num. xxiv. 3, 4, 15. Apocryphal writers claim inspiration for their works, and thus seek to put a *pia fraus* on a level with the canonical books. The character and source of the vision entitles it to the appellation *holy*. The sudden change from the third to the first person is not rare in this book; cf. 12 : 1–3 (37 : 1, 2; 70 : 1–3; 71 : 6); 92 : 1; 108 : 4. Changes of similar character are found Gen. xxii. 12; Isa. i. 29; iii. 26; v. 8; xxii. 16; xxxi. 7; xlii. 20; in Gr. Thucyd. i. 128, 7; Xen. *Hell.* 5, 1, 31; and frequently in the Koran. The difference here noted between *this generation* and *the far-off generations* is not the הזה העולם and the העולם הבא, which in later Jewish theology designate the strictly pre and post Messianic times, but in general terms designates those that will live "in the days of the sinners."— 3. The speaking and conversing with God is the author's interpretation of Gen. v. 24. The designation of God as the Holy and the Great One is strictly confined to this portion of the book, and is found neither in the Parables nor in the Noachic fragments; cf. 10 : 1; 14 : 1; 25 : 3; 84 : 1; 92 : 2; 97 : 6; 98 : 6; 104 : 9; simply *Holy*, 93 : 11; and *Great*, 14 : 2; *God of the world*, 12 : 3; 81 : 10; 84 : 2, and once in the Parables 58 : 4. *He will come from his abode*, which, like Isa. xxvi. 21; Mic. i. 3, indicates him as coming to judge. — 4. *Sinai*, as the mount from which the law was given, will be the place upon which the Lord will descend to judge according to this law; cf. Deut. xxxiii. 2; Ps. lxviii. 17. God, who as יהיה צבאות is the God of the heavenly hosts (cf. Delitzsch, *Zeitschrift für luth. Theol. u. K.*, 1874, p. 217–222), is here accompanied by his host, who assist in the judgment, 1 : 9;

10 : 4 ; 90 : 21 ; 100 : 4 ; cf. also 1 Kings xxii. 19 ; Ps. ciii. 21.
— 5. *Watchers*, cf. notes on chap. 12–16. *Them*, i.e. the
inhabitants of the earth ; cf. Jer. xxv. 30, 31. *Ends of the
earth*, Isa. xlii. 10 ; Ps. lxxii. 8 ; 1 Sam. ii. 10 ; Ps. xxii. 27 ;
lxvii. 7 ; xcviii. 3 ; Isa. xlv. 22 ; lii. 10 ; Zech. ix. 10. — 6. Cf.
Ps. xviii. 7 ; xcvii. 5 ; Hab. iii. 6 ; Judith xvi. 15. These
sentiments expressed similarly in *Assumptio Mosis*, c. 10. —
7. Here the two judgments, the temporary one or the deluge,
and the final one, are blended into one, just as in 10 : 15 sqq.
the period after the deluge and the Messianic times are combined. — 8. The blessedness of the just is not a reward for their
firmness, but, as is taught in the Old Testament, a gift of God.
The שלום is the highest degree of bliss. God's light shines
for them, 38 : 2, and often, similar to Dan. xii. 3 ; cf. Isa.
ii. 5 ; li. 4 ; Prov. vi. 23 ; Ps. cxix. 105. — 9. *The myriads of
angels*, more minutely explained 14 : 22 ; 40 : 1 ; 71 : 8, 13,
are like those in Dan. vii. 10. All flesh shall be judged, Jer.
xxv. 31. This is the verse that is quoted in a free manner in
the Epistle of Jude 14 and 15.

CHAP. 2, 1. Solomon directs the sluggard to the animal
kingdom ; Enoch, the sinners to the inanimate, as could be
expected from an author who knows the secrets of nature, and
writes a "book of the luminaries," 72–82. *These* obey God's
laws, but rational man does not ; cf. Ps. civ. 19 ; Eccl. i. 5. A
similar contrast is found in *Testamentum Naphtali*. — 3. The
division of the year into two seasons is after the manner of the
Old Testament ; cf. Gen. viii. 22 ; Ps. lxxiv. 17 ; Isa. xviii. 6.

CHAP. 3. What fourteen evergreen trees are here meant is
uncertain. Cf. Dillmann ad loc.

CHAP. 4. *Opposite*, i.e. in such a position that the heat can
be best felt.

CHAP. 5, 1. *For you*, i.e. for your instruction. — 4. Cf. Isa.
1–3. Here he applies the lesson of the preceding. *Blaspheme*,
or *slander* is a sin often rebuked in this portion of the
book ; cf. 27 : 2 ; 81 : 8 ; 91 : 7, 11 ; 94 : 9 ; 96 : 7 ; 97 6 ;
98 : 15 ; 99 : 1 ; 100 : 9 ; 101 : 3 ; but is not mentioned

6*

in 37–71; cf. Ps. xii. 4; Dan. vii. 8, 11, 20; Ps. cxxxix. 20, etc. — 5. Their unhappy fate will induce them to curse their day as Job did when in misfortune, Job iii. 1 sqq.; Jer. xx. 14. — 6. The just who had been oppressed by the sinners will curse them in the last times. *You together with the sinners,* i.e. you and the other sinners. — 7. The author's doctrine of retribution stands substantially on the Old Testament basis; for the reward for steadfastness consists in the blessings of this world; cf. Ex. xx. 12; Lev. xxv. 18, 19; xxvi. 4 sqq.; Deut. iv. 40; v. 33; vi. 18 sqq.; 1 Chron. xxviii. 8; Ps. xxv. 13; xxxvii. 19; lxix. 35, 36; Isa. lvii. 13; lxv. 9; Ezek. xxiii. 24–26. — 8. The wisdom to be given to the just in the Messianic kingdom plays an important role in this part, and is one of the characteristics of the glorious time, 91 : 10; 93 : 10. Its throne is God's throne, 84 : 3; and is personified, 91 : 10; and what he means by the word can be seen from 93 : 8, where forgetting wisdom is synonymous with departure from the divine law. In the Parables it is not a distinctive feature of the just or of the Messianic kingdom, but is an attribute of the Messiah himself, 49 : 3. The Messianic times will be free from sin, 92 : 5, — a moral perfection, as is found Isa. iv. 3; xi. 9; xxxii. 1–6; 15–18. — 9. Old age, according to the Old Testament idea, was a special blessing, Gen. xv. 15; xlvii. 9; Ex. xx. 12; Job v. 26; xiv. 5; and as a blessing of the Messianic times, Isa. lxv. 20, 22; Zech. viii. 4; and especially Isa. xxv. 8. Taught also in the book of the Jubilees.

SECTION II.

CHAP. 6. — And it came to pass, after the children of men had increased in those days, beautiful and comely daughters were born to them. 2. And the angels, the sons of the heavens, saw and lusted after them, and said one to another: " Behold, we will choose for ourselves wives from among the children of men, and will beget for ourselves children." 3. And Semjâzâ, who was their leader, said to them : " I fear that perhaps ye will not be willing to do this deed, and I alone shall suffer for this great sin." 4. Then all answered him and said : " We all will swear an oath, and bind ourselves mutually by a curse, that we will not give up this plan, but will make this plan a deed." 5. Then they all swore together, and bound themselves mutually by a curse ; and together they were two hundred. 6. And they descended on Ardîs, which is the summit of Mount Hermon ; and they called it Mount Hermon, because they had sworn on it and bound themselves mutually by a curse. 7. And these are the names of their leaders : Semjâzâ, who was their leader, Urâkibarâmêêl, Akibêêl, Tâmiêl, Râmuêl, Dânêl, Ezêqêêl, Sarâqujâl, Asâêl, Armers, Batraal, Anânî, Zaqêbê, Samsâvêêl, Sartaêl, Turêl, Jomjâêl, Arâzjâl. 8. These are the leaders of the two hundred angels, and the others all were with them.

CHAP. 7.—And they took unto themselves wives, and each chose for himself one, and they began to go in to them, and mixed with them, and taught them charms and conjurations, and made them acquainted with the cutting of roots and of woods. 2. And they became pregnant and brought forth great giants whose stature was three thousand ells. 3. These devoured all the acquisitions of mankind till men were unable to sustain themselves. 4. And the giants turned themselves against mankind in order to devour them. 5. And they began to sin against the birds and the beasts, and against the creeping things, and the fish, and devoured their flesh among themselves, and drank the blood thereof. 6. Then the earth complained of the unjust ones.

CHAP. 8.—And Azâzêl taught mankind to make

swords and knives and shields and coats of mail, and taught them to see what was behind them, and their works of art: bracelets and ornaments, and the use of rouge, and the beautifying of the eye-brows, and the dearest and choicest stones and all coloring substances and the metals of the earth. 2. And there was great wickedness and much fornication, and they sinned, and all their ways were corrupt. 3. Amêzârâk taught all the conjurers and root-cutters, Armârôs the loosening of conjurations, Baraq'âl the astrologers, Kôkâbêl the signs, and Temêl taught astrology, and Asrâdêl taught the course of the moon. 4. And in the destruction of mankind, they cried aloud, and their voices reached heaven.

Chap. 9. — Then Michael and Gabriel and Surjân and Urjân looked down from heaven and saw the great amount of blood which had been spilled on the earth, and all the wickedness which had been committed over the earth. 2. And they said to one another: "The emptied earth re-echoes the sound of their [i.e. mankind's] cries up to the gates of heaven. 3. And now to you, O ye holy ones of heaven, cry the souls of men, saying: 'Secure us judgment before the Most High.' 4. And they spoke to their Lord, to the King: 'O Lord of lords, God of gods, King of kings, the throne of thy majesty is among all the generations of the world, and thy name, holy and glorious, among all the generations of the world. Thou art blessed and praised! 5. Thou hast made all things and all power is with thee, all things are open before thee and uncovered, and thou seest all things and nothing can hide itself from thee. 6. See then what Azâzêl has done, how he has taught all wickedness on earth and has revealed the secrets of the world which were prepared in the heavens. 7. And Semjâzâ to whom thou hast given the power to be chief of his associates has made known conjurations. 8. And they have gone together to the daughters of men and have slept with them, with those women, and have defiled themselves, and have revealed to them these sins. 9. And the women have brought forth giants, and thereby the whole earth has been filled with blood and wickedness. 10. And now, behold, the souls which have died cry and lament to the gates of heaven, and their groans ascend, and they are not able to escape from the wickedness which is committed on the earth. 11. And thou knowest everything before it comes to pass, and thou knowest this and their circumstances, and yet thou dost not speak to us. What shall we therefore do in regard to this?"

CHAP. 10. — Then the Most High, the Great and Holy One, spoke and sent Arsjalâljûr to the son of Lamech, and said to him: 2. "Tell him in my name: 'Hide thyself!' and reveal to him the end which is to come. For the whole earth will be destroyed, and the water of the deluge is about to come over the whole earth, and what is upon it will be destroyed. 3. And now instruct him that he may escape and his seed remain on the whole earth." 4. And again the Lord spoke to Rufael: "Bind Azâzêl hand and foot, and put him in the darkness; make an opening in the desert, which is in Dudâêl, and put him there. 5. And lay upon him rough and pointed rocks, and cover him with darkness that he may remain there forever, and cover his face that he may not see the light! 6. And on the great day of judgment he will be cast into the fire. 7. And heal the earth which the angels have defiled, and announce the healing of the earth that I will heal it, and that not all the sons of men shall be destroyed through the mystery of all the things which the watchers have spoken and have taught their sons. 8. And the whole earth was defiled through the example of the deeds of Azâzêl; to him ascribe all the sins." 9. And God said to Gabriel: "Go against the bastards and those cast off and against the children of fornication, and destroy the children of fornication and the children of the watchers from among men; lead them out, and let them loose that they may destroy each other by murder; for their days shall not be long. 10. And they will all supplicate thee, but their fathers will secure nothing for them, although they expect an everlasting life, and that each one of them will live five hundred years." 11. And God said to Michael: "Announce to Semjâzâ and to the others who are with him, who have bound themselves to women, to be destroyed with them in all their contamination. 12. When all their sons shall have slain one another, and they shall have seen the destruction of their beloved ones, bind them under the hills of the earth for seventy generations, till the day of their judgment and of their end, till the last judgment has been passed for all eternity. 13. And in those days they will be led to the abyss of fire, in torture and in prison they will be locked for all eternity. 14. And then he will burn, and be destroyed; they will be burned together from now on to the end of all generations. 15. And destroy all souls of lust and the children of the watchers, because they have oppressed mankind. 16. Destroy all oppression from the face of the earth, and all wicked deeds shall cease, and the plant of justice and righteousness shall appear, and deeds will become a blessing: justice and righteousness will be planted in joy forever. 17. Then all the just will bend the knee, and they will remain alive till they beget a thousand children, and they will complete all the days of their youth and their sabbath in peace. 18. And in those days the whole earth will be worked in justice, and will all be planted with trees, and will be full of blessings. 19. And all the trees of desire will be planted on it, and vines will be planted on it; the vine planted on it will bear fruit in abundance. And of all the seed sown on it one measure will bear ten thousand, and one measure of olives will make ten presses of oil. 20. And cleanse thou the earth of all oppression and all injustice and all sin and all wickedness and all uncleanness which are produced on the earth: eradicate them from the earth. 21. And all the children of men shall become just, and all the nations shall worship me as God, and bless and all will worship me. 22. And the earth will be cleansed of all corruption and all sin and all punishment and all torment, and I will never again send a flood upon it, from generation to generation, to eternity."

CHAP. 11. — "And in those days I will open the store-rooms of blessings which are in heaven, in order to bring them down upon the earth, upon the deeds and labor of the children of men. 2. Peace and rectitude will become associates in all the days of the world, and in all the generations of the world."

CHAP. 6. With this chapter the book proper begins, and in the recital of the fall of the angels, with other attending circumstances, gives to chap. 16 the historical basis of the whole. This is based on the author's interpretation of Gen. vi. 1 sqq., and is the same as is found in Josephus *Antiqq.* i. 3, 1, and in Philo, *De Gig.* 1, 2. — *Sons of heaven*, being an imitation of the appellation *sons of God* applied to angels Job i. 6 ; ii. 1 ;

xxxviii. 7 ; Ps. xxix. 1 ; lxxxix. 7 (cf. Heb. text), is common
to both portions of this book and to the Parables ; cf. 13 : 8 ;
14 : 3 ; 39 : 1, and is explained by the author himself, 15 :
1–7. *Lust* is throughout the whole book represented as the
great sin of the angels, 9 : 8 ; 10 : 11 ; 12 : 4 ; 15 : 3 ; and
this union with the daughters of men became a fruitful source
of speculation for later Jewish writers. Cf. Langen, p. 321.
— 3. *Semjaza* ; cf. below. — 4. The belief that such an oath
would prove true seems not to have been unpopular among
the Hebrews, as is testified by the implicit faith put in the *bitter
water* in case a man suspected the chastity of his wife; cf.
Num. v. 18 and Josephus, *Antiqq.* iii. 11, 6. — 5. The number
two hundred is repeated verse 8. Origen, *Contra Celsum*,
remarks that Celsus had heard that about sixty or seventy
angels had descended and become wicked. Syncellus also
gives the number as two hundred. — 6. *Ardis* is a corrupt
reading, and probably contracted from the Ἰάρεδ εἰς of Syncellus ; the translator omitting the words ταῖς ἡμέραις ; for the
Greek has οἱ καταβάντες ἐν ταῖς ἡμέραις Ἰάρεδ εἰς τὴν κορυφὴν
Ἐρμονιείμ ὄρους. Fama always placed the fall of the angels in
the time of Jared. *The book of the Jubilees* (chap. 4, ed. Dillmann, p. 17) remarks that Jared was so called because in his
days the angels descended (ירד, to descend) on the earth ;
and Origen (*Comm. in Joan.* tom. viii. p. 132, ed. Hurt.) mentions an explanation of the word Jordan as *the descending*, by
bringing it in connection with the name Jared, and adds :
ὡς ἐν τῷ Ἐνὼχ γέγραπται..... ταῖς ἡμέραις τῆς τῶν υἱῶν τοῦ
θεοῦ καταβάσεως ἐπὶ τὰς θυγατέρας τῶν ἀνθρώπων. Epiphanius
(*adv. Haer.* i. 4, ed. Petav. tom. i. p. 4) puts the origin of
magic in the days of Jared. *Hermon* here taken from החרים
or חֶרֶם. Hilarius (*Comm. in Ps.* cxxxiii. 3) remarks : Hermon mons est in Phoenice cujus interpretatio *anathema* est:
quod enim nobis anathema nuncupatur, id hebraice Hermon
dicitur. Fertur autem id, de quo etiam nescio cujus liber
extat, quod angeli concupiscentes filias hominum, cum de caelo
descenderunt, in hunc montem maxime convenirent excelsum.

This *liber* is undoubtedly the Book of Enoch; cf. Jerome on Ps. cxxxiii. 3. This passage proves that the original was written in one of the Semitic languages. — 7. This verse mentions eighteen leaders; the Gr. has twenty; and 69 : 2 sqq. has twenty-one; and the difference in the names in these three lists is considerable. The disharmony between 6 : 7 and 69 can easily be explained by the fact that these lists were furnished by different authors, for 69 is a portion of the Noachic fragments; and in so uncertain a subject as the names of these angels, which had to be drawn from imagination alone, this lack of agreement is natural and of little moment. The departure of the Ethiopic text from that of Syncellus is probably owing to a gradual corruption of the Ethiopic. Dillmann's unnecessary attempt to harmonize these three lists is more ingenious than successful. Cf. his Notes, p. 93 sqq.

CHAP. 7. In this and the following chapter the Greek and the Ethiopic texts do not harmonize; the former presenting the longer, and in general, although not always, the better, reading. — 1. Syncellus dates the events here recorded as ἐν τῷ χιλιοστῷ ἑκατοστῷ ἑβδομηκοστῷ ἔτει τοῦ κοσμοῦ, and says it continued ἕως τοῦ κατακλυσμοῦ, which certainly never was found in the original book of Enoch, as this, after the manner of apocryphal writings, avoids such specific limitations. On the use of roots as instruments for magic Hoffmann (p. 116–120) treats extensively, and draws especial attention to the instances recorded by Josephus, *Bel. Jud.* vii. 6, 3, and *Antiqq.* viii. 2, 5. — 2. The number three thousand, reduced by one MS. to three hundred and omitted in the Greek, is probably an interpolation. The *great giants* are stated by Syncellus to have been of three kinds, γένη τρία — a statement that must have been in the original, as it is presupposed in 86 : 4; 88 : 2, verses written by the same author. *The book of the Jubilees* (chap. 7, ed. Dillmann p. 31) divides them into Jerbâch, Naphâl, and Eljô. — 4. *The book of the Jubilees* l. c. says that only the third class of giants destroyed mankind. — 5.

7

That the giants (not men) sinned with the birds, etc. is mentioned in almost the same words in *the book of the Jubilees.* *Their* flesh, i.e. that of man, as, unlike the book just quoted where the contest between the giants themselves goes on before the attack on man, the book of Enoch places this contest *after* the destruction of mankind. The terrible crime of drinking blood finds its most vivid expression in *the book of the Jubilees :* " Take heed with blood, take much heed. Bury it in the earth, and eat no blood, for it is the soul ; never eat blood ! " — 6. Like Gen. iv. 10 ; cf. En. 8 : 4 ; 9 : 2.

CHAP. 8, 1. *Azazel ;* cf. Lev. xvi. 8, 10, 26 ; and Gesenius, *Thesaurus* 1012–13 ; and Herzog-Plitt, II. p. 23. That Azazel ὁ δέκατος τῶν ἀρχόντων (interpolation ? of Syncellus), is mentioned first is in harmony with 9 : 6 ; 10 : 4 ; 13 : 1. *To see what was behind them*, correctly explained by S. de Sacy : Edocuit artem specula faciendi. The Greek text and Tertullian (quoted by Laurence, *Prelim. Disc.* p. xvi.) omit this phrase. Cf. *Test. Ruben*, 5. — 2. Cf. *Book of the Jubilees*, 7.— 3. *Amezarak* is undoubtedly a corruption of one of the names in chap. 6, possibly of Semjaza ; cf. Dillmann and Syncelius. Here, probably, the Ethiopic text has omissions, and, not being able to render the distinction between ἀστροσκοπία, the art of Baraqal, and ἀστρολογία, that of Kokabel, he translates the latter *signs*, i.e. of heaven, 48 : 3. This verse is freely quoted by Clemens Alex. in *Eclog. Proph.*, ed. Sylburg, p. 808. — 4. Cf. note on 7 : 6.

CHAP. 9. *Surjan* and *Urjan* are Suriel and Uriel, four of the highest angels. The canonical books (Dan.) know of Michael and Gabriel, but Suriel and especially Uriel are well known in later rabbinical theology as מלאבי הפנים ; cf. e.g. *Talm. Babyl.* Berachoth, fol. 51ᵃ. Generally, however, these four are Michael, Gabriel, Uriel, and Raphael ; cf. Buxtorf, Lex. p. 27 ; and Syncellus gives this passage twice with these last names, and undoubtedly correctly. These angels being constantly near God are the proper ones to report the terrible fate of mankind to him. — 2 is not in the Gr. but must have been in the original. *Emptied,* i.e. of mankind, 67 : 2; 84 : 5. — 3. *Holy ones,* also a biblical name for angels; cf. Job v. 1; xv. 15; Zech. xiv. 5; Dan. iv. 14; viii. 13; cf. note on 15 : 2. *Most-High* or *Highest God* is found in the whole book. — 4. A similar prayer is found 84 : 2 sqq., and is probably an enlargement of the Trisagion. The character and wording of the prayer is strictly determined by the immediate wants; cf. Schürer in *Zeitschrift für prot. Theol.,* 1876, p. 176. — 6. From 9 : 8; 10 : 7, and especially 16 : 3 we are allowed to understand that these secrets are the ones referred to 8 : 1. Without the assistance of the fallen angels men would never have learned charms and conjurations. — 7. Here the Gr. omits the most important words, *made known conjurations.* — 8. How they defiled themselves is stated 15 : 3 sqq. — 10. *They are not able,* i.e. the souls; the plural in the Ethiopic is decidedly better than the singular δύναται with στεναγμός as subject. The cries of those that died can be heard in heaven, 22 : 5 sqq.

CHAP. 10. Arsjalâljûr, for which the Gr. has Uriel, is probably, as Dillmann remarks, a combination of אליאור and חדסיאל (sun-god, light-god), and is about the same as the name Uriel. The *son of Lamech,* as the Gr. states, is Noah. The record here of an event that occurred after the death of Enoch does not demand that this chapter be ascribed to a new author; such chronological mistakes could easily happen to one writing thousands of years later than the events here mentioned. — 2. *Hide thyself* is a command to Noah, as Moses hides on receiving a revelation, Ex. iii. 6; cf. En. 12 : 1; chap. 81. — 3. The additions to the Gr. in this verse are probably by Syncellus himself. — 4. Rufael, the same as Raphael, mentioned here for the first time, is an angel introduced by apocryphal literature, being found first Tob. xii. 15. Azazel, as the chief of these sinful beings, receives a separate punishment. *Dudael* is הדּיאל אֵל, i.e. God's kettle; cf. Jude 6; 2 Pet. ii. 4; Irenaeus, *adv. Haer.* iv. 30. The *desert* as the place of his punishment

is taken from Lev. xvi. 10, 22. The desert was frequently
pictured as the abiding-place of demons; cf. LXX on Isa. xiii.
21; xxxiv. 13, 14; and Tob. viii. 3. This judgment is not
the last, but only a temporary one, as the next verse already
indicates. This first judgment, although stated in verse 5 as
one *forever*, is modified in verse 12 as seventy generations,
and in 14 : 5, as *for all the days of the world.* — 5. As light
is the picture of happiness (1 : 8, etc), darkness signifies
misery. One of the chief horrors of Sheol is darkness; cf.
Lam. iii. 6; Ps. cxliii. 3; Job x. 21, 22; xviii. 18; and in
general, Ps. cvii. 10, 14; Isa. xlii. 7. — 6. *Great day*, i.e.
the final judgment, 22 : 11. The punishment by fire, vs.
13; 18 : 11; 21 : 7–10, and often. — 7. *Heal*, in the sense of
Isa. vi. 10, as could be expected from one whose name is from
רפא. The action of the angel and that of God here run together as in Gen. xix. 17–22; xxxi. 3, 11, 13; Ex. xiii. 21
with xiv. 19. This healing, however, can only take place by
first ridding the earth of the ulcerous giants. — 8. All wicked
deeds are *recorded*, 81 : 2, and the angels learn them, 100 : 10.
— 9. *Bastards*, i.e. the giants, the product of the union of two
different kinds of beings, 15 : 3–7. The manner of this destruction shall be self-slaughter, as is also stated in the book
of the Jubilees (ch. 5, p. 20) : " And he sent among them his
sword that each one should kill his neighbor; and they commenced to kill each other, till they all fell by the sword, and
were destroyed from the earth. But their fathers looked on,
and after that were bound in the abysses of the earth till the
day of the great judgment"; cf. En. 12 : 6; 14 : 6; 87 : 1;
88 : 2. From men, i.e. born of men. — 10. The petition of
the fallen angels is in vain, 12 : 6; 13 : 4 sqq.; 14 : 4, 7.
Eternal life, i.e. long life, as the five hundred shows. — 11.
Michael, as the greatest of the angels, is to punish Semjaza
and the rest of the fallen, with the exception of Azazel. — 12.
This punishment consists in first seeing the destruction of their
children, and then being bound under the hills for seventy

generations; cf. note on verse 4 and chap. 91 and 93. The idea here expressed does not require to be derived from the Greek fables of the Titans, but could very easily have been deduced by a Hebrew mind from passages like Job xi. 8; xxvi. 5; cf. Isa. xiii. 16. This punishment is exceptionally heavy, as the family-ties were especially strong among the Jews. — 13. *Abyss of fire,* 90 : 25, 26. The final punishment is eternal, 14 : 4, 5; 22 : 11; 25 : 4; 27 : 3, etc.; cf. Jude 6; 2 Pet. ii. 4. — 15. *Souls of lust,* 67 : 8, 10; and both the angels and the women are meant; cf. 19 : 2. — 16. *The plant of righteousness* is the people of Israel; cf. 93 : 2, 5, 8, 10, a term frequently found in apocryphal writings. The picture here gradually blends into a portrait of the Messianic times. — 17. Long life was one of the greatest blessings in the Old Testament; cf. note on 5 : 7, and En. 25 : 5, 6; 58 : 3, 6; 71 : 17, etc. *Sabbath,* the last years of their lives, as the Sabbath is the last and resting-day of the week. A numerous progeny was also a great blessing; cf. Deut. xxviii. 4; Ps. cxxviii. 3; Prov. xvii. 6; and barrenness a result of sin, En. 98 : 5. — 18. Cf. Hos. xiv. 8; Amos ix. 14; Jer. xxxi. 5; lxv. 21; Ezek. xxviii. 26, etc. This is the opposite from the condition pictured chap. 8 and 9. Justice is always joined with the happy time of the future; cf. note on 5 : 8. — 19. The Old Testament frequently refers to the vine and the olive and fruitfulness as a source of blessing in the reign of the Messiah; cf. Amos ix. 13; Hos. ii. 22, 23; Isa. xxx. 23–25; Ezek. xxxiv. 26, 27; xxxvi. 8, 29, 30; Zech. viii. 12; Ps. lxxii. 16, and especially Isa. v. 10, of which this verse is an imitation; cf. also Harnack on *Papias Frag.,* p. 87. — 20. This refers to the deluge. — 21. A sudden transition to the times of the Messiah, containing a well-known hope frequently expressed by the Old Testament prophets. In 90 : 37 the same is said of the Messiah, and in the Parables chap. 57. — 22. Cf. Gen. ix. 11, 15. *Sin;* cf. note on 5 : 8.

CHAP. 11, 1 Is simply a combination of the preceding; cf.

7*

Deut. xxviii. 12. The idea that there are store-rooms or receptacles for things good and bad runs through the whole book. — 2. Cf. Ps. lxxxv. 10 ; Isa. xxxii. 17.

SECTION III.

CHAP. 12. — And previous to all *these* things Enoch was hidden, and not one of the children of men knew where he was hidden, and where he was, and what had become of him. 2. And all his deeds were with the holy ones and with the watchers in his days. 3. And I, Enoch, was praising the great Lord and the King of the world, and, behold, the watchers called to me, Enoch, the scribe, and said to me : 4. " Enoch, thou scribe of justice, go, announce to the watchers of heaven, who have left the high heaven and the holy, eternal place, and have contaminated themselves with women, and have done as the children of men do, and have taken to themselves wives, and are contaminated in great contamination upon the earth. 5. But upon earth they shall have no peace, nor forgiveness of sin ; for they will not enjoy their children. 6. They will see the murder of their beloved ones, and they will lament over the destruction of their children, and will petition to eternity, but mercy and peace will not be unto them."

CHAP. 13. — And Enoch, departing, said to Azâzêl : " Thou wilt have no peace ; a great condemnation has come upon thee, and he [i.e. Rufael, cf. 10 : 4] will bind thee ; 2. and alleviation and intercession and mercy will not be unto thee, because thou hast taught oppression, and because of all the deeds of abuse, oppression, and sin which thou hast showed to the children of men."

3. And then going, I spoke to them all together; and they were all afraid, fear and trembling seized them. 4. And they asked me to write a memorial petition for them that they thereby might attain forgiveness, and to carry their memorial petition before God into heaven. 5. For they could not, from now on, speak *with him*, nor could they raise their eyes towards heaven from shame on account of their sins for which they were being punished. 6. Then I wrote this memorial petition, and prayed with reference to their souls and for each of their deeds, and for that which they had asked of me, that they thereby might obtain forgiveness and patience. 7. And going I sat down near the waters of Dan in Dan, which is to the right [i.e. south] of the evening side [i.e. west] of Hermon, and read their memorial petition till I fell asleep. 8. And, behold, a dream came to me, and visions fell upon me, and I saw the vision of chastisement to show to the sons of heaven, and to upbraid them. 9. And having become awake I went to them, and they were all sitting assembled lamenting at Ublesjâêl, which is between the Lebanon and Sênêsêr, with their faces covered. 10. And I related before them all the visions that I had seen in my sleep, and commenced to speak those words of justice and to upbraid the watchmen of heaven.

CHAP. 14. — This writing is the word of justice and the admonition of the watchers, who are from eternity, as the Holy and Great One commanded it in this vision. 2. I saw in my sleep what I now will relate with a tongue of flesh and with my breath, which the Great One has given to the mouth of men that they might converse with it and understand it in their hearts. 3. As he has created and given to men *the power* to understand the word of knowledge, thus also he has created me and given to me *the power* to upbraid the watchers, the sons of heaven. 4. "I have written your petition, and in my vision it appeared to me thus, that your petition will not be granted in all the days of the world, and that judgment has been passed over you, and nothing will be granted unto you. 5. And from now on ye will not ascend into heaven to all eternity, and upon earth, it has been decreed, they shall bind you for all the days of the world. 6. But before this ye will have seen the destruction of your beloved children, and ye will not be able to possess them, but they shall fall before you by the sword. 7. Your petition for them will not be granted unto you, nor the one for yourselves; and while ye are weeping and praying ye cannot speak a single word from the writing which I have written." 8. And the vision appeared to me thus: behold, clouds in the vision invited me and a fog invited me; and the course of the stars and lightning drove and pressed me, and the winds in the vision gave me wings and drove me. 9. And they lifted me up into heaven, and I went till I approached near a wall which was built of crystals and a tongue of fire surrounded it; and it began to cause me to fear. 10. And I went into the tongue of fire and approached near to a large house, which was built of crystals, and the walls of this house were like a floor inlaid with crystals, and the groundwork was of crystals. 11. The ceiling was like the course of the stars and of the lightning, and Cherubim of fire were between them, and their heaven was water. 12. A flaming fire surrounded the walls, and its doors burned with fire. 13. And I went into this house, and it was hot like fire and cold like ice, and there was nothing pleasant and no life in it: fear covered me, and trembling seized me. 14. And as I was shaking and trembling, I fell down on my face and saw in a vision. 15. And behold, *there was* a second house, larger than the other, all whose doors stood open before me, and it was built with a tongue of fire. 16. And in all things it excelled in grandeur and magnificence and size, so that I cannot describe to you its magnificence and its size. 17. Its floor was fire, and above it was lightning and the course of the stars, and its ceiling was also a flaming fire. 18. And I looked and saw therein a high throne; its appearance was like the hoar-frost, and its circuit like a shining sun and voices of the Cherubim. 19. And from under the great throne came streams of flaming fire, and it was impossible to look at it. 20. And he who is great in majesty sat thereon; his garment shone more brilliantly than the sun, and was whiter than any hail. 21. None of the angels were able to enter, nor any flesh to look upon the form of the face of the Majestic and Honored One. 22. Fire of flaming fire was round him, and a great fire stood before him, and none of those who were around him could approach him; ten thousand times ten thousand were before him; but he required not any holy counsel. 23. And the holy ones who were near him did not leave day or night, nor did they depart from him. 24. And I had had so long a veil upon my face, and I trembled; and the Lord called me with his own voice and said to me: "Come hither, Enoch, and to my holy word!" 25. And he caused me to arise and I went to the door; but I bent my face downwards.

CHAP. 15. — And he answered and spoke to me with his word: "Hear, and fear not, Enoch, thou just man and

scribe of justice, approach hither, and hear my words. 2.
And go, say to the watchers of heaven, who have sent
thee, that thou shouldst petition for them : ' Ye should
petition for men, and not men for you. 3. Why have
ye left the high, holy, and everlasting heaven, and lain
with women, and defiled yourselves with the daughters
of men, and taken wives unto yourselves, and acted like
the children of earth, and begotten giants as sons ? 4.
While ye were spiritual, holy, having eternal life, ye defiled yourselves with women, and with the blood of flesh
have begotten children, and have lusted after the blood
of men, and have produced flesh and blood as they produce who die and are destroyed. 5. Therefore I have
given them wives that they might impregnate them and
children be born by them, as it is done on earth. 6. Ye
were formerly spiritual, living an eternal life without
death to all the generations of the world. 7. Therefore
I have not made for you any wives, for spiritual beings
have their home in heaven. 8. And now the giants, who
have been begotten from body and flesh, will be called evil
spirits on earth, and their dwelling-places will be upon
the earth. 9. Evil spirits proceed from their bodies ;
because they are created from above, their beginning
and first basis being from the holy watchers, they will
be evil spirits upon the earth, and will be called evil
spirits. 10. But the spirits of heaven have their dwelling-places in heaven, and the spirits of the earth, who
were born on the earth, have their dwelling-places on
earth. 11. And the spirits of the giants, who cast
themselves upon the clouds, will be destroyed and fall,
and will battle and cause destruction on the earth, and
do evil ; they will take no kind of food, nor will they become thirsty, and they will be invisible. 12. And these

spirits will not (?) rise up against the children of men and against the women, because they have proceeded from them. In the days of murder and destruction.

CHAP. 16. — and of the death of the giants, when the spirits have proceeded from the bodies, their flesh shall decay without judgment; thus they shall be destroyed till that day when the great judgment over all the great world shall be completed over the watchers and the impious. 2. And now to the watchers who have sent thee that thou shouldst petition for them who were formerly in heaven *say :* 3. 'Ye have been in heaven, and though the secrets were not yet revealed to you, still ye knew illegitimate mysteries, and these ye have, in the hardness of your hearts, related to the women, and through these mysteries women and men increase wickedness over the earth.' 4. Tell them therefore : 'Ye have no peace !' "

CHAP. 12. Enoch was hidden, probably to receive the revelation that now follows, as Noah was to hide himself for a similar purpose, 10 : 2 ; based upon Gen. v. 24. The Targums of Jonathan ben Uziel and of Jerusalem both interpret the לקח as a retiring from the earth and associating with higher beings. — 2. *Holy ones,* cf. note on 9 : 3, and is found in all the three parts of this book. *Watchmen,* a standard name for all classes of angels, good and bad (for the fallen angels are also called thus, 1 : 5 ; 10 : 9, 15 ; 12 : 4 ; 13 : 4, 10 ; 14 : 1, 3 ; 15 : 2 ; 16 : 1, 2 ; 91 : 15), and strictly confined to this portion of the book, the nearest approach to it in the Parables being *those that do not sleep,* 39 : 12, 13 ; 61 : 12 ; 71 : 7. They are mentioned first in Dan. iv. 17. For the writer of the Parables the term seems to indicate exclusively one class of angels, viz. the archangels ; cf. 71 : 7 ; while in the first part it is used in this limited sense in 20 only, a chapter of doubtful authenticity. Cf. the Old Testament statements concerning the prophets as watchmen, Isa. xxi. 11, 12; lii. 8; lxii. 6; Jer. vi. 17; Ezek. iii. 17; xxxiii. 7; Hab. ii. 1; cf. 1 Clem. *ad Corinth*, 56 1. — 3. *King of the world;* cf. note on 1 : 3. *The scribe;* cf. verse 4; 15 : 1; 92 : 1. The book of the Jubilees remarks that Enoch was the first to teach men writing. This was probably a kind of official title, which is modified 12 : 4 and 92 : 1. as *scribe of justice,* he being just himself, 15 : 1; 71 : 14–16; and announcing the just judgment, 39 : 2; 81 : 6; 82 : 1; 108 : 1; and writing books for this purpose, 104 : 13; 108 : 9; cf. the interesting remarks of Dillmann, in *Allg. Enleitung,* p. xli. sq. — 4. Cf. Jude 6 and En. 15 : 3 sqq. — 5. Cf. 10 : 9–12. The forbidden union between an Israelite and a heathen could be forgiven, Ezra x. 19, but not that between angel and woman. — 6. Cf. on 10 : 9.

Chap. 13. Azazel alone is here addressed, in harmony with 10 : 4 sqq. — 3. *To them all,* i.e. to Semjaza and the other angels. — 4, 5. The greatness of the fall is expressed by the fact that they who are of heaven cannot now raise even their eyes upwards out of shame for their deeds, 14 : 7; 15 : 3 sqq. Being cut off from the communion with God is one of the most terrible things an Israelite could conceive of, and thus this separation is one of the horrors of the Sheol; cf. Job vii. 7–10; Ps. lxxxviii. Writing was comparatively rare in the Old Testament, but was evidently a common thing in the time of the author of this book, and the statement here undoubtedly refers also to Enoch's literary character. Writing instead of speaking the petition is the tribute of reverence paid to the majesty of God, and is taken from the customs of earth's royalty. Furthermore, it seems that even Enoch could not speak to God, for none of his numerous questions are addressed to him, although God speaks to him, 14 : 24; 15 : 1. — 6. *Patience,* i.e. that God should have patience with them. The angels, originally spiritual, 15 : 4, 6, are represented here after their fall as possessing soul and body, like man; cf. 19 : 1 — 7. He goes in a south-western direction to the river Dan in the country of Dan. This river, a tributary of the Jordan, is also called the smaller Jordan, Josephus, *Antiqq.* i. 10, 1 ; v. 3, 1 ; viii. 8, 4. The banks of flowing water were favorite places for prayer, Dan. viii. 2; x. 4. As Hermon was a desecrated place, Enoch could not expect to receive a revelation there. — 8. *Sons of heaven;* cf. note on 6 : 2. Revelations through dreams were frequent in the Old Testament; Gen. xx. 3 ; xxxi. 10 sqq.; xlvi. 2 ; 1 Sam. xxviii. 6 ; 1 Kings iii. 5 ; Job xxxiii. 15, etc.; and Josephus, *Bel. Jud.* iii. 8, 3. Philo wrote a special work on this subject, περὶ τοῦ θεοπέμπτους εἶναι τοὺς ὀνείρους. — 9. *Ublesjael,* being stationed between Lebanon and Sênêsêr, must have been a real, not imagined place, but what one is uncertain. The same must be said of Sênêsêr. As a mark of their lamentation, they have their faces covered; cf. 2 Sam. xv. 30 ; Isa. xxv. 7 ; Esth. vi. 12. — 10. *Words of justice,* i.e. the just punishment. Being important, this vision is farther explained in chap. 14–16.

CHAP. 14, 1. As the following is to be a minute description of the vision, it is very properly preceded by its own superscription. The angels are *from eternity,* in the sense of the biblical מעולם, i.e. not eternity absolutely and metaphysically, but only subjectively, from a time hidden (עלם) to the author; cf. Orelli, *Heb. Synonyma d. Zeit und Ewigkeit,* p. 69 sqq. and note on 10 : 4, 10 and 15 : 3, 4, 6, 7, 10 ; 12 : 4 ; 15 : 3. — 2. *Tongue of flesh,* to emphasize his privilege as a human being, who is of flesh, to rebuke the angels who are spiritual. The contrast is strengthened by the fact that the author here evidently, as in 15, especially verse 8, and as it is probably done Gen. vi. 3. and Ps. lxxviii. 39, and certainly in the New Testament (cf. Wendt, *Fleisch und Geist,* p. 42, sqq.), attaches to the idea of flesh the ethical idea of moral weakness; cf. also 84 : 1; cf. the similar idea in Isa. viii. 1. — 4. *The judgment has been passed,* i.e. decided

upon by the unchangeable God, 65 : 10, like the biblical כלה.
— 5. Cf. note on 13 : 4, 5. — 6. note on 10 : 9. — 7. Cf. note
on 10 : 10. *Speak*, probably from falsely reading λαλεῖν for
λαβεῖν, and should be : ye will not *receive*. The *writing* is of
course Enoch's petition. To this and the following Irenaeus
refers in *adv. Haer.* iv. 30, when he says : Sed et Enoch sine
circumcisione placens Deo, cum esset homo, legatione ad
angelos fungebatur et translatus est et conservatur usque nunc
testis judicii Dei, quoniam angeli quidam transgressi decide-
runt in terram in judicium, homo autem placens translatus est
in salutem. — 8. The picture here is evidently taken from
passages like Isa. xix. 1 and the places where God is said to
descend on a cloud, Ex. xix. 9 ; xxxiv. 4 ; Lev. xvi. 2 ; Num.
xi. 25 ; xii. 5. In the *Ascensio Isaiae*, chap. vii., viii., in which
Isaiah ascends up to the seventh through the other six heavens,
the manner of the ascent is not stated, except that the angels
caused it. The statements here are certainly connected with
Isa. vi. ; Ezek. i. and x.: Dan. vii. 9, 10. — 9. These holy
places are surrounded by walls of the purest substances. In
Zech. ii. 5 the Lord is himself a wall of fire, and fire is the
symbol of purity, Prov. xxv. 22 ; Jer. xxiii. 29 ; Mal. iii. 2.
— 10. The picture is taken from the shape of an earthly
temple : behind the wall is the אילם or πρόναος. — 11. *Water*,
because transparent. — 13 is an expression of his awful feelings
in seeing these astounding phenomena. — 14. Cf. Ezek. i. 28 ;
Dan. viii. 17, 18 ; x. 9 ; *Ascensio Isaiae*, ix. 1, 2. — 15. Now
he sees the holy of holies, whose doors are open, which is to
explain how in the following he can narrate what was within,
although he did not enter ; cf. the similar description in *Pirke
Elieser*, c. 4. His not entering is explained by Ex. xxxiii.
20 ; Judg. vi. 22 sq. ; xiii. 22 ; 1 Sam. vi. 19 sq. — 16. *You*,
i.e. the readers. — 17. Cf. verse 11. — 18. *Hoar-frost*, to
express the intensity of the whiteness ; cf. Dan. vii. 9. *Throne*,
the prophet Isaiah in his ascent finds a throne in each one of
the seven heavens ; cf. *Ascensio Isaiae* vii. 14 sqq. and Isa. vi.

1 sqq. — 19. Cf. Dan. vii. 10. — 20. *Ascensio Isaiae* ix. 27. Et vidi quendam stantem, cujus gloria superabat omnia, et gloria ejus magna erat et mirabilis. — 21. Cf. note on verse 2. That God's residence cannot be entered by man is stated also 3 Macc. ii. 14 sqq.; cf. *Ascensio Isaiae* iii. 8 sqq. — 22. The angels are servants, not advisers of God, hence they are not required in his βουλή; cf. note on i. 9. — 24. *Word*, not the λόγος, but probably the ῥῆμα or command of God personified. Dillmann says it is equal to: Come here to hear my holy word; cf. Langen, p. 268, and the personification of the word of God in Ps. cxlvii. 15; Isa. lv. 11. — 25. *To the door*, according to verse 21.

CHAP. 15, 1, 2. *Scribe of justice;* cf. 12 : 3. Angels interceding for men is biblical; cf. Job v. 1; xxxiii. 23; Zech. i. 12 sqq. (Tob. xii. 12–15; 2 Macc. iii. 25 sqq.; Philo, *De Gig.* § 4.); Apoc. viii. 3, and in En. 9 : 3; 40 : 6, 7; 47 : 2; 89 : 76; 104 : 1. — 3. Cf. 12 : 4; Jude 6. — 4. The contrast lies here between spiritual and eternal on the one hand, and flesh and mortality on the other. The angels, being eternal, did not require propagation as a means of the preservation of their kind, and thus their lust had caused them to step out of their sphere. Their guilt was increased by the result of this unnatural union, the wicked giants. — 5. Man, being mortal, did not sin by propagating his kind; cf. *Test. Naphtali,* 3. — 6. That the angels are spiritual is not definitely stated in the Old Testament, but repeatedly in the New; cf. 1 Cor. xiv. 12, 32; Heb. i. 14; Apoc. xxii. 6; Acts viii. 26, 29, 39. — 8, 9. Giants were the product of this lustful connection, and being the children of spiritual fathers, but begotten in sin, they are evil spirits. Syncellus has also 15 : 8–16 : 1, and gives a good text. Justin Martyr (*Apol. brev.* ii. 5) remarks: Οἱ δ᾽ ἄγγελοι παραβάντες τήνδε τὴν τάξιν γυναικῶν μίξεσιν ἡττήθησαν, καὶ παῖδας ἐτέκνωσαν οἵ εἰσιν οἱ λεγόμενοι Δαίμονες, but in his *Apol. pro Christ. ad Anton. Pium* he calls these angels themselves Δαίμονες φαῦλοι. Tertul. *Apol.* 22 adopts the first view:

Quomodo de angelis quibusdam sua sponte corruptis corruptio
gens daemonum evaserit, etc.; as also do the *Pseudo-Clement.*,
8, 18. — 10 is omitted in the Gr., but was undoubtedly in the
original, as it suits the connection. — 11, 12. The Ethiopic
text is evidently not pure here, and departs considerably from
the Gr., the latter having the transitive ἀφανίζειν, instead of
the intransitive *be destroyed*, and instead of the strange word
clouds (νεφέλας) νεμόμενα, and the negative in verse 12 must
be erased, as the sense and the Gr., which has simply ἐξανασ-
τήσονται, demand. The sense is, according to the Gr.: The
spirits of the giants destroy, practise injustice, cause destruction,
make attacks, fight and struggle, throw down on the earth and
assault, but eat nothing, assume ghostly forms or produce
them, but become thirsty and rush upon mankind. But the
acc. of the Ethiopic is better than the καὶ τῶν γυναικῶν of the
Gr. On the view of later authorities on the subject of
demons, cf. Hoffmann, p. 203 sqq.; Langen, pp. 322, 323.

CHAP. 16, 1. Evidently simply continuation of the preceding. The Ναφηλείμ οἱ ἰσχυροὶ τῆς γῆς οἱ μεγάλοι ὀνομαστοί
of Syncellus, which Dillmann calls a *müssige sinnsstörende
Glosse*, does not belong to the text. In this book the judgments, both the first and the final, have many different names,
e.g. the great judgment, 19:1; 22:4; 25:4; 100:4; 103:
8; or day of the great judgment, 84:4; 94:9; 98:10; 99:
15; 104:5; or great day of the judgment, 10:6; 22:11; day
of completion, 10:12; while the Parables have, the great day,
54:6; or day of trouble, 45:2. — 2. Clemens Alex. refers to
this strange statement in his remarks, *Strom.* V. p. 550 (ed.
Sylburg. 1641), cf. Justin. *Apol. B.*; Epiph. *adv. Haer.*, 1:4;
Tertul. *De Cultu Fem.* 1:10.

SECTION IV.

CHAP. 17. — And they took me to a place where there were *images* like flaming fire, and when they wished they appeared like men. 2. And he led me to the place of the whirlwind, and on a hill, the point of whose summit reached to heaven. 3. And I saw shining places, and the thunder at the ends *thereof;* in the depths thereof a bow of fire, and arrows and their quiver, and a sword of fire, and all lightning. 4. And they took me to the so-called water of life, and to the fire of the west, which receives every setting of the sun. 5. And I came to a river of fire, whose fire flows like water, and is emptied into a great sea which is towards the west. 6. And I saw all the great rivers, and came to a great darkness, and went there where all flesh wanders. 7. And I saw the mountains of the black clouds of winter, and the place whither all the waters of the deep flow. 8. And I saw the mouths of all the rivers of the earth and the mouth of the deep.

CHAP. 18. — And I saw the repositories of all the winds, and I saw how he had ornamented all the creation and the foundations of the earth with them. 2. And I saw the corner-stone of the earth, and I saw the four winds which support the earth and the firmament of the heavens. 3. And I saw how the winds expand the lights of the heavens; and they remained between heaven and earth, and they are pillars of heaven. 4. And I saw the winds which turn the heavens, which lead down the course of the sun and all the stars. 5. And I saw the winds upon the earth which carry the clouds, and I saw the paths of the angels; I saw at the end of the earth the firmament of the heavens above. 6. And

I proceeded towards the south; and it burns day
and night there where seven hills of precious stones
are, three towards the east, three towards the south.   7.
But of those towards the east, one of colored stone, one
of pearls, and one of antimony; and those towards the
south of red stone.   8. But the middle one reached up
to heaven, like the throne of God, of alabaster, and the
summit of the throne of sapphire.   9. And I saw a
burning fire which was in all the hills.   10. And there
I saw a place, beyond the great earth; there the waters
collected.   11. And I saw a great abyss in the earth,
with columns of heavenly fire; and I saw among them
columns of heavenly fire, which fall, and are without
number, either towards the light or towards the depth.
12. And over that abyss I saw a place which had no
firmament of heaven above it, and no foundation of earth
beneath it, and no water above it, and no birds upon it;
it was a void place.   13. And there I saw a terrible thing:
seven stars, like great burning mountains and like spirits,
that petitioned me.   14. The angel said: " This is the
place of the consummation of heaven and earth; it is a
prison for the stars of heaven, and for the host of heaven.
15. And the stars that roll over the fire are they who
have transgressed the command of God before their rising, because they did not come forth in their time.   16.
And he was enraged at them, and bound them till the
time of the consummation of their sins in the year of
the mystery."

CHAP. 19. — And Uriel said to me: " Here will stand
the souls of those angels who have united themselves
with women, and having assumed many different forms,
have contaminated mankind, and have led them astray
so that they brought offerings to the demons as to gods,

namely on the day when the great judgment, on which they will be judged, shall be consummated. 2. And their women having led astray the angels of heaven, will be like their friends." 3. And I, Enoch, alone saw this vision, the ends of all ; and no man has seen them as I have seen them.

CHAP. 20. — And these are the names of the holy angels who watch : 2. Uriel, one of the holy angels, the angel of thunder and of trembling ; 3. Rufael, one of the holy angels, the angel of the spirits of men ; 4. Raguel, one of the holy angels, who takes vengeance on the earth and the luminaries ; 5. Michael, one of the holy angels, namely set over the best portion of men, over the people ; 6. Saraqâel, one of the holy angels, who is over the spirits of the children of men who induce the spirits to sin ; 7. Gabriel, one of the holy angels, who is over the serpents and over the Paradise and the Cherubim.

CHAP. 21. — And I went around to a place where not one thing took place. 2. And I saw there something terrible, no high heavens, no founded earth, but a void place, awful and terrible. 3. And there I saw seven stars of heaven, tied together to it, like great mountains, and flaming as if by fire. 4. At that time I said : " On account of what sin are these bound, and why have they been cast hither ? " 5. And then answered Uriel, one of the holy angels, who was with me, conducting me, and said to me : " Enoch, concerning what dost thou ask, and concerning what dost thou inquire, and ask and art anxious ? 6. These are of the stars who have transgressed the command of God, the Highest, and are bound here till ten thousand worlds, the number of the days of their sins, shall have been consummated." 7. And from there I went to another

place which was still more terrible than the former.
And I saw a terrible thing: a great fire was there,
which burned and flickered and *appeared* in sections;
it was bounded by a complete abyss, great columns of
fire were allowed to fall into it; its extent and size
I could not see, and I was unable to see its origin. 8.
At that time I said: " How terrible this place is, and
painful to look at! " 9. At that time answered Uriel,
one of the holy angels, who was with me; he answered
and said to me: " Enoch, why such fear and terror in
thee concerning this terrible place and in the presence
of this pain? " 10. And he said to me: " This is the
prison of the angels, and here they are held to
eternity."

CHAP. 17. With this chapter commences the account by
Enoch of a trip through heaven and earth in company with
angels. 1. With the word *they* the writer joins his account to
the previous, referring to agents in the preceding narrative as
the subject. As the following clearly shows, the subject of
took are the angels, chap. 12. What is stated, Gen. v. 24, of
God is said here of the angels, for our verse has evidently
been fashioned after that passage. These fiery images are, notwithstanding Dillmann's objections, probably angels. In 14:11
we also have the Cherubim, and 19:1 states that angels can assume different forms, and in the Old Testament the angels are
seldom known as such when they first appear; and adding to this
the general indefinite character of the angelology of this first
portion of the book, and the passages Dan. x. 16; Tob. xii. 19,
Hoffmann's interpretation of angels is undoubtedly correct. —
2, 3. *He*, indefinite subject; *Place of the whirlwind*, probably
from Job xxxvii. 9. — 3. As thunder is joined with lightning the places here are *shining*. The writer's views are
principally based on Job xxxvi. 30–37; v. 15; xxxviii. 25; cf.

En. 41 : 3 ; 44 : 59 (60 : 13–15). *Bow*, with which the *arrows*, i.e. the lightning, are shot, according to Ps. vii. 12, 13 ; Hab. iii. 9 ; Lam. ii. 4 ; iii. 12, and the *arrows* as in Ps. xviii. 14 ; lxxvii. 17, 18 ; and cxliv. 6 ; the *quiver*, Lam. iii. 12, 13 ; the *sword*, Ps. vii. 12 ; Deut. xxxii. 41. — 4. *Water of life*, cf. the fountain of life, in Prov. x. 11 ; xiii. 14 ; xiv. 27 ; xvi. 22 ; but water of life, Apoc. xxii. 17. The fire in the west is the great mass of fire from which the sun daily receives its necessary portion, 23 : 4 ; 72 : 4. — 5, 6. It is curious that a writer whose object it is to oppose the entrance of Greek ideas should resort to Greek myths himself for his ideas, for that his statements here are not based on Old Testament premises is self-evident. *The river of fire* is the πυριφλεγέθων, *Od.* 10, 513. That he mentions only this one stream by name, and that one, too, being an unimportant one in the lower world of the Greeks (cf. Preller. *Gr. Mythologie*, 3d ed., p. 671 sq.) finds its explanation in its name, as suiting the connection. This stream of fire empties into the Okeanos, an idea indeed strange to the Greeks, who, however, locate Hades near the Okeanos; cf. Hesiod, Theogony, 744, 760, 767, 779 (all later interpolations in Hes. cf. Flach, *Die Hes. Gedichte*, p. 58). Enoch's description is very much like Virgil's, Aen. vi. 259, 323, 549 sqq. *All the great rivers*, i.e. probably the other rivers of the lower world. *Where all flesh wander* is Hades, cf. chap. 22. The Old Testament pictures Sheol as the receptacle of all the dead, in 1 Kings ii. 2 ; Job xxx. 23 ; Ps. lxxxix. 48.—7. What is meant by these *mountains* is uncertain, as nothing like it is found in the Old Testament.

CHAP. 18, 1. The winds are kept by God in *repositories*, on which cf. Job xxxvii. 9–13 ; Jer. x. 13 ; li. 16 ; Ps. cxxxv. 7, and En. 34–36 ; 41 : 4 ; 60 : 11, 12 ; and the object of such repositories is given Job xxxviii. 22 sqq. *The foundations of the earth* is a frequent biblical expression, cf. Isa. xxiv. 18 ; Jer. xxxi. 37 ; Mich. vi. 2 ; Ps. xviii. 15 ; lxxxii. 5 ; Prov. viii. 29. — 2. *Corner-stone of the earth*, cf. Job xxxviii. 6, and in

general Ps. xxiv. 2; lxxxix. 11; Prov. iii. 19; xxx. 4; Isa.
xlviii. 12. The four winds carrying the earth is probably the
author's explanation of Job xxvi. 7, with the assistance of Job
ix. 6 and Ps. lxxv. 3. — 3. The pillars of heaven, Job xxvi. 11,
are here declared to be the winds, for by their expansion they
support the heavens. — 4. Distinct from the winds that support the heavens are those that turn the heavens and the luminaries; cf. 72 : 5; 73 : 2. — 5. A third class of winds are those
that carry the clouds; evidently an explanation of Job xxxvi.
29; xxxvii. 16. *The paths of the angels* on which they as servants of God and mediums of revelation descend from the
heavenly home, 15 : 10, on the earth, as in Jacob's dream, Gen.
xxviii. 12 sqq. It is aptly brought in here in connection with
the winds. — 6. From the west, whither he had gone, 17 : 4,
Enoch now proceeds to the south. *It burns*, being in the south.
The seven hills are in a group, six of them forming an angle.
In the division of the earth between the sons of Noah, so
minutely recorded in the book of the Jubilees, chap. 8, it is
stated, p. 37, that the hills of fire formed a portion of Ham's
inheritance. — 7. Those to the south are *red*, probably because
the heat is more intense there. — 8. In the angle formed by
the six others stands the seventh, *like the throne of God*, of
sapphire, after Ezek. i. 26. — 10. In the south he again sees
the great Okeanos. — 11. He is still in the south, where naturally the pool of fire, as the place of punishment for the angels,
could be expected. *Without number*, in the sense of *which cannot be numbered*, a clause modifying the following words.
Heavenly fire, the same as in Gen. xix. 24; Ps. xi. 6; Ezek.
xxxviii. 23. — 12. The place here pictured is a different one
from the preceding, as chap. 21, which enlarges on these topics, shows. — 13. This latter place is occupied by disobedient
stars. The *seven* is simply a round number, cf. 18 : 6; 24 : 2;
32 : 1; 61 : 11; 77 : 4–8; 91 : 16; 93 : 10, and Winer, *Real-
wört.*, under "Zahlen." Under no circumstances dare we bring
in connection here the identification of angels and stars as was

done in later writings (cf. Langen, p. 309), or think of the seven "throne-assistants" in Tob. xii. 15. The writer simply states that the stars, who have their laws, shall also be punished for disobedience, vs. 15, and possibly refers to the ἀστέρες πλανῆται, or comets, of Jude 13. *And like spirits* is not a personification of the stars, but states only that the motions of the stars while being punished was that of petitioning spirits. — 14. *The angel*, i.e. Uriel, cf. 19 : 1, and chap. 20. *The stars* are here termed in Old Testament phraseology *host of heaven.* — 16. The limits of the punishment are unknown to the writer, like 21 : 6.

Chap. 19, 1. Uriel, in conformity with the etymology of the word, is over the luminaries, as is expressly stated 75 : 3, and explains his conduct here and in 21 : 5, 9 ; 27 : 2 ; 33 : 3, 4. This other place of punishment, the one mentioned 18 : 11, is not yet inhabited, but is intended for the fallen angels, who are now temporarily being punished by being bound in the desert or under the hills, chap. 10, but shall at the final judgment be condemned to this place, cf. 10 : 6, 13 ; 21 : 10. *Souls of the angels*, a kind of anthropomorphism, like 13 : 6. With the change of forms cf. 17 : 1 and *Test. Ruben* 5. The statements here have their parallels in Justin Martyr, *Apol. Brev.* (p. 92, ed. Maur.), *Apol. pro Christ*, p. 46 (ed. Maur.), and Tertullian, *De Idol.* 4 : Enoch praedicans, omnia elementa, omnem mundi censum, quae coelo, quae mari, quae terra continentur, in idolatriam versuros daemonas et spiritus desertorum angelorum, ut pro Deo adversus Dominum consecrarentur ; and *ib.* 15 : Haec igitur ab initio praevidens Spiritus Sanctus etiam ostia in superstitionem versura praececinit per antiquissimum prophetam (poetam) Enoch. These demons are, according to chap. 15 and 16, the spirits of the slain giants, and these being children of the fallen angels these latter persuade mankind to worship these demons. That the gods of the heathen are demons finds expression in Baruch iv. 7, and LXX on Ps. xcvi. 5 ; cvi. 37 ; Deut. xxxii. 17 ; Isa. lxv. 11. In *Dialog. cum Tryph.* § 83

Justin Martyr refers to the passage Ps. xcvi. 5 (xcv. 5 according to LXX) as proof for his statement. — 2. The women, too, are to be punished, for they were not passive in the sin of the angels, but they led them astray by their beauty, cf. 6 : 1 sqq. and *Test. Ruben*, 5. — 3. Probably the original of Clemens Alex. *Eclog. Proph.* § 2 (ed. Sylburg, p. 801): καὶ εἶδον τὰς ὕλας πάσας; and of Origen, *De Princ.* iv. 35 : universas materias perspexi.

CHAP. 20. The catalogue of angels in this chapter is an uncalled-for interpolation by a later hand. The number *six* (the same number in Past. Hermae Vis, 3, 4, 1) does not harmonize with the rest of this book, for the writer, when he does have occasion to speak of the number of angels, always chooses one of the sacred figures, three or seven, cf. 90 : 21, 22 ; 81 : 5 ; 90 : 31. In the number (six), but not in the names, the statements here agree with *Targ. Jerush.* on Deut. xxxiv., and Philo, ζήτημ. on Ex. xxv. 22. Another reason to doubt the authenticity of this chapter are the strange functions assigned to these angels. 1. *Who watch*, like the ἐγρήγοροι, or watchmen of later Jewish theology, based on Dan. iv. 10; xiv. 20. Cf. note on 12 : 2. — 2. *Uriel*. The functions here assigned to this angel are not in harmony with his deeds nor with the statements of our book, cf. note on 19 : 1. Uriel, not a biblical name, is also mentioned 4 Ezra iv. 1; v. 20; x. 28. — 3. *Rufael* (i.e. Raphael), who in later works and in En. 10 : 4, 7 is the angel of healing (cf. Buxtorf, *Lex.*, ed. Fischer, p. 27), is here vaguely called *the angel of the spirits of men*, the meaning of which expression is most mysterious.— 4. *Raguel*. The name is not rare in the Old Testament as the appellation of a man, רעיאל, cf. Gen. xxxvi. 10; Ex. ii. 18; Num. x. 29, etc., and Ραγουήλ in Tobit, but as the name of an angel it is post-biblical. The moral accountability of the luminaries, mentioned 18 : 15, is also recognized here. — 5. *Michael* is the angel of the children of Israel, in conformity with Dan. x. 13, 21 ; xii. 1 ; *Assumptio Mosis* x. 2, *Ascensio Isaiae* ix. 13, the Targumim, and later tradition. — *Saraqael*, a name nowhere else found. — 7. *Gabriel*, whose functions are possibly connected with the account Gen. iii. 24.

CHAP. 21, 1. The writer begins a second narration, treated in a somewhat different manner from the above, which covers to a great extent the ground already gone over. This verse is quoted by Origen, *De Princ.* iv. 35, in the words: ambulavi usque ad imperfectum. *Around*, i.e. in a circuit. — 2. He here repeats and enlarges on the place of punishment for the stars already mentioned 18 : 12–16. — 3–6. cf. chap. 18. — 7–10. follows a description of the place of torment for the fallen angels as in 18 : 11 ; 19 : 1 sqq. *Sections;* the word for this is found only in one other passage, viz. *Ascensio Isaiae* iv. 21, where it is used in the sense of section or verse of Scripture.

SECTION V.

CHAP. 22. — And from here I went to another place, and he showed me in the west a great and high mountain-chain and hard rocks and four beautiful places. 2. And beneath them there were *places* deep and broad and entirely smooth, as smooth as if a thing were rolled, and deep and dark to look at. 3. And this time, Rufael, one of the holy angels, who was with me, answered and said to me: " These beautiful places are intended for this, that upon them may be assembled the spirits, the souls of the dead; for they have been created, that here all the souls of the sons of men might be assembled. 4. These places have been made their dwellings till the day of their judgment, and to their fixed period ; and this period is long, till the great judgment *will come* over them." 5. And I saw the spirits of the children of men who had died, and their voices reached up to heaven, and lamented. 6. At that time I asked the angel Rufael, who was with me, and said to him: "Whose soul is that one whose voice thus reaches *to heaven* and laments?" 7. And he answered and said to me, saying: "That is the spirit that proceeded from Abel, whom his brother Cain slew; and it laments on his account till his seed be destroyed from the face of the earth and his seed disappear from among the seed of men." 8. And at that time I therefore asked concerning him, and concerning the judgment of all, and said: "Why is one separated from the other?" 9. And he answered and said to me: "These three *apartments* are made in order to separate the souls of the dead. And thus are the souls of the just separated: there is a spring of water, above it, light. 10. And thus also is one such *apartment* made for the sinners when they die, and are buried in the earth, without a judgment having been passed upon them during their lives. 11. Here their souls are separated in this great affliction until the great day of judgment and punishment and affliction upon the revilers to eternity, and the vengeance for their souls, and here he binds them to eternity. 12. And if it was before eternity, then this *apartment* has been made for the souls of those who lament and those who reveal their destruction when they were killed in the days of the sinners. 13. And thus it has been created for the souls of men who were not just, but sinners, who were complete in their crimes; and they will be with criminals like themselves; but their souls will not be killed on the day of judgment and will not be taken from here." 14. At that time I blessed the Lord of glory, and said: " Blessed is my Lord, the Lord of glory and of justice, who rules all things to eternity!"

CHAP. 23. — And from there I went to another place towards the west, to the ends of the earth. 2. And I saw a flaming fire which ran without resting, and did not cease from its course day or night, but *continued* regularly. 3. And I asked saying: "What is that which has no rest?" 4. At that time answered Raguel, one of the holy angels, who was with me, and said to me: "That burning fire which thou seest running towards the west is *the fire of* all the luminaries of heaven."

CHAP. 24 — And from there I went to another place of the earth; and he showed me a mountain-chain of fire which flamed day and night. 2. And I went towards it and saw seven magnificent mountains, each one different from the other, and magnificent and beautiful rocks, everything magnificent and fine in appearance and of beautiful surface; three towards the east, one founded upon the other, and three towards the south, one founded upon the other, and ravines, deep and winding, not one joining with the other. 3. And the seventh hill was between these; and in their hights they were all like the seats of a throne and surrounded with fragrant trees. 4. And among them was a tree such as I had never smelt before, neither among these nor among others; nor was there a fragrance like its; its leaves and buds and wood do not wither in eternity; its fruit is beautiful, like the fruit of the vine and the palm-tree. 5. And at that time I said: "Behold, this is a beautiful tree and beautiful to look at, and its leaves are fair, and its fruit very pleasant to the eye." 6. At that time answered Michael, one of the holy and honored angels, who was with me, who was over them [i.e. the trees].

CHAP. 25. — And he said to me : " Enoch, what dost thou ask me concerning the fragrance of this tree and dost seek to know ? " 2. Then I, Enoch, answered him, saying : " Concerning all things I desire to know, but especially concerning this tree." 3. And he answered me, saying : " This high mountain which thou hast seen, whose summit is like the throne of God, is the throne where the holy and great God of glory, the Eternal King, will sit when he shall descend to visit the earth with goodness. 4. And this tree of beautiful fragrance cannot be touched by any flesh until the time of the great judgment ; when all things will be atoned for and consummated for eternity, this will be given to the just and humble 5. From its fruits life will be given to the chosen ; it will be planted towards the north, in a holy place, towards the house of the Lord, the Eternal King. 6. Then they will rejoice greatly, and be glad in the Holy One ; they will let its fragrance enter their members, and live a long life upon the earth, as thy fathers lived ; and in their days no sorrow or sickness or trouble or affliction will touch them." 7. Then I blessed the Lord of glory, the Eternal King, because he had prepared such for the just men, and had created such, and said he would give it to them.

CHAP. 26. — And from here I went to the middle of the earth, and saw a place, blessed and fruitful, where there were branches which rooted in and sprouted out of a tree that was cut. 2. And here I saw a holy mountain, and beneath the mountain, towards the east, water which flowed towards the south. 3. And I saw towards the east another mountain of the same height, and between them a deep valley, but not broad : therein also water flowed along the mountain. 4. And towards the west of this was another mountain, lower than the former, not high, and below, between them a valley; and other deep and sterile valleys were at the end of the three. 5. And all the valleys were deep and not broad, of hard rock. And trees were planted upon them. 6. And I was astonished on account of the rocks, and was astonished on account of the valley, and was very much astonished.

CHAP. 27. — Then I said: " For what purpose is this blessed land, which is entirely filled with trees, and this cursed valley between them?" 2. Then answered Uriel, one of the holy angels, who was with me, and said to me: " This cursed valley is for those who will be cursed to eternity, and here will be assembled all those who have spoken with their mouths unseemly words against God, and speak insolently of his glory; here they will be assembled, and here will be their judgment. 3. And in the latter days there will be the spectacle of a just judgment upon them in the presence of the just, in eternity forever; for this reason they who have found mercy will bless the Lord of glory, the Eternal King. 4. And in the days of their judgment they will bless him for his mercy, according to which he has assigned to them *their lot.*" 5. Then I blessed the Lord of glory, and spoke to him, and remembered his greatness, as it is fitting.

CHAP. 28. — And from here I went towards the east, into the midst of the mountains of the desert, and saw only a plain. 2. But it was filled with trees of this seed, and water dropped down over it from above. 3. It was seen that the water which it sucked up was strong, as towards the north, so towards the west, and as in all places, so water and dew also ascended from here.

CHAP. 29. -- And I went to another place, away from the desert, approaching the east of the mountains. 2. And there I saw trees of judgment, especially those that emitted the fragrance of frankincense and myrrh, and they were not like *ordinary* trees.

CHAP. 30. — And above, over these, over the eastern mountain, not far off, I saw another place, valleys with water that does not dry up. 2. And I saw a beautiful tree, and its fragrance was like that of a mastic. 3. And along the edges of these valleys, I saw fragrant cinnamon. And I advanced over these towards the east.

CHAP. 31. — And I saw another mountain in which were trees from which water flowed, and it flowed like nectar, which is called Sarira and Galbanum. 2. And over this mountain I saw another mountain, on which were aloe-trees; and these trees were full of hard substance like almonds. 3. And in taking that fruit it was better than all the odors.

CHAP. 32. — And after these odors, as I looked towards the north, over the mountains, I saw seven mountains full of pleasant nard and fragrant trees and cinnamon and pepper. 2. And from here I went over the summits of those mountains, far towards the east, and passed far above the Erythraean sea, and went far from it and passed over the angel Zutêl. 3. And I came into the garden of justice, and I saw the mingled diversity of those trees; many and large trees are planted there, of attractive beauty and large and beautiful and magnificent, also the tree of wisdom; eating of it one learns great wisdom. 4. It is like the carob-tree, and its fruit is like the grape, very good; the fragrance of this tree goes out and is spread far. 5. And I said: "This tree is beautiful; how beautiful and pleasant to look at!" 6. Then the holy angel Rufael, who was with me, answered and said to me: "This is the tree of wisdom from which thy old father and thy aged mother, who were before thee, ate, and they learned wisdom, and their eyes were opened, and they learned that they were naked, and were driven out of the garden."

CHAP. 33. — And from here I went to the ends of the earth, and saw great animals there, and one differed from the other, and the birds differed as to their appearance, their beauty and voices, one differed from the other. 2. And to the east of these animals, I saw the ends of the earth, where the heavens rest, and the portals of the heavens open. 3. And I saw where the stars come out from heaven, and I counted the portals out of which they come, and I wrote down all their outlets, each one, according to their number and their names, their connections and their positions and their times and their months, as the angel Uriel, who was with me, showed them to me. 4. He showed all things to me and wrote them down for me ; also their names he wrote for me, and their laws and their deeds.

CHAP. 34. — And from here I went towards the north, to the ends of the earth, and there I saw a great and magnificent wonder, at the ends of the whole earth. 2. There I saw three portals of heaven open in the heavens; from each of them proceed north winds; when *one of them* blows, there is cold, hail, frost, snow, dew, and rain. 3. And out of one of the portals it blows for good ; but when it blows from the two *other* portals, it blows with power, and there is misfortune upon the earth, and they blow with great power.

CHAP. 35. — And from here I went towards the west,

to the ends of the earth, and saw there three open portals, as I had seen in the east, similar portals and
similar outlets.

CHAP. 36. — And from here I went towards the south,
to the ends of the earth, and there I saw three open
portals of heaven ; out of them come the south wind
and dew and rain and wind. 2. And from here I went
towards the east to the ends of the heavens, and there
I saw the three portals of heaven open towards the east,
and over them small portals. 3. Through each one of
these small portals the stars of the heavens come and
go every evening on the path which is shown to them.
4. And as I looked, I blessed, and thus each time I
blessed the Lord of glory, who had made the great and
glorious wonders, to show the greatness of his work to
the angels and to the souls of men, that they might
praise his work, and that all his creatures might see the
works of his might, and praise the great work of his
hand, and bless him to eternity.

CHAP. 22. Conducted to the west, Enoch sees a high mountain-chain, which is not the same as the seven hills in 18 : 6,
cf. 24 : 1. As is seen by the following, it is Rufael that leads
him, this angel thus appearing in the same role in which we
find him in Tobit. The number *four* may be an error for *three*,
cf. vs. 9. If *four* is correct, then Dillmann's suggestion that one of
the places is for the class of mankind described 5–7, and 8, 9
the other places are described. — 2. *Dark*, cf. note on 10 : 5.—
3. According to God's own plan these places are assembling
places of all the dead, in other words the Sheol of the Hebrews
or Hades of the Greeks. The expression *souls of the dead* is
absolute, meaning *all* the souls, and in this the writer is in agreement with Old Testament statements, where Sheol, entirely distinct from the grave, is for the souls of the dead who are called

Raphaim, i.e. shades like the εἴδωλα καμόντων or σκιαί of the Greeks, cf. Spiess, *Entwicklungsgeschichte der vorstellungen vom Zustande nach dem Tode*, p. 422 sqq. — 4. Here these souls shall abide to the day of the final judgment. Deliverance from Sheol is a hope frequently expressed in the later books of the Old Testament, e.g. Ps. xlix. 15. — *Lamented*, i.e. as the following shows, not on account of their being there, but because of the injustice they suffered during life. — 6, 7. One voice is especially noticeable, and that is Abel's, according to Gen. iv. 10. As the sins of the parents are visited upon the children, justice will not have been done to Abel until his brother's descendants are destroyed. — 8. We see by this verse that the spirits of the dead are not all in one place, but are separated; and now follows the description of the other apartments. — 9. Of these (other) apartments there are three. The reason for this separation is probably the author's conviction that the difference in the moral character produces a different fate after death, even before the final judgment. The apartment here (if indeed not identical with 7 and 8) is for the souls of the other just, i.e. for those who were just, but unlike Abel did not die a violent and undeserved death. — 10. There are two divisions for the sinners, the first one for those who died without being punished during their lives, and who obtained even an honorable burial. According to the Old Testament (and according to Greek ideas) it was a disgrace of the highest kind to be left unburied. — 11. Here already they suffer affliction to the day of final judgment (with which the *eternity* is identical, cf. note on 14 : 1). — 12, 13. The second class of sinners are those who although sinners nevertheless suffered in the world. *Before eternity*, i.e. before the final judgment. But these, having already been partially punished, shall not again be judged like the other class, which statement shows that the final judgment is to inaugurate for those of vs. 10 and 11 a greater punishment than the terrors of Sheol. The killing of the souls here referred to is not annihilation, as many other passages in Enoch show, but is identical with the eternal death in the punishment of hell. *Will not be taken from here*, i.e. will not rise from the dead. That the *just* shall rise is clearly stated 81 : 4 ; 90 : 33 ; 91 : 10 ; 92 : 3 ; 100 : 5. Cf. on the whole matter what is said of the second death of the sinners in Onkelos on Deut. xxxiii. 6 ; Jonath. on Isa. xxii. 14 ; lxv. 15 ; Jer. li. 39, 57. — 14. As is his manner in receiving a revelation (cf. 24 : 7 ; 27 : 5 ; 36 : 4 ; 39 : 9–12 ; 81 : 3 ; 83 : 11 ; chap. 84, 90 : 40), Enoch blesses the Lord, in which he is imitated in the *Ascensio Isaiae*, chap. 6 sqq. *Lord of glory* (25 : 3, 7 ; 27 : 5 ; 36 : 4 ; 40 : 3 ; 63 : 2 ; 75 : 3 ; 81 : 3 ; 83 : 8) and *Lord of justice* (83 : 11 ; 90 : 40) are proper appellatives of God in this connection, as these two characteristics of his divinity were exemplified in the preceding.

CHAP. 23, 1. He leaves the place of departed spirits, but remains in the west. — 2-4. This is probably the same fire that he mentioned 17 : 4. *Towards the west*, a modifying clause of *fire*, not of *running*.

CHAP. 24, 1. He fails to state just where that *other place* is. but as *the mountain-chain of fire* are the seven hills of 18 : 6–9, this new place must be in the south. — 2. Here these mountains are positively identified with those mentioned in 18, but he enlarges on their aspect. *Not one joining the other*, i.e. they were parallel. — 3. *Fragrant trees*, a proof that it was a blessed place. — 4-6. Of these trees one is especially beautiful, cf. note on 10 : 19. *Michael*, as the special angel of Israel, instructs the seer on the special blessing in store for the true Israelite.

CHAP. 25, 1. The conversation carried on here and above is very much like the one between Isaiah and the angel in their ascent through the seven heavens in the *Ascensio Isaiae*. — 3. The throne that Enoch saw, 24 : 3, is not an illusion, but is in reality the throne of God. Although the location would answer, it is more than probable that the author did not mean Mount Sinai of 1 : 4 here, for God descends on Mount Sinai to judge, but here, as is shown by the context and expressed by the words, *to visit the earth with goodness*, cf. 77 : 1. *Lord of glory*, cf. note on 22 : 14. *Eternal king*, cf. vs. 5, 7, a biblical name of God. — 4. This tree is here preserved until the time of the judgment. *Mortal*, literally *flesh*, cf. note on 14 : 2, and Gen. iii. 22–24. — 5. Now the guide explains that this is the tree of life, Gen. ii. 9 ; iii. 22 ; Prov. iii. 18 ; xi. 30 ; xiii. 12 ; xv. 4, a hope found also 4 Ezra viii. 62 ; Apoc. ii. 7 ; xxii. 2, 14, 19 ; *Testamentum Levi* xviii, and by rabbinnical writings, cf. Schöttgen, *Horae Talmud.* in Apoc. ii. 7. This tree, however, is entirely distinct from the tree of wisdom, 32 : 6. In the Messianic times this tree is to be transplanted from the south, where it is now kept, to the north, to the New Jerusalem, which is to stand on the site of the old, cf. chap. 26, 27. Such is the power of this tree that simply breathing of it gives long life ; cf. Ezek. xxxvii. 9 ; cf. note on 10 : 17, and Isa. lxv. 19, 20.

CHAP. 26, 1. Having mentioned that the tree of life is to be transplanted to the New Jerusalem, he now visits that place. As the Greeks thought Delphi, the centre of their worship, the middle of the earth, the Jewish seer here regards Jerusalem as such, as it is possibly already done, Ezek. xxxviii. 12 ; v. 5 ; Isa. ii. 2, and book of the Jubilees, viii. 2, where Zion is called the *navel of the earth*, like the term ὀμφαλός, used of the round stone in the temple at Delphi as the centre of the earth in Pindar P. 4, 131 ; 6, 3. Early oriental Christians entertained the same views, cf. Tertullian and Jerome on Ezek. v. 5, and the former *Contra Marcion* II. 196. In En. 90 : 26 Gehenna is in the middle of the earth, and in the Ethiopic *Synaxaria, de Melchisedec* (Dill. *Chrest.* p. 16) Mount Calvary is regarded as such. *Fruitfulness* is constantly a characteristic of the Messianic times. *The tree* is Israel ; it was *cut* as a punishment for its sins ; the branches are the faithful, who will enjoy the Messianic kingdom. — 2. The following is simple : the hill is Zion, the water is the brook of Siloah. — 3.

The other hill is the Mount of Olives, which is in reality but a few feet higher than Mount Zion. The deep valley is that of Kedron or of Jehoshaphat, and the water is the Kedron brook. — 4. The Mount of Offence and the valley of Hinnom. — 5. The description is trustworthy, cf. Strabo 16, 2, § 36. — 6. This is the valley of Hinnom, or Gehenna.

CHAP. 27, 1, 2. As this valley is an important element in the Messianic times the author describes it more minutely, especially as the Old Testament statements on the subject are very indefinite. This valley is, according to the first part of Enoch, the place where the sinners are punished, 90 : 26, 27, cf. 4 Ezra vi. 1–3. In the Parables it is indeed mentioned that the kings and the mighty will be punished in a valley, 54 : 1, 2 ; 56 : 4, and in the sight of the just, 48 : 9, 10 ; 62 : 12, but there is no evidence whatever that this writer thought to specify any particular valley. Then the punishment in Gehenna, according to 90 : 23–27, is restricted to the unfaithful in Israel, and the scope of the verse before us is evidently no broader, while in 54 and 56 altogether different persons are punished " in the valley," cf. 38, 1. The author's statements here are at least partially drawn from Old Testament premises. That this valley is the place of punishment rests on the statements Jer. vii. 31 ; xix. 6 ; xxxii. 35, and on the accounts in 2 Kings xxiii. 10, and on Jeremiah's curse, Jer. vii. 32, 33 ; xix. 6 sqq., and partially, perhaps, on the nature of the valley, for according to *Talmud Erabin*, fol. 19, a smoke ascended there, thus indicating a subterranean fire. That a fire destroys the sinners in this valley finds its explanation in Gen. xix. 25 ; Ps. xi. 6 ; Isa. lxvi. 15, 16, 24. — 4. *Lot*, or portion, cf. *Ascensio Isaiae* i. 3. — 5. Cf. note on 22 : 14.

CHAP. 28, 1. From the centre of the earth, the New Jerusalem, the seer goes towards the east, and from among the mountains of the desert he sees a plain.— 2. This plain was, however, filled with trees of this [which ?] seed. What places are here meant is a mystery. Dillmann conjectures the Arabah, or plain of the Jordan, and the mountains as the hilly tract between that river and Jerusalem.

CHAP. 29, 1. He continues on his eastward trip, and there reaches the sweet-smelling trees, the Arabia and India of the ancients, to the הַר הַקֶּדֶם of Gen. x. 30, in which the ancients recognized the place of frankincense and spices. — 2. *Trees of judgment,* i.e. trees that will be given to the just after the judgment to be planted by them, cf. 10 : 19. Also cf. Isa. lx. 6 ; Ps. lxxii. 10.

CHAP. 30. According to the testimony of the ancients cinnamon was an eastern product.

CHAP. 31. *Sarira,* a word not found elsewhere. An Amharic vocabulary says the word means *a black flower,* cf. Dillmann, *Lex.,* col. 343. But the form is probably corrupt. *Galbanum,* cf. Winer, *Realwörterb., in verb.*

CHAP. 32, 1, 2. *Zutel,* a name otherwise not known (at least Buxtorf does not mention him), must be the angel guarding the entrance of Paradise. — 3. The destination of the seer is *the garden of justice,* i.e. the Paradise, called by the same name 77 : 3 ; *garden of the just* 60 : 23 ; *garden of life* 61 : 12. The tree of wisdom is entirely distinct from the tree of life, 25 : 4. As wisdom is to characterize the just in the Messianic times the tree of wisdom is very properly here mentioned. — 4. *Carob tree,* cf. Dillmann, *Lex.,* col. 76. — 6. Here we learn that it is the earthly Paradise that Enoch visits. It is not strange that the author fails to give any hint as to the object and future destiny of this garden. He could not make it the abode of the departed just, for they have their place in one (or two) of the apartments of Sheol, cf. 22 : 6 sqq. ; nor could it be the seat of the Messianic kingdom, for this was to be at Jerusalem, cf. chap. 25 and 26, and therefore the writer must leave it out in the cold. And why the tree of wisdom should not be transplanted to the New Jerusalem like the tree of life, 25 : 5, is not mentioned.

CHAP. 33, 1. Now he gets to the ends of the earth, to the

place of the extraordinary specimens of the animal kingdom. This chapter was probably suggested by the preceding, in which he visits lands favored with mineral wealth, or by the notices in Gen. ii. 19, 20 of the animals in close connection with Paradise. — 2. *Portals.* or exits for the luminaries. *Uriel,* as is required by his office, cf. 19 : 1, instructs the seer in these matters. As Enoch had claimed a higher source for his knowledge of the judgment, 1 : 2, he here claims the same for his special book on the luminaries, chap. 72–82.

CHAP. 34. Evidently he had been at the ends of the earth in the preceding chapter, and now goes to the extreme north. As there could be no portals for the luminaries in the north, he finds some there for the winds, joined with phenomena of nature such as could be expected in that region. As the north winds are usually injurious, but not always, he says there is one portal from which it blows for good, but two for evil. Cf. the system in chap. 76.

CHAP. 35. The portals are of course for the setting luminaries, the outlets for the winds, as the latter expression, in the *west,* suits only the winds.

CHAP. 36, 1. The symmetry of the narrative demands that he goes to the south also. Here, as in the north, he sees only portals for the winds, but none for the luminaries. — 2. He returns to the east, where he sees three portals for the winds which he had failed to mention 33 : 2, 3, and above these were smaller portals for the stars. — 4. Cf. Ps. ciii. 20–22; cxlviii.; cf. 22 : 14.

SECTION VI.

CHAP. 37. — The second vision of wisdom which Enoch, the son of Jared, the son of Mahalaleel, the son of Cainan, the son of Enos, the son of Seth, the son of Adam, saw. 2. And this is the beginning of the words

of wisdom, which I commenced to speak and to relate
to those who dwell on the earth: hear, ancestors, and
see, descendants, the holy words which I will speak before the Lord of the spirits! 3. It is proper to name
the former first, but from the descendants too we will
not keep back the beginning of wisdom. 4. And up to
the present time there was not given from before the
Lord of the spirits the wisdom which I have received
according to my knowledge, according to the pleasure
of the Lord of the spirits, by whom the portion of life
everlasting was given to me. 5. Three Parables were
given to me; and I commenced to relate them to those
who dwell on the earth.

CHAP. 37. The reasons for assigning 37–71 to a different
author and time will be found in the Special Introduction. 1.
The second, or other, *vision of wisdom* distinguishes it in plain
terms from the first part, and like the heading 1 : 1 sqq. gives
the object of the following. By wisdom, 82 : 1 ; 92 : 1, the writer
understands the knowledge and appreciation of God's revelation (cf. vs. 4) concerning the true state of affairs in the time
of the Messiah, in whom dwells the spirit of wisdom, 49 : 3,
and it will be given by him to the just, 49 : 1. This wisdom
could be obtained only by revelation, as wisdom resides in
heaven, chap. 42. The genealogy here given certainly points
to an entirely new element in the book. — 2. After the heading in the preceding, Enoch addresses his readers directly : they
are all mankind in all generations. The words are *holy*, cf. 1 : 2.
As proof that they are true he speaks to them as if he were in
the very presence of the *Lord of the spirits*. This name for
God is peculiar to the three Parables, being found 38 : 2, 6 ; 39 :
7–9, 12 ; 40 : 1, 2, 4–7 ; 41 : 2, 6, 7 ; 43 : 4 ; 46 : 3, 6–8 ; 47 : 1, 2 ;
48 : 2, 3, 5, 7, 10 ; 49 : 2, 4 ; 50 : 2, 3, 5 ; 51 : 3 ; 52 : 5, 9 ;
53 : 6 ; 54 : 5–7 ; 55 : 3, 4 ; 57 : 3 ; 58 : 4–6 ; 59 : 1, 2 ; [60 :

6, 8, 25;] 61 : 3, 5, 8, 9, 11, 13; 62 : 10, 12, 14, 16; 63 : 1, 2, 12, [65 : 9, 11; 66 : 2; 67 : 8, 9; 68 : 4; 69 : 24;] 29; 71 : 2, 17; and is in the closest harmony with the contents of this portion of the book, cf. 39 : 12 sqq.; 41 : 8. — 3. The reason for speaking to the ancestors first is, probably, not the reverence paid to old age, a virtue so characteristic of the true Jew to the present day, but rather, as the second clause indicates, their moral superiority over the later generations, which did not deserve such revelations. *The beginning of wisdom* in verse 2 and here, is in conformity with the whole object of the book as an instructor in true wisdom, used as in Ps. cxi. 10; Prov. i. 7; ix. 10. — 4. Although it is stated in the first part that the just shall rise from the dead (cf. note on 22 : 12, 13), and that the Messianic reign shall endure forever (cf. 91 : 17; 92 : 4; 105 : 2), the distinctly expressed hope of eternal life is found only in the Parables; cf. also 39 : 8, 9; 40 : 9; 58 : 3; 71 : 14–17. — 5. The author divides his tract into three parts. *Parables;* the word used in the original corresponds to the Heb. מְשָׁלִים, παραβολαί (cf. Gesenius, *Thesaur.* p. 828); Dillmann, following the proposal of Hoffmann, Einleit., p. 13, translates *Bilderreden*; Maurice Vernes, *Histoire des Idées Messianiques,* has *Paraboles*, or *Similitudes; Ascensio Isaiae* iv. 21 it is used in quoting David's Psalms; Drummond uses *Similitudes.*

SECTION VII.

CHAP. 38. — First Parable. When the congregation of the just shall appear, and the sinners are condemned because of their sins, and expelled from the face of the earth, 2. and when the Just One shall appear in the presence of the just who are chosen, whose deeds hang on the Lord of the spirits, and the light shall appear to the just and to the chosen, who dwell on the earth, — where will be the habitation of the sinners, and where the resting-places of those who have denied the Lord of the spirits? It were better had they not been born. 3. And when the secrets of the just shall be revealed, then the sinners will be judged, and the impious will be expelled from the presence of the just and chosen. 4. And from that time those who hold the earth will not be powerful and exalted, nor will they be able to behold the face of the just, for the light of the Lord of the spirits is seen on the face of the holy and just and chosen. 5. And the mighty kings will perish at that time, and will be given over into the hands of the just and holy. 6. And from that time on no one can ask for mercy from the Lord of the spirits, for their lives have ended.

CHAP. 39. — And it will come to pass in these days that the chosen and holy children will descend from the high heavens, and their seed will become one with the children of men. 2. In those days Enoch received books of zeal and of anger, and books of disturbance and of expulsion, and " mercy will not be upon them," said the Lord of the spirits. 3. And at that time, a cloud and a whirlwind seized me from the face of the earth, and carried me to the end of the heavens. 4. And here I saw another vision, the dwellings of the just and the resting-places of the holy. 5. Here my eyes saw their dwellings with the angels, and their resting-places with the holy, and they asked and petitioned and prayed in behalf of the children of men, and justice like water flowed before them, and mercy like dew on the earth; thus it is among them to all eternity. 6. And in those days my eyes saw the place of the chosen of justice and of faith [fidelity], and how justice will be in their days, and the just and chosen without number before him to all eternity. 7. And I saw their dwellings under the

10*

wings of the Lord of the spirits; and all the just and chosen before him are ornamented as with the light of fire, and their mouths are full of blessings, and their lips praise the name of the Lord of the spirits, and justice before him will not cease. 8. Here I desired to dwell, and my soul longed for this place; here my portion has been before, for such is established concerning me before the Lord of the spirits. 9. And in those days I blessed and exalted the name of the Lord of the spirits with blessings and praise, for he has strengthened me in blessing and praise according to the will of the Lord of the spirits. 10. For a long time my eyes looked at this place, and I blessed him, saying: "Bless him, and let him be blessed from the beginning and to eternity! 11. Before him there is no ceasing; he knows, before the world was created, what the world is, and will be from generation to generation. 12. Thee they praise who do not sleep; they stand before thy glory, and bless and glorify and exalt thee, saying: 'Holy! Holy! Holy! the Lord of the spirits fills the earth with spirits.'" 13. And here my eyes saw all those who do not sleep, standing before him and blessing him, and they say: " Blessed art thou, and blessed the name of the Lord to all eternity." 14. And my face was changed until I could see no more.

Chap. 40. — And after that I saw a thousand times thousand, and ten thousand times ten thousand *beings*, an innumerable and immense multitude, who stood before the glory of the Lord of the spirits. 2. I looked, and on the four sides of the Lord of the spirits I saw four faces, different from those standing, and I learned their names, which the angel who came with me announced as their names to me, and showed me all the secrets. 3. And

I heard the voices of those four faces as they blessed before the Lord of glory. 4. The first voice blessed the Lord of the spirits to all eternity. 5. And I heard the second voice praising the Chosen One and the chosen ones, who hang on the Lord of the spirits. 6. And I heard the third voice asking and praying for those who dwell on the earth, and petitioning in the name of the Lord of the spirits. 7. And I heard the fourth voice keeping off the satans, and not allowing them to come before the Lord of the spirits to accuse those who dwell on the earth. 8. After that I asked the angel of peace who went with me, who showed me all things that were hidden, and said to him: " Who are these four faces that I see, and whose voices I hear and have written them down ? " 9. And he said to me: " The first is the holy Michael, merciful, slow to anger; and the second, who is over all sicknesses and over all the wounds of the children of men, is Rufael; and the third, who is over all the powers, is the holy Gabriel; and the fourth, who is over penitence and the hope of those who inherit everlasting life, is Fanuel." 10. And these are the four angels of God, the Most High, and the four voices I heard in those days.

CHAP. 41. — And after this I saw all the secrets of heaven, and the kingdom as it is divided, and how the deeds of men are weighed upon scales. 2. There I saw the dwellings of the chosen, and the dwellings of the holy, and my eyes saw there how all the sinners were cast from there, they who had denied the name of the Lord of the spirits, and they are dragged away, and there is no rest for them because of the punishments which proceed from the Lord of the spirits/ 3. And there my eyes saw the secrets of the lightning and of the thunder, and the secrets of the winds, how they are divided to blow over the earth, and the secrets of the clouds and of the dew, and there I saw also from what place they proceed, and from whence they satisfy the dust of the earth.] 4. And there I saw the closed repositories, and from them the winds are divided out, and the repository of hail and the repository of fog and of the clouds; and his cloud hovers over the earth from the beginning of the world. 5. And I saw the repositories of the sun and of the moon, from whence they come and to which they return, and their glorious return, and how one is more glorious than the other, and their fixed course, and how they do not leave their course, and how they add nothing to their course and take nothing from it, and preserve their fidelity one with the other, remaining steadfast in their oath. 6. And first the sun goes out, and makes his way according to the command of the Lord of the spirits, and strong is his name to all eternity; 7. and after this the hidden and the revealed course of the moon, completing the course of her way in that place by day and by night, one looking at the other [i.e. opposite each other] before the Lord of the spirits; and they give thanks and praise and do not rest, for their thanksgiving is rest for them. 8. For the shining sun makes many changes for a blessing and for a curse, and the course of the path of the moon is light to the just, and darkness to the sinners in the name of the Lord who created *a separation* between light and darkness, and divided the spirits of men, and strengthened the spirits of the just, in the name of his own justice. 9. For neither does an angel hinder, nor is any power able to hinder, for the Judge sees them all, and judges them all before him.

CHAP. 42. — Wisdom did not find a place where she might live, and a dwelling-place was *given* to her in the heavens. 2. Wisdom came to dwell among the children of men, and found no dwelling-place; wisdom returned to her place and took her seat among the angels. 3. And injustice came forth from its repository; whom it did not seek, them it found, and dwelt with them, like the rain in the desert, and like dew in the thirsty land.

CHAP. 43. — And again I saw lightning, and the stars of heaven, and I saw how he called them all by their names, and they heard him. 2. And I saw that they were weighed on the scales of justice, according to their light, according to the width of their places, and the day of their appearance, and their course; one flash of lightning produces another, and their course according to the number of angels, and their fidelity they preserved among themselves. 3. And I asked the angel, who went with me, who showed me what was secret: "What are these?" 4. And he said to me: "The Lord of the spirits has showed thee a picture of them: these are the names of the just, who dwell on the earth and believe on the name of the Lord of the spirits to all eternity."

CHAP. 44. — Also other things I saw in reference to *the flashes of* lightning; how they arise from the stars, and become lightning, and can leave nothing behind with them.

SECTION VIII.

CHAP. 38, 1. The writer, who shows himself as much more systematic in everything than the author of the first book, states that what now follows is the first parable; and this con-

tinues to chap. 44. He immediately enters *in medias res*, showing both how important he considers his revelation and making
it certain that at the author's time the hope for the Messianic
times must have been especially prominent, else he would certainly have needed some explanatory words as introduction.
Congregation of the just is explained in verse 3, 39 : 6 ; 53 : 6 ;
62 : 8, and is an expression entirely peculiar to the Parables ;
shall appear, i.e. when the Messianic rule shall be inaugurated.
Expelled: the Parables teach that the sinners shall be destroyed, 53 : 5, in some unknown valley, 56 : 3, 4, for it is
neither in heaven nor on earth, 45 : 2, 5, 6 ; 53 : 2, but the
first book teaches emphatically that the place of eternal punishment is in the valley of Hinnom near Jerusalem, cf. notes
on chap. 27. — 2. Contemporaneous with this is the appear-
rance of the Messiah, the Just One, a name applied to him
because he is a just judge, and is found also 53 : 6. *Just and
chosen*, one of the many names for the inhabitants of the Messianic kingdom ; others are simply *just*, or *chosen*, or *chosen
just, holy and chosen, just and holy, just and good, children of
God, children of heaven.* It has been claimed that the expression *it were better had they not been born* was based on Matt.
xxvi. 24, and that the Parables consequently were written
after that Gospel, but this is without any foundation whatever, as
the Old Testament presents sufficient premises for this statement
in Job iii. 3 ; Jer. xx. 14 ; Psalt. Salom. iii. 11 ; cf. the חלי בי in
Pirke Aboth, Perek ה, and in *Kiddushim*, Perek א, and the classical writers have any amount of similar expressions ; cf. Spiess,
l. c. pp. 38, 39, and Delitzsch in *Zeitschrift für Luth. Theol.*,
1876, p. 405, Hermae Pastor iv. 2, 6.—3. *The secrets of the just*,
i.e. the Messiah and his kingdom, for even in the days of the sinners he had been revealed to the just, 48 : 7 ; 62 : 7. — 4. The
important role that the *mighty of the earth* play in the Parables
will soon appear. *Light*, in a moral and physical sense, cf. Num.
vi. 25 ; Ps. civ. 2 ; cxxxix. 11, 12 ; Isa. ix. 1, 2 ; lx. ; Zech.
xiv. 6 sqq. ; Dan. xii. 3, and often in Enoch. — 5. *Mighty·*

kings are the object of the writer's threats, instead of the sinners in general, as is the case in the first part, cf. 46 : 4–8;
48 : 8–10; 53 : 5; 62 : 1–12, 63, while they are only casually
mentioned as one kind of sinners 96 : 8; 104 : 3. — 6. The
judgment is irrevocable.

CHAP. 39. The contrast with the children of men compels
us to believe the children of heaven to be the angels; cf. note
on 6 : 1. Although the angels are not called *chosen* by the Old
Testament or by Enoch elsewhere, but first by 1 Tim. v. 21, the
name could easily be applied to them, partly from the οἱ ἐκλεκτοί
of Tob. viii. 15, partly from the fact that it is the general appellation of those with whom their fate is to be united. A parallel
statement is that even the Messiah shall dwell with men during his reign, 45 : 4; 62 : 14, and thus "heaven shall be on
earth," cf. Jonath. *ad Zach.* iii. 7. *Their seed will be one*, of
course not in the sinful manner of the fallen angels and the
women, but rather as in 62 : 14. — 2. The sudden change of
subjects is somewhat surprising, but as the writer has announced in general terms the wonderful changes introduced
by the Messiah he must explain how these are to be effected,
viz. by a judgment. *Books*, i.e. books containing an account
of the judgment, but to specify further as to what books he
refers is impossible. It is even possible that the word *books* is
chosen simply on account of Enoch's literary character, but cf.
93 : 1–3. — 3. Cf. note on 14 : 8. — 4. The sudden change
again to the subject of the first verse almost forces the belief
that something is wrong with verse 2, unless it is an adverbial
clause specifying the time of his vision concerning the home
of the just. — 5. The vision is entirely prophetic, for the writer
has as little to say concerning the happiness of saints in heaven as
the Old Testament has; the Messianic kingdom is, as it were,
now yet in heaven. In view of this, that it is not yet determined
who shall belong to that kingdom, the angels petition (cf. note
on 15 : 1, 2) for mankind, and in view of chap. 50; 90 : 29–38;
91 : 14 (cf. notes) that many may take part. With these angels

are justice and mercy. with the side idea that these shall be brought down with them when they descend, vs. 1. *Water* and *dew* are symbols of plenty, cf. Isa. xi. 9; Micah v. 6. — 6. *Faith* (cf. note on 58 : 5), certainly not in a Christian sense; the word *haimanoth* means also *fidelity*, i.e. to God. Then it is very easily possible that the Christian translator uses a word here that may not exactly express the original, cf. Herzog *R. E.* xii. p. 310 (ed. 1). — 7. *Under the wings*, a symbol of protection, Ex. xix. 4; Deut. xxxii. 11, 12; xxxiii. 12; Matt. xxiii. 37; cf. note on 38 : 2. — 8. Cf. 71 : 14–17; 90 : 31. — 9. Cf. 37 : 4. — 11. The eternity and foreknowledge of God is extolled because they have been exemplified in vs. 8. — 12, 13. *Who do not sleep*, cf. note on 12 : 2. The change of the Trisagion (Isa. vi. 3) in this passage is according to the contents of the Parables, and especially because God is here the Lord of the spirits. — 14. *Could not see*, i.e. was blinded by the glory he saw; cf. 14 : 24, 25; *Ascensio Isaiae* ix. 38.

CHAP. 40. Cf. note on 1 : 9. The transition from the description of the Messianic kingdom to the glories of heaven is easily explained by the connection between the two as laid down in the previous chapter. — 2. Distinct from the multitude before the Lord are the four special angels, whose special name being מַלְאֲכֵי הַפָּנִים, a name taken from Isa. lxiii. 9, are here accordingly represented as faces. The same distinction is observed 71 : 1, and rigidly by rabbinical writers, cf. Buxtorf, *Lex.* (ed. Fischer), p. 27, and Herzog *R. E.* iv. p. 20 sqq. (ed. 1). This verse is used in *Pirke Elieser* c. 4. *The angel who came with me* is the *angel of peace* in verse 8; cf. 52 : 5; 53 : 4; 54 : 4; 56 : 2, where he receives this name, and 43 : 3; 46 : 2; 52 : 3, 4; 61 : 2, 3; 64 : 2. Who he is, is not mentioned, but Hoffmann's conjecture of Uriel is not improbable, especially as the Parables, unlike the almost unanimous verdict of later Judaism (cf. Buxtorf, l. c.), do not make him one of the four chief angels, but put Fanuel in his place; cf. **vs. 9** and 71 : 8. His name is taken from his functions as the opposite of the satans, or possibly as the well known angel of death, cf. Jonath. on Hab. iii. 5. — 4. The first one praises the Lord, an idea probably taken from Isa. vi. 3, and according to verse 9 this is Michael. His name is taken from his work, for his cry is מִי כָאֵל (cf. Buxtorf, l. c.). He is here already, like in later works (cf. Herzog, *R. E.*, l. c. p. 27), the שַׂר הַפָּנִים, or the Metatron, and as such he has attributes which are generally assigned to God alone. — 5. The second praises the Chosen One, i.e. the Messiah, the most frequent name for him, found also 45 : 3–5; 49 : 2; 51 : 3, 5; 52 : 6–9; 53 : 6; 55 : 4; 61 : 5, 8; 62 : 1. He is so called because he has been chosen by the Lord of the spirits, 46 : 3. The name taken from Isa. xlii. 1 is peculiar to the Parables, and is found in no other apocryphal book. The estimate put on the Messiah here in making him the object of praise by one of the highest angels is seriously diminished by having the chosen ones put into the same category, and further by the fact that nothing more is meant here than that they are both objects of the special concern of this angel; and as 61 : 10 the Chosen One is included in the host of those that praise the Lord, the idea of a Christian origin cannot be entertained for a second. This angel is, vs. 9, Rufael; cf. notes on 10 : 7; 20 : 3, and the healing by Rafael in Tob. iii. 17. — 6. The third is Gabriel, over all the powers, his name being from גבר and אל. — 7. The fourth wards off the satans. These beings, altogether unknown to the writer of the first part, and entirely distinct from the fallen angels or their children, are conceived by the writer of the Parables as the powers of an anti-divine kingdom under the leadership of a prince, who is Satan, κατ' ἐξοχήν, 53 : 3. These satans existed before the fall of the angels, for these sinned by becoming subjects of Satan, 54 : 6, and they, unlike the watchers, 13 : 5; 14 : 5, have access to heaven, on the basis of Job ii. 1; Zech. iii. To this kingdom of Satan belong also the angels of punishment, cf. notes on 53 : 3. Satans are mentioned in the Noachic additions, 65 : 6; cf. *Ascensio Isaiae*

11

ii. 2. The fourth angel is Fanuel, and as he keeps off the satans he thereby protects those who inherit everlasting life, cf. note on 37 : 4. — 8. *Angel of peace,* cf. vs. 2.

CHAP. 41, 1. As the writer of the first part was initiated into the secrets of the physical world as well as the spiritual, the author here also gives a treatise on natural philosophy, but not without first again having spoken of his favorite topic, of the dwellings of the just. The *kingdom* is scarcely the Messianic (Dillmann), but rather the kingdom of this world, which is to be divided, i.e. the faithful separated from the sinners, when the deeds of all are weighed in the final judgment. Interpreting thus it is easily seen why he mentions the fate of both the just and the sinners in the next verse. *Weighed,* cf. 61 : 8 ; Prov. xvi. 2 ; xxi. 2 ; xxiv. 12 ; Job xxxi. 6 ; Ps. lxii. 9 ; Dan. v. 27 ; 4 Ezra i. 35 (ed. Laurence), and Homer, *Il.* 8, 69 sqq.; 22, 209 sqq. — 2. *Expulsion of the sinners,* cf. note ch. 27. *Deny,* a sin often mentioned in the Parables, cf. 38 : 2 ; 45 : 1, 2 ; 46 : 7 ; 48 : 10, (denying the just judgment, 60 : 6, or the heavenly sphere, 45 : 1, or the Messiah, 48 : 10, or the spirit of God, 67 : 10). It is pictured as the chief and principal sin.— 3. The introducing clause is different from the one employed in the first part, where the writer always says : "And I went and saw." *How they are divided,* cf. Job xxxviii. 24, 25, 35. — 4. The repositories of the wind are *closed* as the winds are allowed to escape only at certain times ; cf. Job xxxviii. 22, 25–28, 34, 37, 38 ; xxxvii. 11, 12. *His cloud* ; Dillmann thinks of the *Shechinah,* Langen, p. 293, of " the spirit hovering over the deep," but the statement is so vague that no conclusion can be attempted. — 5. These repositories must, then, be near the portals of 33 : 3 sqq. ; cf. Ps. xix. 6. *Glorious return,* i.e. their secret return from west to east. *More glorious,* i.e. the sun than the moon ; cf. chap. 72 sqq. *Oath ;* the luminaries have taken oaths among themselves to be true to each other, 43 : 2, a figure probably taken from the marriage vow ; cf. 69 : 20, 25. — 6. *Strong,* for even the mighty sun obeys him ; cf. Ps. lxxiv.

16 ; civ. 19 ; Eccles. i. 5. — 7. *Hidden course of the moon,* the time when she is not seen in the heavens ; cf. chap. 73 and 74. *Praise,* cf. Ps. xix. 2 sqq. ; cxlviii. 3 sqq. ; Job xxxviii. 3. — 8. The writer plays on the biblical expression, children of light and of darkness ; cf. Job xxiv. 13–17 ; xxxviii. 15 ; En. 59.

CHAP. 42, 1. Drummond (p. 62) is certainly right in calling this "a detached fragment," for it apparently interrupts the sense. The only possible connection it could have would be that wisdom was in the hands of God his means of strengthening the just, 41 : 8, or that wisdom and injustice have repositories like the powers of nature of which he is here speaking ; cf. vs. 3. Wisdom found no place to dwell, i.e. on earth, and returns to heaven ; cf. Job xxviii. 12–14, 20–24 ; Baruch iii. 31. Wisdom is here personified as in Prov. viii. and ix. — 2. Cf. Prov. i. 20 sqq. ; viii. 1 sqq. ; ix. 1 sqq. ; Son of Sirach xxiv. 7. In the Messianic times, however, she will return, 48 : 1 sqq. ; 49 : 1 sqq. ; 91 : 10. — 3. As wisdom in the author's mind is the biblical wisdom, its opposite here is injustice ; cf. Zech. v. 8. The contrast here is a success. Although the expression here *sounds* somewhat like John's prologue to his Gospel, the connection goes no further, and does not betray a Christian source ; cf. Langen, p. 44 sq. *Dew and rain* are symbols of plenty, cf. on 39 : 5 ; Job xxxviii. 26, 27 ; Isa. xxxv. 6 ; xli. 18 ; xliii. 20.

CHAP. 43. 1, 2. He continues the topic of chapter 41 with the stars. *Called,* cf. Isa. xl. 26 ; Ps. cxlvii. 4 ; Baruch iii. 34. *Weighed,* as the context shows, means simply that their mass, course, etc. is assigned to them in a manner pleasing to a higher power. They are guided by angels. Neither here nor above is any personality or moral accountability attributed to them, although their conduct is to be an example for men, cf. in general Dan. viii. 10 with En. 46 : 7, and Dan. xii. 3 with En. 104 : 2, and thus the stars can represent the names of the just. With this we can understand the strange answer of the angel in verse 4. *Believe,* the opposite of *denying,* cf. note on

41 : 2, believing being the great characteristic of the faithful ; cf. 58 : 5. *Name*, for the being or person it represents, as often in the Parables.

CHAP. 44. Here he certainly means nothing but the shooting stars.

SECTION VIII.

CHAP. 45. — And this is the second Parable concerning those who deny the name of the dwelling-place of the holy and of the Lord of the spirits. 2. They will not ascend to heaven, and will not come on the earth ; such will be the portion of the sinners who deny the name of the Lord of the spirits, who are thus preserved to the day of suffering and sorrow. 3. On that day the Chosen One will sit upon the throne of glory, and will choose among their [i.e. men's] deeds and places without number, and their spirit will become strong in them when they see my Chosen One and those who have called upon my holy and glorious name. 4. And on that day I will cause my Chosen One to dwell among them, and will transform heaven and make it a blessing and a light eternally. 5. And I will transform the earth and make it a blessing, and will cause my chosen ones to dwell thereon ; and those who have committed sins and crimes will not step on it. 6. For I have seen and satisfied with peace my just ones, and have placed them before me ; but for the sinners there awaits before me a judgment, that I may destroy them from the face of the earth.

CHAP. 46. — And there I saw one who had a head of days [i.e. was old], and his head was white like wool ; and with him was a second whose countenance was like the appearance of a man, and his countenance was full of agreeableness, like one of the holy angels. 2. And I asked one of the angels, who went with me, and who showed me all the secrets, concerning this son of man, who he was and whence he was, and why he goes with the Head of days? 3. And he answered and said to me: "This is the Son of man, who has justice, and justice dwells with him, and all the treasures of secrecy he reveals, because the Lord of the spirits has chosen him, and his portion overcomes all things before the Lord of the spirits in rectitude to eternity. 4. And this Son of man, whom thou hast seen, will arouse the kings and mighty from their couches, and the strong from their thrones, and will loosen the bands of the strong, and will break the teeth of the sinners. 5. And he will expel the kings from their thrones and from their kingdoms, because they do not exalt him and praise him, and do not acknowledge humbly whence the kingdom was given to them. 6. And he will expel the countenance of the strong; and shame will fill them: darkness will be their dwelling-place and worms will become their couches, and they will have no hope of rising from their couches, because they do not exalt the name of the Lord of spirits. 7. And these are they who master the stars of heaven, and raise their hands against the Most High, and tread the earth and live thereon, and all their doing is injustice and their doing manifests injustice, and their power is in their riches, and their faith is in gods which they have made with their hands, and they have denied the name of the Lord of the spirits. 8. And they will be cast out of the houses of his congregations, and of the faithful who hang on the name of the Lord of the spirits."

11*

CHAP. 47. — And in those days the prayer of the just, and the blood of the just one ascend from the earth before the Lord of the spirits. 2. In these days the holy ones, who dwell in high heaven, will unite in one voice, and will petition and pray and praise and thank and bless the name of the Lord of the spirits, on account of the blood of the just which has been spilled, and the prayer of the just, that it may not be in vain before the Lord of the spirits, that judgment may be held over them, and they not suffer to eternity. 3. And in those days I saw the Head of days, as he sat upon the throne of his glory, and the books of the living were opened before him, and his whole host, which is in high heaven and around him, stood before him. 4. And the hearts of the holy ones were filled with joy, because the number of justice was fulfilled and the prayers of the just had been heard and the blood of the just one had been demanded before the Lord of the spirits.

CHAP. 48. — And at that place I saw an inexhaustible fountain of justice; and around it many fountains of wisdom, and all the thirsty drank out of them and were filled with wisdom, and their dwelling-places were with the just and holy and chosen. 2. And at that hour that Son of man was called near the Lord of the spirits, and his name before the Head of days. 3. And before the sun and the signs were created, before the stars of heaven were made, his name was called before the Lord of the spirits. 4. He will be a staff to the just and the holy, upon which they will support themselves and not fall, and he will be the light of the nations, and he will be the hope of those who are sick in their hearts. 5. All who live upon the earth will fall down before him and bend the knee to him, and will bless and praise him and will sing psalms to the name of the Lord of the spirits. 6. For this purpose he was chosen and hidden before him before the world was created, and he will be before him to eternity. 7. And the wisdom of the Lord of the spirits has revealed <u>him</u> to the holy and the just, for he preserves the portion of the just, because they have hated and despised this world of injustice, and have hated all its deeds and ways in the name of the Lord of the spirits; for in his name they will be saved, and he will be the revenger of their lives. 8. And in those days the countenances of the kings of the earth, and of the mighty who possess the earth, will be *bent* down on account of the deeds of their hands, for on the day of their terror and trouble their souls will not be saved. 9. And I will put them into the hands of my chosen, like straw in fire and like lead in water; thus they will burn before the face of the just, and sink before the face of the holy, and no trace of them will be found. 10. And on the day of their trouble, there will be rest on the earth; before him they will fall and not rise again, and there will be no one to take them with his hands and lift them up, because they have denied the Lord of the spirits and his Anointed. The name of the Lord of the spirits be blessed!

CHAP. 49. — For wisdom is poured out like water, and glory does not cease before him to all eternity. 2. For he is powerful in all the secrets of justice; and injustice, like a shadow, will end, having no stability, because the Chosen One has arisen before the Lord of the spirits and his glory is to all eternity, and his power to all generations. 3. In him dwells the spirit of wisdom, and the spirit of him who imparts understanding, and the spirit of doctrine and of power, and the spirit of those asleep in justice. 4. And he will judge the secrets, and no one will be able to speak a vain word before him, because he is the Chosen One before the Lord of the spirits, according to his will.

CHAP. 50. — And in those days there will be a change for the holy and chosen, and the light of the days will dwell over them, and glory and honor will be turned over to the holy. 2. And on the day of trouble, evil will gather over the sinners, but the just will overcome through the name of the Lord of the spirits; and he will show it to the others, that they may repent, and cease the work of their hands. 3. And they will have no honor before the Lord of the spirits, but in his name they will be saved, and the Lord of the spirits will have mercy on them, for his mercy is great. 4. And he is just in his judgment, and before his glory, and injustice will not stand in his judgment: whosoever will not repent shall be destroyed. 5. Henceforth I will not have mercy on them, says the Lord of the spirits.

CHAP. 51. — And in those days the earth will return that entrusted to it, and Sheol will return that entrusted to it, which it has received, and hell will return what it owes. 2. And he will choose the just and holy from among them, for the day has come that they be saved. 3. And the Chosen One in those days will sit upon his throne, and all the secrets of wisdom will proceed from the thoughts of his mouth, for the Lord of the spirits has given it to him and has honored him. 4. And in those days the mountains will skip like rams, and the hills spring like lambs satisfied with milk, and they will all be angels in heaven. 5. Their faces will shine in gladness, because the Chosen One has arisen in those days, and the earth will rejoice, and the just will live thereon, and the chosen will walk and move thereon.

CHAP. 52. — And after those days, at that place, where I had seen all the visions of that which is hidden — for I was taken up by the whirling of the wind and carried toward the west — 2. there my eyes saw the secrets of heaven, all things that will be on the earth, a mountain of iron, and a mountain of copper, and a mountain of silver, and a mountain of gold, and a mountain of soft metal, and a mountain of lead. 3. And I asked the angel who went with me, saying: " What are those things which I have seen in secret?" 4. And he said to me: " All these things which thou hast seen are for the power of his Anointed, that he may command and be powerful on the earth." 5. Then this angel of peace answered and said to me: " Wait a little, and thou wilt see, and there will be revealed to thee every secret that the Lord of the spirits has planted. 6. These mountains which thou hast seen, the mountain of iron, and the mountain of copper, and the mountain of silver, and the mountain of gold, and the mountain of soft metal, and the mountain of lead, all these will be before the Chosen One like wax in the presence of fire, and like the water which falls down from above on these mountains, and will be weak before his feet. 7. And it will come to pass in those days that no one will save himself, not with gold and not with silver: no one will be able to save himself or to flee. 8. And there will be no iron for war and no clothing for a breast-plate; metal will not aid and zinc will not aid, and will not be beaten out, and lead will not be desired. 9. And all these things will disappear and be destroyed from the face of the earth, when the Chosen One shall appear before the face of the Lord of the spirits."

CHAP. 53. — And there my eyes saw a deep valley, whose mouth was open, and all those who dwell upon the earth and sea and islands will bring him gifts and presents and tokens of submission, but that deep valley will not be filled. 2. And they commit crimes with their hands, and everything they make they devour criminally, they, the sinners; but they will be destroyed in the presence of the Lord of the spirits, they, the sinners, and will be chased from off the face of his earth continually to all eternity. 3. For I have seen the angels of punishment, going and preparing all the instruments for Satan. 4. And I asked the angel of peace who went with me: "These instruments, for whom have they been prepared?" 5. And he said to me: "These are prepared for the kings and the mighty of this earth that they be destroyed with them. 6. And after this the Just and Chosen One will cause the house of his congregation to appear; henceforth it will not be hindered in the name of the Lord of the spirits. 7. And these mountains will be in his presence like the earth, and the hills will be like a fountain of water, and the just will rest from the oppression of the sinners."

CHAP. 54. — And I looked and turned toward another side of the earth, and I saw there a deep valley with a burning fire. 2. And they brought the kings and the powerful, and put them into the deep valley. 3. And there my eyes saw how they make instruments for them, iron chains of immense weight. 4. And I asked the angel of peace, who went with me, saying: "These chain instruments, for whom have they been prepared?" 5. And he said to me: "These have been prepared for the hosts of Azâzêl, to imprison them and put them into the lowest hell: and their jaws will be covered with rough stones, as the Lord of the spirits has commanded. 6. Michael and Gabriel, Rufael and Fanuel, they will overpower them on that great day, will throw them on that day into the oven of burning fire, that the Lord of the spirits may avenge himself on them on account of their injustice, because they became subject to Satan, and have led astray those who dwell on the earth." 7. And in those days the punishment from the Lord of the spirits will come, and all the repositories of water, which are above in the heavens, and also the fountains of water, which are under the heavens, and which are under the earth, will be opened. 8. And all the waters will be joined with the waters which are above in the heavens; but the water which is in high heaven is the masculine, and the water which is beneath on the earth is the feminine. 9. And then will be destroyed all those who dwell on the earth, and those who dwell under the ends of heaven. 10. And through this they know their injustice, which they have done on the earth, and therefore they are destroyed.

CHAP. 55. — And after that the Head of days repented and said: "In vain have I destroyed all who dwell on the earth." 2. And he swore by his great name: " Henceforth I will not do thus to all those who dwell on the earth, and I will place a sign in the heavens; and it will be *a token of* fidelity between me and them to eternity, as long as heaven is above the earth. 3. And then it will be according to my command; when I desire to overpower them by the hand of the angel on the day of trouble and suffering, before this my anger and my punishment, my anger and my punishment will remain over them," says the Lord of the spirits. 4. "Ye mighty kings, who will dwell on the earth, ye shall be about to see my Chosen One, as he sits on the throne of my glory, and judges Azâzêl and all his associates, and all his hosts in the name of the Lord of the spirits."

CHAP. 56. — And I saw there the hosts of the angels of punishment walking and holding chains of iron and of metal. 2. And I asked the angel of peace, who went with me, saying: "To whom are these going, holding *them* [i.e. the chains]?" 3. And he said to me: "Each one to his chosen and his beloved, that they be thrown into the deep abyss of the valley. 4. And then that valley will be filled with their chosen and beloved, and the day of their lives will be ended, and the day of their error will, from that time on, not be counted." 5. And in those days the angels will assemble, and turn their heads toward the east, towards the people of Parthia and Media, in order to excite the kings, and that a spirit of disturbance come over them, and disturb them from off their thrones, that they come forth from their resting places like lions, and like hungry wolves amidst their flocks. 6. And they will ascend and step upon the land of their chosen, and the land of his chosen will be before them a threshing-floor and a path. 7. But the city of my just will be a hinderance to their horses, and they will take up a battle amongst themselves, and their right will become strong against themselves, and a man will not know his neighbor or his brother, nor the son his father or his mother, until there shall be sufficient bodies by their death and their punishment over them, — it will not be in vain. 8. And in those days the mouth of Sheol will be opened, and they will sink into it; and their destruction, Sheol, will devour the sinners from the presence of the chosen.

CHAP. 57. — And it came to pass after this that I saw again a host of wagons, upon which men were riding, and they came upon the wind from the east and from the west to the south. 2. And the noise of their wagons was heard, and as this commotion took place, the holy ones from heaven noticed it; and the pillars of the earth were moved from their place, and it was heard from the ends of the earth to the ends of the heavens in ONE day. 3. And they will all fall down and bend the knee before the Lord of the spirits. And this is the end of the second Parable.

CHAP. 45, 1. With this chapter commences the most interesting and most important part of the whole book, the second parable, which extends to chapter 57, and gives an account of the Messiah, — his person, his judgment, with its consequences for both righteous and unrighteous. The first verse, which is manifestly intended as a superscription, has been the cause of some trouble, as it does not seem to indicate the contents of the parable, and Drummond, p. 63, has made use of this apparent discrepancy for his curious theory of interpolation. Yet a proper understanding of the word *concerning* will probably clear up the matter. The original word is *dîba,* and is a preposition very frequently used in an adversative and inimical sense, like εἰς, *adversus, contra, in.* It is so used in our own book 10 : 9; 56 : 7, and often in the Ethiopic version of the Bible, e.g. Ex. xvii. 3; Num. xvi. 3; Deut. xv. 9; Ps. xiv. 4; Ezek. xxxii. 9, 10; Matt. xii. 32; xxiv. 7; Acts xxiii. 5, 30; Mark iii. 29, etc; cf. Dillmann, *Lexicon Aethiopico-Latin.* col. 1104, and *Aethiopis. Gramm.* p. 313. The author does not so much desire to give a description of the unhappy fate of the unjust, but rather in a general manner directs his polemics against those who will not believe in a Messianic rule and judgment; it is his defence of העולם הבא against those who accept only

הזה הזלם. That this object as stated here is in strict conformity with the contents of the parable is apparent at first glance. — 2. Cf. notes on 38 : 1; 41 : 2. — 3. *Chosen One*, the most frequent name of the Messiah in the Parables; cf. note on 40 : 5. *Throne of glory*, 51 : 3; 62 : 1–9; 69 : 27–29, also *throne of God*, 47 : 3; 55 : 4; 62 : 1–9. In the first part God himself is judge, but here it is the Messiah, 51 : 3; 55 : 4; 69 : 27; but according to 47 : 3; 62 : 2 it may seem as if God himself will judge. The difficulty is solved in 69 : 27, where we learn that although God is in reality the judge he has empowered the Messiah to act in his name; what is done by God's deputy is virtually done by himself; cf. note on 10 : 7. *Choose*, cf. note on 41 : 1. *Without number*, 39 : 6; probably to indicate that many shall enjoy this happy time. *Strong*, i.e. hopeful and encouraged because the day of their oppression is over. — 4. Cf. notes on 1 : 2 and 39 : 1. — 5. *Heaven ana earth changed* is a characteristic of the Messianic times portrayed by both the first and this part of Enoch, based on Isa. lxv. 17 and lxvi. 2; cf. 2 Pet. iii. 13; Apoc. xxi. 1. This kingdom is to be established on earth, probably in Palestine; cf. chap. 56. His idea of this kingdom is one with a visible prince, although, unlike some of the later prophets, he does not find this prince in the house of David.

CHAP. 46. The following is largely based on Dan. vii., and the Ancient of days becomes here *the Head of days*, 47 : 3; 48 : 2; 55 : 1; (60 : 2;) 71 : 10, 12, 13, and is consequently peculiar to the Parables. He is called thus as the one who was from the beginning, and as in the first parable the eyes of the seer are mainly directed to the completed Messianic kingdom, and not to its process of development, the omission of this designation of God in that portion is easily understood. *White*, cf. Dan. vii. 9. With this Ancient of days there is joined, as in Dan. vii. 13, one who is like a son of man (not like *the* son of man, as the Authorized Version gives it). Whatever may be the true interpretation of Daniel's expression, be it the personality of the Messiah, or be it the ideal Israel, it is certain that our author, perhaps from Ps. cx. 1, understood by that difficult clause a certain person, and that person was the Messiah. *Son of man* the Messiah is frequently called in the Parables ; cf. 46 : 2, 3, 4 ; 48 : 2 ; 62 : 7, 9, 14 ; 63 : 11 ; 69 : 26, 27 ; 70 : 1 ; 71 : 17. His countenance is like an angel's ; cf. 1 Sam. xxix. 9 ; Tob. v. 5, 11, 14 ; Acts vi. 15 ; Gal. iv. 14 ; Col. ii. 18. — 2. As Daniel, vii. 16, asks for an explanation of his mysterious vision Enoch here asks his guide ; cf. note on 40 : 2. — 3. As his chief office is that of a judge, his most important attribute is that of justice ; he is idealized justice, for he possesses it as his own, and abides with it, based on passages like Isa. ix. 6 ; xi. 3–5 ; Jer. xxiii. 5, 6 ; xxxiii. 15 ; Isa. liii. 11 ; Zech. ix. 9 ; Ps. xlv. 4–8 ; lxxii. In this capacity as just judge he will reveal *all the treasures of secrecy*, a clause primarily referring to the fact that he will know all secrets so as to judge aright, but manifestly here used as referring to everything that his coming will reveal, but which is unknown at present. *Chosen,* cf. note on 40 : 5 ; he does not, then, hold his office by any right of his own, but God has chosen him, 51 : 3. — 4. *Overcomes ;* none shall be superior to him, or be able to oppose him ; cf. 48 : 5 ; 49 : 1, 2 ; 51 : 4, etc. — 5. Having received such a destiny from God, even the mighty of this earth (against whom the author is continually directing his polemics) shall be overcome. The idea of a last attack and defeat of the combined enemies of the new kingdom, an idea based on statements in Ezekiel and Daniel, and promulgated by many apocryphal writers, and also by the writer of the first part in 90 : 16, does not lie in this or the following verses, nor in 52 : 4–9, but these rather picture the effect of the Messianic judgment on these sinners, and any other interpretation would not be in harmony with the strictly forensic character of this judgment as taught in the Parables ; cf. note on 41 : 1, and Schürer, p. 587 ; cf. Isa. xiv. 9, 11 ; Job xvii. 13, 14. *Bonds,* cf. Ps. cvii. 14 ; cxvi. 16 ; Jer. ii. 20 ;

xxx. 8; Nahum i. 13.   *Teeth*, cf. Ps. iii. 7; lviii. 6; Lam. iii.
16.   Their sin is again the one that is here so frequently condemned, that of unbelief, which here, according to the subjects,
takes the form of ingratitude and unwillingness to acknowledge the source of power; cf. Sap. vi. 2; Rom. xiii. 1.   But
against whom is this sin committed, God or the Messiah? and
who is the source of this power?   It would be strange if it
were the latter person, and as in verses 6, 7, and 8 this unbelief is directed against God, we are constrained to believe that
the *him* after *exalt*, and the *he* implied in *whence* is God and
not the Messiah.   *Then he will expel*, from 47 : 3; 62 : 2,
would also indicate God as the subject, for it seems as if the
Messiah is to have the purely forensic part of the judgment,
but the punishment is inflicted either by God or through the
agency of his angels. — 6. *Darkness*, cf. note on 10 : 5. *Worms*,
cf. Job xvii. 14; xxi. 26; Isa. xiv. 11. — 7. *Stars*, cf. Dan.
viii. 10, 11, 13, 25; En. 43 : 4.   *Riches*, cf. Ps. xlix. 6; lii. 7.
— 8. *Houses*, for which in 53 : 6 we have the singular.

CHAP. 47, 1. As the following verse shows, the *just one*
here and verse 4 is used collectively for the *just*. — 2. The
angels petition for men; cf. note on 15 : 1, 2. — 3. *Books of the
living*, cf. Ex. xxxii. 32 sq; Ps. lxix. 29; Mal. iii. 16; Isa. iv.
3; Dan. xii. 1; Book of Jubilees c. 30, and En. 103 : 2; 104 :
1, and are probably the same as the books mentioned 89 :
61–64, 68, 70, 71, 76, 77; 90 : 17, 20; 98 : 7, 8; 104 : 7; cf.
Harnack's note on Pastor Hermae, Vis. 1, 3, 2.   As judgment
is to be passed over both good and bad, the author evidently
pictured these books of life as containing the lives of all to be
judged.   *Host;* in Dan. vii. 10 God has his host with him in
the judgment; cf. note on 1 : 4.   Although God is here and
elsewhere present at the judgment, it is not said that he judges;
but other passages show that this function was assigned to the
Messiah.   Cf. note on 45 : 4. — 4. *Number;* the words *eternity*,
vs. 2, and *demanded* here show that the *number* signifies the
number of years which God had determined should pass before
the judgment should be held; cf. 18 : 16.

CHAP. 48, 1. Having just mentioned the justice that characterizes the judge and the judgment, he now states that justice or righteousness, the lack of which on earth he so deplores, will be given in abundance to the saints. This justice, 39 : 5; 91 : 10, they shall drink from a fountain, and from fountains of wisdom; cf. Prov. xvi. 22; Sir. i. 5; Bar. iii. 12; 4 Ezra xiv. 28, and in general Isa. lv. 1. *Place,* cf. 46 : 1. — 2. *At that hour,* i.e. at the time when Enoch was seeing and hearing these things. — 3. Almost the very words here are found also *Targum Jonath.* on Zech. iv. 7. There can be no doubt of the fact that the writer here as in *Targum Jonath.* on Isa. ix. 6; Mic. v. 1 plainly teaches the pre-existence of the Messiah. In verse 6 he existed before the world was created, and will continue to be to eternity, and in 62 : 7 he has been hidden, but revealed to the just; cf. 69 : 26, and *Targum Jonath.* on Mic. iv. 8; and in 70 : 1 this pre-existence is presupposed. This idea the author beyond all doubt develops from Dan. vii. 13 sqq. and Mic. v. 1 [b] (in the Heb.). Gfrörer (cf. Drummond, p. 290) sees the pre-existence of the Messiah taught in the LXX on Ps. lxxi. 5; cix. 3; Isa. ix. 6, but with doubtful results. A more successful appeal, however, can be made to 3 Sibyl. 186 sqq. and to 4 Ezra xii. 32; xiii. 26; cf. Schürer, p. 584; cf. also Prov. viii. 22–30; Sir. i. 4; xxiv. 9. *Signs,* of course those of heaven, the astronomical; cf. 8 : 3; 72 : 13, 19, and Gen. i. 14; Jer. x. 2; Epist. Jer. 67. — 4. This Messiah is to be the light of the nations; cf. Jer. xlii. 6; xlix. 6; 3 Sibyl. 710–726. The blessings in store are, then, by no means restricted to the people of Israel. — 5. *All will acknowledge him,* 10 : 21; (53 : 1 ;) 90 : 33–38, even his enemies, 62 : 6, 9, 10, and chap. 63. Cf. what is said Isa. xlix. 22; lx. 4, 9; lxvi. 20; Psalt. Salom. xvii. But as this Messiah is such only by God's will, their praise ultimately seeks him as its object. — 6. *For this purpose.* i.e. for the one just stated. *Was chosen,* in explanation of his name as the *Chosen One. Hidden,* 62 : 7, 8, exactly as in 4 Ezra xiii. 52. This Messiah, being pre-existent, shall also abide to eternity. — 7. Although hidden from the world the Messiah was revealed to the just in order that their portion may not fail them; they received the revelation that they might remain firm in their trials, and not miss their final blessedness. God revealed him through wisdom, 62 : 7, i.e through the revealed wisdom of the prophets. — 8. But he that brings happiness to the faithful has punishment for their oppressors; cf. 46 : 4–8. *Day of terror*, i.e. day of judgment. *Will not be saved*, as the opposite of the *saved* in verse 7; cf. Job v. 4; Ps. vii. 2; lxxi. 11; Isa. xlii. 22. — 9. *Put*, cf. 38 : 5, and in 50 : 2. they will conquer. This appears to indicate a final struggle before the real inauguration of the judgment, for according to 50 : 3, 4 some will then repent. But the great punishment is by fire; cf. Ex. xv. 10 and 7; Isa. v. 24; xlvii. 14; Obad. xviii. Or could not the *chosen* here possibly refer to the angels of punishment (cf. 53 : 3), who throughout the Parables are the punishers of these kings? The name *chosen* does not speak against this idea, as these angels are beyond all doubt under the rule of God, and have been selected and chosen for this special office. — 10. *Rest*, cf. 53 : 7; 62 : 13. *Before him*, i.e. before the Messiah. *Fall*, as opposite of verse 4; cf. Ps. xxxvi. 12. *Denied the Lord and his Anointed* is taken from Ps. ii. 2. *Anointed*, found also 52 : 4; Apoc. Baruch xxix. 3; xxx. 1; xxxix. 7; xl. 1; lxx. 9; lxxii. 2; 4 Ezra vii. 28, 29; (according to the Arabic and Arm.) xii. 32; and in Psalt. Salom. xvii. 36 and xviii. 6, 8 Χριστὸς κύριος (or rather it should be κυρίου).

CHAP. 49. The ability to effect all this lies in the nature of the Messiah. On 1 cf. Isa. xi. 9, 10. *For* connects with the previous, and thus the verse is to show the reason for the statements just made. *Wisdom*, in the sense of knowledge and fear of God; cf. 37, 2. — 2. *Secrets of justice*, in explanation of which in verse 4 it is stated that he will judge the secrets; cf. Isa. xi. 2. As shadow flees when light arrives thus injustice disappears when the Messiah, who is justice itself, vs. 3, appears;

cf. Job xiv. 2. *Has arisen*, cf. Mic. v. 2. *Eternity*, cf. Isa. ix. 5, 6 ; Mic. v. 3. — 3. This verse is shaped after Isa. xi. 2, and the connection points to the interpretation of the clause, *those asleep in justice*, as referring to the spirits of the prophets, concretely used for the spirit of prophecy ; cf. Langen, p. 45. — 4. Cf. Isa. xi. 3, 4.

CHAP. 50. The state of affairs will be entirely changed when the Messiah comes : the exalted shall be humiliated, and the humble exalted. The political aspects of the Messianic kingdom will be the reverse of the present. *Light of days*, i.e. daylight, explained well 58 : 5, 6. For the just the rule of the unjust had been night ; cf. Ps. cxxxix. 11. — 2. In addition to this political change there will be punishment in store for the wicked. *Day of trouble*, usually employed only of the day of final judgment, could possibly refer to a last struggle ; cf. note on 48 : 9. That the final judgment is not meant is clear, for the day of grace is not yet over, and the *others* will repent. Who the *others* are is uncertain (except, indeed, that they are sinners), for it is uncertain whether the contest is to be between the faithful and the renegades, or between the former and the heathen nations. If it is allowed to use 90 : 30, 33, 34 ; 91 : 14, the former would be the case, and the others would be the hitherto neutral heathens. — 3. But as these *others* did not endure the trials of the faithful their position in the Messiah's kingdom will not be as honorable. How could a Christian with Matt. xx. 1 sqq. before him have written these words ? *His name*, i.e. God's. — 4. Although God is merciful he is also just, and therefore all who do not repent in the time of grace will be destroyed. It seems, then, that the Messianic kingdom is not to come all of a sudden, but shall undergo a certain development.

CHAP. 51, 1. The resurrection of the dead, first plainly announced by Dan. xii. 2, is to the author a universal one, thus agreeing with 2 Macc. vii. 9, 14, 23, 36 ; xii. 43, 44 ; Psalt. Salom. iii. 16 ; xiv. 2 ; Josephus, *Antiqq.* xviii. 1, 3 ; *Bel. Jud.*

ii. 8, 14 ; Baruch xxx. 1–5 ; l. 1–li. 6 ; 4 Ezra vii. 32.   The
first part of Enoch clearly teaches the resurrection of the *just*
(cf. notes on 22 : 12, 13), but also that certain sinners shall
not rise, while here the writer says that earth, Sheol, and hell
will return their contents.   The Old Testament idea of Sheol
is here split into two notions — a place of departed spirits and
of hell.   The original of the latter term is *haquel*, i.e. destruction, and is consequently the same as the *Abaddon* used by the
Old Testament as synonymous with Sheol, e.g. Job xxvi. 6 ;
xxviii. 22 ; Prov. xv. 11.   But then it is possible that the
word *hell* here has been added by the translator, as hell, the
place of fiery torment, is, according to both Part I. and the
Parables, uninhabited until after the judgment.   The passage
61 : 5 does not contradict the idea of a universal resurrection.
Whether the bodies will rise with the souls is not said, but
seems probable from the use of the word *earth*. — 2. Out of
this multitude he (i.e. the Messiah) will chose his holy ones.
The wording is adapted to the forensic character of the judgment. — 3. *Wisdom*, cf. note on 49 : 1, 3.   This verse is to
characterize him as regent and potentate, a role he is to assume after the judgment is over.   The just will be the recipi-
ents of this wisdom, 48 : 1 ; 49 : 1 ; 61 : 7, 11.   Here again it
is said that he has these powers only as a gift of God. — 4.
Skip, cf. Ps. cxiv. 4, 6.   The happiness will be like that of
the heavenly angels ; cf. 104 : 4, 6. — 5. Cf. Ps. xxxvii. 3, 9,
11, 29, 34.

CHAP. 52, 1. He is for the present done with the Messianic
kingdom as such, but still desires to give some facts concerning it that could not well have been interwoven in the above,
and with this partial change of subjects the scene of observa-
tion is somewhat shifted towards the west.   He is carried to
his destination by the wind, according to the sentiments of
both authors ; cf. 14 : 8 and 39 : 3.   *At that place*, i.e. from
heaven, for there he was. — 2. The metal hills belong to the
secrets of heaven, i.e. it is known only in heaven that hills

which now, indeed, have no existence shall exist in the Messianic times. *Soft metal*, or flowing metal; Dillmann has *Tropfmetal*, but just what is meant is uncertain; but cf. 65 : 7, 8. Hoffmann thought of quicksilver, but Dillmann rightly opposes this idea. — 3. *In secret*. I, and no one else. — 4. The application of the allegory and object of the metallic hills follows. They are for the benefit of the Anointed; but not for the increase of his power and wealth, as 6–9 exegetically explain. *Anointed*, 48 : 10. — 5. Patience is enjoined on Enoch that he may learn still more secrets; a promise which is fulfilled in chap. 53 sqq. — 6. Now follows the true object of these mountains. They are symbolical of the enemies of the Messiah, and his power will be shown by their complete disappearance. The term *mountains* probably plays on the fact that the chief offenders in the Parables are the mighty of the earth. These mountains will melt; cf. Mic. i. 3 ; Ps. xcvii. 5, and like water that flows, cf. Mic. i. 4, and become weak that they cannot stand in his presence. — 7. Therefore, too, these metals will have no value to save in the time of the Messiah, as the judgment then will be according to other standards; cf. Zeph. i. 18 ; Ezek. vii. 19 ; Ps. xlix. 7–10 ; Jer. iv. 30 ; Isa. xiii. 17. *Flee;* it will be impossible to escape justice by buying the judge. — 8. Nor will the coarser metals be of any value whatever in defence against this judgment; no human weapons of defence can ward off the sure destruction. — 9. In plain words, says the author, these instruments of war will disappear when the prince of peace arrives; cf. Hos. ii. 20 ; Isa. ii. 4 ; ix. 6 ; Zech. ix. 10 ; Ps. xlvi. 10 ; Mic. v. 9.

CHAP. 53. In beginning a second parabolical sketch Enoch says he saw a deep valley whose mouth was open, to which all mankind bring offerings. These presents are, to judge from 63 : 10 ; 98 : 10 ; 94 : 7 ; 97 : 7–10, brought to buy release from the judgment of the Messiah, the author connecting this thought with 52 : 7. The term *valley* is chosen only to show the vast amount of presents brought. *Him* i.e. the Messiah. *Not full,* do not suffice. — 2. *They* shows that the subject in verse 1 must be restricted to the sinners. The reason these presents cannot be received is because their givers are criminal, and therefore, in spite of their offerings they will be destroyed. *They make,* i.e. what the *just* make, for only thus can the clause be intelligently understood. Cf. note on 38 : 1. — 3. *Angels of punishment,* a name mentioned here for the first time, but found also 56 : 1; 62 : 11; 63 : 1; (66 : 1). As in 53 : 5, and in nearly all these passages (with the *possible* exception of 56 : 1), these angels are preparing to punish the kings and the powerful. Cf. 46 : 4. It seems that the author, who states that the fallen angels as special sinners had special tormentors in the higher angels, 54 : 6, conceived that the mighty of this earth should find their special tormentors in the persons of these angels of punishment. They are in the service of Satan (cf. note on 40 : 7), and may possibly be identical with the satans, cf. Dillmann, p. 147. — 6. *House,* cf. 38–39 and 46 : 8. — 7. All things shall be changed, is probably the meaning of this verse. Cf. Isa. xxix. 17; xxx. 25; xl. 4. It is highly probable that the author, on the basis of Ezek. xl.–xlviii.; Isa. liv. 11 sqq.; lx.; Hag. ii. 7–9; Zech. ii. 6–17, thinks of the new Jerusalem to be brought down from heaven, although he nowhere, except possibly in chap. 56, definitely states that the Messianic kingdom shall have its centre in Jerusalem. Cf. Schürer, p. 588 and En. 56 : 6; 61.

CHAP. 54. In the third sketch he sees the execution of the judgment. This valley with the burning fire is hell. It is not the valley of Hinnom; cf. notes on 27 : 1 sqq. and 38 : 1. — 3. *Instruments,* cf. 53 : 3, intended for Azazel and his host, for the *for them* in vs. 2 refers forward and backward. — 5. The Messiah is also judge of the angels, 55 : 4; 90 : 24. This is their final punishment, after the temporal one described chap. 10. — 6. As the expression *oven of fire* shows, these verses refer not to the first, but to the final judgment. The same sin that occasioned the temporal will also occasion the final punishment, and the same agents will inflict both; cf. 40:7. — 7. With this verse commences an interpolation, and ends at 55:2. It is one of the Noachic fragments; cf. Introd. The occasion of its introduction was the mention made of the fallen angels just previous. It treats of the deluge. The designation of the waters above as masculine and the waters below as feminine is altogether unlike the sentiments in either of the two main parts, but suits the gnostically tainted ideas of this fragmentist; cf. 60:7, 8, 16. — 10. Interpreting *they* as referring to men gives the best sense.

CHAP. 55. As we have positive evidence, 68:1, that the Noachic fragmentist made use of the Parables, we can understand why he here changes the subject in Gen. viii. 21, and uses the term *Head of days* instead of God. — 2. The sign is, of course, the rainbow. — 3. This continues the account of 54: 6, and therefore *angel* is here collectively used. — 4. To increase the torments of the punishment the kings must first behold the terrors of the fallen angels, as these had to see the death of their own children, 10:12. If he judges the angels and overpowers them, how much more easily will the kings of the earth be punished by him?

CHAP. 56. *Angels of punishment*, cf. note on 53:3, from which it also appears that those here punished are the kings themselves, for that their turn is next follows from chap. 55. *There*, cf. 54:3, 1. — 3. The chosen and beloved of these angels are then probably the mighty kings, as it would be too extravagant to suppose that *all* the sinners were to be bound by special officers. — 4. *Will not be counted*, because they have ended. — 5. This verse is important as it may furnish an historical hint as to the time when the Parables were written. The whole description is certainly prophetical, and pictures the last struggle of the new kingdom with its enemies, on the basis of passages like Joel iv.; Zech. xii. and xiv.; Ezek. xxxviii. and xxxix. In summoning up these enemies as Parthians and Medes, the author indicates that he regarded these as dangerons to the new Israel, but whether the basis of his prophecy is a concrete case, the invasion of Palestine by the Parthians about 40 B.C., mentioned by Joseph. *Antiqq.* xiv. 13 ; *Bel. Jud.* i. 13 must, as the statements are so *very* vague, remain doubtful. Hilgenfeld strangely finds here an indication of the belief that Nero would return from the east! *Lions,* symbol of strength and bravery, Judges xiv. 18 ; 2 Sam. i. 23 ; xvii. 10 ; Prov. xxviii. 1 ; xxx. 30 ; *wolf,* symbol of a robbing disposition, Gen. xlix. 27 ; Ezek. xxii. 27 ; Zeph. iii. 3 ; Hab. i. 8. He avoids an anthropomorphism by substituting the angels in the place of God, as it stands in Isa. xix. 2 sqq. ; Ezek. xxxviii., xxxix ; cf. Zech. vi. 1–8 ; Dan. x. 13, 14, 20, 21 ; xi. 1, 2 ; xii. 1. The motive that prompted this change was probably the idea that God who had established the new kingdom through his Chosen One could not aid in its embarrassment. This passage makes it probable that Palestine is to be the country where the Messianic kingdom will be established. *Threshing-floor,* partly from Isa. xxi. 10. Cf. Isa. xli. 15 ; Jer. li. 33 ; Mic. iv. 12 sq. ; Amos i. 3. — 7. But the attempt will fail, Zech. xii. 2, 3. and revolution will break out among themselves, Ezek. xxxviii. 21 ; Zech. xiv. 13 ; Hag. ii. 22. The ties of relationship are disregarded, Isa. iii. 5 ; ix. 19, 21. *Sufficient,* i.e. for the satisfaction of justice. *Opened,* Num. xvi. 31 sqq. ; Isa. v. 14.

CHAP. 57. The result of this repulse is of importance for the new kingdom, for all the nations, Isa. xiv. 1 ; xliv. 6 ; lv. 5 ; lvi. 3 sqq. ; Zech. viii. 21 sqq. ; Ezek. xlvii. 22 sqq., (and not simply scattered Israel, *Dillmann*) come to take part in it. That it must be taken in this wide sense is apparent from vs. 3, where all worship him, an expression used in other parts of the book for the coming of the heathens. And then too it is a suitable ending for this important Parable. *Came upon the wind* indicates their eager longings and haste ; cf. Isa. v. 28 ; Jer. iv. 13 ; Ezek. x. 13. — 2. Cf. Hag. ii. 6, 7 ; Zech. i. 11 sqq. ; Isa. xxvii. 13 ; xliii. 5, 6 ; xlix. 12, 13, 22, 23 ; **xxiv.** 18 ; Ps. lxxxii. 5 ; Prov. viii. 29.

SECTION IX.

CHAP. 58. — And I began to speak the third Parable concerning the just and concerning the chosen. 2. Blessed are ye, the just and chosen, for your portion is glorious! 3. And the just will be in the light of the sun, and the chosen in the light of everlasting life; and there will be no end to the days of their life, and the days of the holy will be without number. 4. And they will seek the light and will find justice with the Lord of the spirits; *there will be* peace to the just with the Lord of the world. 5. And after that it will be said to the holy, that they should seek in heaven the secrets of justice, the portion of faith [fidelity], for it has risen like the sun on the earth, and darkness has disappeared. 6. And there will be an unceasing light, and in the number of days they will not enter, because darkness will be destroyed first, and the light will be mighty before the Lord of the spirits, and the light of rectitude will be strong in eternity before the Lord of the spirits.

CHAP. 59. — And in those days my eyes saw the secrets of the lightning, and the masses of light, and their judgments; and they flashed for a blessing and for a curse, as the Lord of the spirits desired. 2. And there I saw the secrets of the thunder, and how when it resounds above in the heavens its sound is heard; and they showed me the dwelling-places of the earth, and the thunder, either for peace or a blessing or for a curse, according to the word of the Lord of the spirits. 3. And after that all the secrets of the luminaries and of the lightning were shown to me, as they flash for a blessing and for satisfaction.

CHAP. 58. 1. As the author states himself, this chapter commences the third Parable. This extends to chap. 71, with the exception of 60 and 65 : 1–69 : 25, which are Noachic interpolations; cf. Introd. The Parable is to treat, at least mainly, of
the blessedness of the chosen and the just. Intimately connected with this is the description of the judgment with its
consequences for the wicked, and therefore he treats these topics
also. *I began to speak*, as in 37 : 2. — 2. In contradistinction
from the curse pronounced on the wicked, the just will have a
blessed portion. — 3. *Light*, cf. note on 38 : 4. *Everlasting life*,
cf. note on 37 : 4. *Without number*, i.e. numberless. — 4. But
light is their element, therefore they seek it, 50 : 1. They
will also seek justice, as the Messiah is personified justice; cf.
48 : 1; 46 : 3. *Lord of the world*, cf. note on 1 : 3. — 5. *The
secrets of justice in heaven*, 49 : 2; 51 : 3, i.e. the glorious lot
stored up in heaven by the just judge, and realized only in the
Messianic times, but before that hidden to the world; cf. note
on 49 : 2. *Faith*, cf. 39 : 6; 46 : 8; 61 : 4. As *denying*, 41 : 2,
is the cardinal sin of the wicked, its opposite — belief, faith, or
trust in God's promises during the period of the sinners' rule —
is the most shining virtue of the just. We need not go to the
New Testament for the origin and use of this word. *It has
risen*, in general terms, like *it has become light.* — 6. As this
state is permanent, and not transitory, no one will attempt to
number the days.

CHAP. 59. 1. As he has repeatedly done before, the author
has interwoven here brief remarks on the secrets of the physical world. His statements rest on Job xxxvi. 30–37; v. 13;
xxxviii. 24–27. *Their judgment*, not in the sense that they
are to be judged, but rather that they are instruments in the
hands of God to effect judgment when they flash for a curse or
a blessing. His object is, then, to give here the moral object
of these phenomena of whose origin he has spoken above,
chap. 41. — 2. Cf. Job xxxvii. 1–5. Enoch, being in heaven,
is now allowed to see the dwellings of men, as these are

affected by what he sees in heaven; cf. Job xxxvii. 13. This
is all further explained in the Noachic fragment, 60:13–15.—
3. Cf. 41:8; Job xxxviii. 24–27.

SECTION X.

CHAP. 60. — In the year five-hundred, and in the
seventh month, on the fourteenth day of the month,
of the life of Enoch. In that Parable I saw that the
heaven of heavens shook tremendously, and the host of
the Most High, and the angels, a thousand times thousand, and ten thousand times ten thousand, were disturbed exceedingly. 2. And then I saw the Head of
days sitting upon the throne of his glory, and the angels
and the just ones stood around him. 3. And a great
trembling took hold of me, and fear seized me; my
loins were bent and were loosened, and my whole being
melted together, and I fell down on my face. 4. And
the holy Michael sent another holy angel, one of the
holy angels, and he raised me up. And as he raised me
my spirit returned, for I had not been able to endure
the sight of this host and of that trembling and shaking
of heaven. 5. And the holy Michael said to me: "On
account of what vision is such trembling? Up to to-day
was the day of his mercy, and he was merciful and slow
to anger over those who dwell on the earth. 6. But
when the day and the power and the punishments and
judgments come, which the Lord of the spirits has prepared for those who bow to the judgment of justice, and
for those who deny the judgment of justice, and for
those who take his name in vain — that day has been
prepared a covenant for the chosen, and a test for the

sinners.   7. And on that day two monsters will be dis-
tributed, a female monster, named Leviathan, to dwell in
the depth of the sea, over the fountains of the waters.
8. But the masculine is named Behemoth, who occupies,
with his breast, a void desert called Dêndâin, in the east
of the garden where the chosen and holy will dwell,
where my grandfather was taken up, the seventh from
Adam, the first of men whom the Lord of the spirits
made.   9. And I asked that other angel that he should
show me the power of those monsters, how they were
separated on ONE day, and that one descended into the
depths of the sea and the other to the desert land.   10.
And he said to me: "Thou son of man, thou desirest to
know here that which is a secret."   11. Then the other
angel, who went with me, spoke to me, and showed me
that which was secret, the first and the last, what is in
the heavens on high, and in the earth in the deep, and
on the ends of the heavens, and on the foundations of
heaven, and in the repositories of the winds; 12. and
how the spirits are divided, and how weighing is done,
and how the fountains and the winds are counted
according to the power of the spirit, and the power
of the lights of the moon, and that is it a power of
justice, and the divisions of the stars according to their
names, and how each division is divided; 13. and peals
of thunder according to the places where they fall, and
all the divisions that are made among the flashes of
lightning that lightning may take place, and their hosts
obey.   14. For the thunder has places of rest for the
awaiting of its peal, and thunder and lightning are in-
separable, and although not one, both go together
through the spirit and are not separated.   15. For
when the lightning flashes, the thunder utters its voice,

and the spirit causes a rest during the flash, and divides
equally between them, for the treasury of their flashes
is like the sand; and each one of them, in its flash, is
held with a bridle, and turned back by the power of the
spirit, and is pushed forward, according to the number
of the directions on the earth. 16. And the spirit of
the sea is masculine and strong, and according to the
strength of his power, he draws it [i.e. the sea] back
with a bridle, and in like manner it is pushed forward,
and scattered in all the mountains of the earth. 17.
And the spirit of the hoar-frost is his *own* angel, and
the spirit of hail is a good angel. 18. And he has left
go the spirit of the snow on account of its strength, and
it has a special spirit, and that which ascends from it
is like smoke, and its name is frost. 19. And the
spirit of the fog is not joined with them in their repositories, but it has a special repository, for its course is
in clearness and in light and in darkness and in winter
and in summer, and its repository is the light, and it
[i.e. the spirit] is its angel. 20. And the spirit of the
dew has its dwelling-place at the ends of the heaven,
and is connected with the repositories of the rain, and
its course is in winter and in summer; and its clouds
and the clouds of the fog are connected, and one gives
to the other. 21. And when the spirit of rain moves
out of its repository the angels come and open the
repository, and lead it out, and when it is scattered over
all the earth, and also as often as it is joined to the
waters of the earth. 22. For the waters are for those
who live on the earth; for they are the nourishment
for the earth from the Most High, who is in heaven;
therefore rain has its measure, and angels receive it.
23. All these things I saw towards the garden of the

just. 24. And the angel of peace, who was with me, said to me: "These two monsters are prepared to be fed, according to the greatness of God, that the punishments from God be not in vain, and sons will be killed with their mothers, and children with their fathers. 25. When the punishments from the Lord of the spirits shall rest over them it will rest, so that the punishments from the Lord of the spirits may not come in vain over those; after that there will be a judgment in his mercy and his patience."

Chap. 61. — And I saw in those days that long cords were given to those angels, and they took to themselves wings, and flew, and went towards the north. 2. And I asked the angel, saying: "Why have these taken the long cords, and have gone away?" And he said to me: "They went out to measure." 3. And the angel, who went with me, said to me: "These bring the measures of the just and the ropes of the just, that they may support themselves on the name of the Lord of the spirits to all eternity. 4. And the chosen will begin and dwell with the chosen, and these measures will be given to faith [fidelity], and will strengthen the word of justice. 5. And these measures will reveal all the secrets of the depths of the earth, and those who have been destroyed by the desert, and those who have been devoured by the fish of the sea, and by the beasts, that they return and support themselves on the day of the Chosen One, for none will be destroyed before the Lord of the spirits, and none can be destroyed. 6. And then received a command all who dwell in the hights of heaven, and ONE power, and ONE voice, and ONE light, like the fire, was given to them. 7. And that one first they blessed and exalted and glorified with wisdom, and showed themselves wise in speech and in the spirit of life. 8. And the Lord of the spirits placed his Chosen One on the throne of his glory, and he will judge all the deeds of the holy ones in high heaven, and will weigh their deeds on scales. 9. And when he shall raise his countenance to judge their paths that are secret by the word of the name of the Lord of the spirits, and their path in the way of the just judgment of the highest God, then they will all speak with ONE voice, and bless, and praise, and exalt, and glorify the name of the Lord of the spirits. 10. And then will cry out all the host of the heavens, and all the holy ones above, and the host of God, Cherubim and Seraphim and Ophanim, and all the angels of power, and all the angels of supremacies, and the Chosen One, and the other powers on the earth, above the water, on that day; 11. and will raise ONE voice, and will bless, and glorify, and praise, and exalt, in the spirit of faith [fidelity], and in the spirit of wisdom and of patience, and in the spirit of mercy, and in the spirit of judgment and of peace, and in the spirit of goodness, and will all say with ONE voice: ' Blessed is he, and blessed be the name of the Lord of the spirits, in eternity, and to eternity.' 12. And all who do not sleep in high heavens will bless him; all his holy ones, who are in heaven, will bless him, and all the chosen, who dwell in the garden of life, and every spirit of light, who is able to bless, and glorify, and exalt, and say : ' Holy,' to thy sacred name, and all flesh, which will exceedingly praise and bless thy name to all eternity. 13. For great is the mercy of the Lord of the spirits, and he is slow to anger, and all his doing, and all his power, as much as he has made, he has revealed to the just and to the chosen, in the name of the Lord of the spirits.

CHAP. 62. — And thus the Lord commanded the kings and the powerful and the exalted and those who dwell on the earth, and said : " Open your eyes, and lift up your horns, if ye are able to recognize the Chosen One." 2. And the Lord of the spirits sat on the throne of his glory, and the spirit of justice was poured out over him, and the word of his mouth slew all the sinners and all the impious, and they were destroyed before his face. 3. Then will stand up on that day all the kings and the powerful and the exalted and those who hold the earth, and will see him and will know that he sits on the throne of his glory, and that the just are judged in justice before him, and that there is no word spoken in vain before him. 4. And pain will come over them, like a woman who is in travail, and to whom the birth is hard, when the son enters the mouth of the mother, and she has pain in giving birth. 5. And one portion of them will look upon the other, and will tremble and cast down their countenances, and pain will seize them, when they see this Son of the woman sitting on the throne of his glory. 6. And the powerful kings, and all who hold the earth, will honor, and bless, and exalt him who rules over all, who was hidden. 7. For formerly the Son of man was hidden, and the Most High preserved him before his power, and has revealed him to the chosen. 8. And the congregation of the holy and the chosen will be sown, and all the chosen will stand before him on that day. 9. And all the powerful kings and the exalted and they who rule the earth will fall before him upon their faces, and will worship and will hope in this Son of man, and will petition him and ask him for mercy. 10. And that Lord of the spirits will only press them, that they hasten to leave his presence and their countenances will be filled with shame, and darkness will be heaped upon their countenances. 11. And the angels of punishment will receive them to take vengeance on them, because they have abused his children and his chosen. 12. And they will be a spectacle for the just and for his chosen; they will rejoice over them, because the wrath of the Lord of the spirits rests upon them, and the sword of the Lord of the spirits is drunk with them. 13. And the just and chosen will be saved on that day, and will henceforth not see the face of the sinners and of the unjust. 14. And the Lord of the spirits will dwell over them, and they will dwell with this Son of man, and will eat and lie down and rise again *with him* to all eternity. 15. And the just and the chosen will have risen from the earth, and will have ceased to cast down their faces, and will be clothed with the garments of life. 16. And these will be the garments of life before the Lord of the spirits; and your garments will not become old, and your glory will not decrease before the Lord of the spirits.

CHAP. 63. — And in those days the powerful kings, who hold the earth, will petition the angels of punishment, to whom they are delivered, that they should give them a little rest, so that they could fall down and worship before the Lord of the spirits, and could acknowledge their sins before him. 2. And they will bless and glorify the Lord of the spirits, and will say: "Blessed is the Lord of the spirits, and the Lord of kings, the Lord of the powerful, and the Lord of the rulers, and the Lord of glory, and the Lord of wisdom, and every secret is clear. 3. And thy power is to all generations, and thy glory to all eternity: deep are thy secrets all and without number, and thy justice without reckoning. 4. Now we know that we should praise and bless the Lord of kings, and him who rules over all the kings." 5. And they will say: "Who will give us rest, that we might praise and thank and bless him, and be believers before his glory? 6. And now we long for a little rest, and do not find it; we are driven away, and do not receive it; the light has ceased before us, and darkness is our dwelling-place to all eternity. 7. For before him we have not believed, and have not honored the name of the Lord of the kings, and we have not praised the Lord in all his doing, and our hope was in the sceptre of our kingdom and in our glory. 8. And in the day of our trial and our trouble he did not save us, and we do not find rest to believe that our Lord is faithful in all his deeds and in all his judgments and his justice, and that his judgment does not respect persons. 9. And we shall disappear before his face on account of our deeds, and all our sins are counted in justice." 10. Now they will say to them: "Our souls are satisfied with unjust goods, but it does not prevent our going to the flames of the pain of hell." 11. And after that their countenances will be filled with darkness and shame before that Son of man, and they will be expelled from his presence, and a sword will dwell in their midst before his countenance. 12. And thus said the Lord of the spirits: "This is the ordinance and judgment of the mighty and the kings and the exalted and those who hold the earth before the Lord of the spirits."

CHAP. 64. — And I saw other faces in that place in secret. 2. I heard the voice of the angel saying: "These are the angels who descended from heaven upon the earth, and have revealed to the children of men that which was secret, and have led astray the sons of men that they committed sin."

CHAP. 60. 1. This whole chapter is one of the Noachic fragments, as is shown by the contents, cf. Introd. The date being given here points to a new author; as in the other portions there is never the least hint given as to the time when the vision was received, except in an indefinite way in 83:2 and 85:3, and as the verse is, beyond all doubt, constructed after Gen. v. 32, and Noah, not Enoch, is the recipient of the vision in the following; and as the contents point to the time of its reception after the death of Enoch, it is an absolute certainty that for *life of Enoch* we should read *life of Noah*. Its introduction here can be explained by the fact that Noah as well as Enoch received revelations, Gen. vi. 13, and its object was probably to supplement the brief statements of the rest of the book concerning the first judgment, as the second had received such a minute description. All these additions treat of the flood. *Parable*, i.e. the following vision. The effort of the interpolator to connect his fragments with the Parables is also clear from 68:1. *Shaking of the heavens* is a sign of a coming revelation of judgment, 1:9; 14:22; 40:1; 71:8, 13. *Host*, cf. note on 1:9. — 2. *Head of days*, in imitation of the Parables, cf. 55:1, as is also the *sitting on the throne of glory*, as a sign of judgment, cf. 47:3 and *passim*. By remarking that the *just ones* stand around the throne the fragmentist blends the two judgments into one, unless, indeed, he understands by the *just ones* the patriarchs who had died before the time of the deluge. It is scarcely possible that he would have used the word as synonymous with angels. — 3. Cf. 14:13; 14:24. *Loins*, cf. Isa. xlv. 1; Ps. lxix. 23. — 4. Cf. Dan. viii. 17 sqq.; x. 9, 10. Michael here is the first and highest angel, strictly in accordance with 40:4, and not like 20:5, where he is fourth in rank. As one to whom almost divine attributes are ascribed, 40:9, he does not raise Noah himself,

but sends another angel, whose occupation is similar to that of
the angel of peace (vs. 24) in the Parables; cf. note on 40:2.
— 6. *Power*, because the day of the deluge will develop God's
power. After the manner of 37–71, mankind is divided into
two classes, those who bow to, i.e. believe in, the judgment
and those who deny it. The writer here clearly adapts the
description of the second judgment in the Parables to the first.
— 7, 8. This judgment shall consist in a flood, as is shown by
the mention of the two monsters, Behemoth and Leviathan, of
Job xl. and xli., and are also, according to Jewish interpreters,
to be found in Gen. i. 21; Ps. xl. 10; Isa. xxvii. 1. On this
strange fancy of later Judaism, cf. Drummond, p. 352 sqq. As
they are male and female, and at least one of them dwells in
the water, it is probable that they are in some way connected
with the masculine and feminine water of 54:8, perhaps per-
sonifications of the destructive elements in the waters above
and below; cf. verse 24. On the subterranean fountains, cf.
Gen. vii. 11; Job xxxviii. 16. *Dendain* דּין דַּיָּן " the judgment
of a judge," is probably a fictitious place, cf. 10:4. *The garden* is, of course, Eden. It is very strange that the desert
should be in this garden. Probably better, *to the east of the
garden*, as the preposition *ba* is frequently used in the sense of
ad, apud. juxta, cf. Dillmann, *Lex.*, col. 478. Whether the
souls of the departed saints shall dwell there from their death
to the last judgment, or after that, is not clear, although the
former is the more probable; cf. 70:3. Enoch was in reality
the great-grandfather of Noah, but cf. 65:2, 5, 9; 67:4; 68:
1. *Taken up*, cf. Dillmann, ad loc. *Seventh from Adam*, cf.
Jude 14. — 9. *That other angel*, cf. vs. 4. *How*, in the sense
of *why*. — 10. *Son of man*, the mysterious name with which
Ezekiel is constantly addressed; cf. En. 71:14. — 11. With
the other angel, cf vs. 4; the writer connects the following with
the previous, and with his statement *and showed me that which
was secret* enlarges on the secrets of the physical world before
he answers Noah's question, for the answer does not follow till

vs. 24. *The first and the last,* i.e. all, *Repositories of the winds,* cf. 18 : 1. — 12. *Spirits are divided,* i.e. to what phenomena of nature special spirits are given ; cf. vs. 16–21. This peculiar, gnostic way of allotting spirits or angels is a certain proof of the comparatively late origin of these additions. The notion is frequently developed in later Jewish books, e.g. *Book of the Jubilees,* chap. 5. Augustine (*Quest.* 83, 79) remarks: unaquaeque res visibilis in hoc mundo habet potestatem angelicam sibi praepositam. Cf. also Sir. xxxix. 28, 29 and Langen, p. 306 sqq. *Weighing,* not in the moral and judicial sense, but rather, as in 43 : 2, to indicate that these phenomena receive each only a certain mass of substance and degree of power, as in Job xxviii. 25. *Power of the lights of the moon,* i.e. in the different phases of her appearance ; cf. 43 : 2. *Power of justice,* i.e. that even these natural phenomena, and not only the moral world, are guided by a certain power of justice. *Divisions* and the following are still objects of showed in vs. 11 ; cf. 82 : 9 sqq. — 13. Cf. Job xxxvii. 1–5. — 14. *Places of rest* are not repositories. Thunder and lightning originate together, but the former must wait a certain time before it can resound, and this waiting is done in the places of rest. — 15. The whole government of these two phenomena is in the hands of their angel. *Divides equally* allows them to appear only in a certain number and at a certain time. — 16. This explains the tide and ebb of the sea. — 17. *Is his (own) angel,* i.e. has his own peculiar (ἴδιος) angel (Dillmann). The spirit of hail is good to show that this generally injurious phenomenon is not under a demon. — 18. *Left go,* i.e. allowed him to be independent, but strangely *on account of its strength!* — 19. The fog he especially enlarges on, on account of its frequent occurrence. It can appear both in clear and in dark weather, and at all times. The rest of the sentence is mysterious. — 20. That the dew is closely connected with both rain and fog is easily understood. — 21. As the rain is so important for the world, even ethically (Job xxxvii. 12, 13), its guidance is en-

trusted not to its own spirit, but to the angels; cf. Job xxviii.
26; xxxviii. 25–27, 33–38. — 24. Now first comes the answer
to Noah's question, vs. 9. These monsters will be fed by those
destroyed in the deluge, as God has determined, according to
his greatness, and thus the punishment will not be in vain.
According to other apocryphal and rabbinical writings these
two monsters are to be the food of the just in the Messianic
times; cf. Drummond, p. 355. — 25. Cf. Gen. viii. 21, 22; En.
50:3; 61:13.

CHAP. 61. 1. The author of the Parables continues with an
account of how the future Messianic kingdom was measured.
The account is, then, in full harmony with the object of the third
Parable, 58:1, and rests on Zech. ii. 5–9; also cf. Ezek. xl. 3
sqq. and xlvii. 3 sqq. *Those angels*, i.e. those well-known angels, already mentioned so frequently. *Took wings* is especially added because the Old Testament does not represent
angels as possessing wings. *Towards the north*, of uncertain
meaning; but cf. 25:5. — 2. The angel here asked is the angel
of peace; cf. 40:2. *Went out to measure*, the object is supplied
further on in stating that they will measure the future home
of the just. — 3. Therefore they are called the measures of the
just. The result will be that the just will lean firmly on the
Lord. — 4. After the future Messianic kingdom has been measured out, then the chosen will dwell there with the chosen, no
longer mixed and interfered with by the unjust; cf. 38:1; 53:
6; 62:8; the reward promised to fidelity will be given them,
and righteousness during the time of oppression will now receive its reward, and be manifested as being well founded. — 5.
On the day of the Chosen One, which is the day of the realization of the prophecies just stated, the departed saints shall
return and take part in the happiness. As he speaks here
only of the bliss of the saints, and not of the condemnation of
the sinners, he mentions only the resurrection of the former,
but thereby in no wise contradicts his previous doctrine of a
general resurrection, 51:1. *By the sea and by beasts*, to show

that God will fulfil his promises to all, even to those who according to human ideas could not possibly rise again. If we were allowed to believe that the author taught the resurrection of the body as well as of the soul, the force of this clause would be greatly increased. Unless the word *earth* in 51 : 1 is simply used rhetorically to round off the sentence we might believe that the earth there is the receptacle for the bodies and Sheol and hell for the souls, and that the bodily resurrection is there taught also. — 6. *All who dwell in heaven*, i.e. the angels. *Received command*, as the following shows, to praise and to exalt. — 7. *That one*, i.e. the Messiah. It may be that instead of *Kâl* we should read *bakâla*, i.e. *jussu*, agreeing with verse 6, and thus translate: And that one, according to the command, they praised first; cf. 40 : 5. *Spirit of life*, undoubtedly an expression for their enthusiasm. — 8. Modelled after Ps. cx. 1. The words as they stand indicate that the Messiah is to judge the angels also, as they alone are called *holy ones in the high heavens*. But in verse 10 those here judged are distinctly separated from the host of heavens, and then it is against the spirit of the book that the good angels should be judged. *In high heavens* is, beyond all doubt, an addition of the translator. The idea of angels was still in his mind from vs. 6 and 7, and he did not notice the change of subjects in this verse. But that the just shall be judged is in perfect harmony with the strictly forensic character of the judgment in the Parables, and suits remarkably well to the connection. *Weighed*, cf. note on 41 : 1. — 9. *Secret ;* as all the secret wickedness of the sinners shall be judged, thus too shall the secret and unappreciated virtue and firmness of the just receive their reward. *By the word,* i.e. either in the name of the Lord, as if the Lord himself pronounced the judgment, or, taking *nagar* in the sense of *mandatum* (Judith ii. 1 ; Gen. xxiv. 9), by the command of, thus commenting on verse 8. — 10. At the sight of this final justice and happiness accorded to the saints by God through the Messiah, all the hosts of heaven, and even the Messiah himself,

will praise and glorify God. *Host of God*, distinguished from
the general *host of heavens*, are the archangels, divided here
and 71 : 7 into the three scriptural classes of Cherubim, Seraphim, and Ophanim. The last name is from Ezra i. and x.
Angels of power and supremacy. cf. Col. i. 16 ; Eph. i. 21. As
no anticlimax can be thought of, it cannot be decided whether
these are co- or sub-ordinate to the archangels ; cf. *Test. Levi*, 3.
Other powers, i.e. the lower classes of angels. *Chosen One*, cf.
40 : 5. — 11. The motives that prompt to this praise are of the
highest spiritual character. On the doxology, cf. 39 : 10. —
12. *Who do not sleep*, cf. note on 12 : 2. *Garden of justice.*
In 70 : 4 Enoch finds the first patriarchs there. According to
the first part, when he visited Paradise (cf. note on 32 : 6) it
was apparently empty. These expressions can scarcely be
harmonized with the rest of the book ; cf. note on 60 : 7, 8.
Spirit of light is founded on passages like Job xxiv. 13 sqq. ;
xxxviii. 15. *All flesh* shows that most assuredly not all
flesh dwells in the Paradise. The author evidently thinks
that it is the place of the departed saints, where they shall
remain to the coming of the Messiah. — 13. They praise those
attributes of God which he has chiefly exhibited in the judgment.

CHAP. 62. 1. This is one of the most interesting and important chapters in the whole book: interesting, because it so
well portrays the forensic character of the last judgment, important, because it affords the best hold for those who claim,
for the Parables at least, a Christian origin ; and Hilgenfeld
has taken some of his sharpest javelins from this chapter in
his *Die jüdische Apokalyptik*, etc., 1857. — After the judgment
of the just comes that of the kings and the mighty, together
with those who dwell on the earth. There is a temporal, but
no local, difference between these judgments, as in verse 3
the kings must behold the just judgment of the saints. It is
no tautology to bring in this judgment here as in 46 : 4–8 ; 48 :
8–10 ; 53–54 : 3, only certain phases of this judgment are re-

corded, but here the very act with its connecting circumstances are recorded. Just when the resurrection of the dead sinners, made necessary from 51:1 before this judgment, shall take place is not stated, but verse 2 of that chapter almost forces the idea that it is to be contemporaneous with the resurrection of the just, mentioned 61:5. There no mention of the rising of the wicked was needed; but, as in the author's mind the two classes will rise together, he makes no mention here of the resurrection. *Kings and powerful*, cf. 38:4; 46:7; 62:3, 6, 9; 63:1, 12; 67:8, 12. His polemics are against the rich and exalted who are happy in the possessions of this world, trust them only, and care not for the future. Now these proud ones will not even be able to lift up their eyes, out of shame and fear on account of their former conduct. They had denied the Messiah, but now must see that he has come as judge. *Horns*, cf. Ps. lxxv. 4, 5. As a curiosity it may be mentioned that Hilgenfeld, p. 174, claims that the word *recognize* implies that they had seen the Messiah before, and this must have been in the time when Christ became man!—2. As this verse is modelled after Isa. xi. 4, and the expression *the spirit of justice was poured out over him* suits only the Messiah, and not God, the *over him* must refer to the Messiah. To interpret it of God breaks the whole force of this and the following verses; cf. Psalt. Salom. xvii. 39; 4 Ezra xiii. 10 sqq. The perfect is used here because Enoch *saw* these things. — 3. Now he continues prophetically to his readers, and speaks in the future tense. In looking at the word *know* here and *recognized* verse 1, it seems that those judged here are those who had heard of the coming Messiah through the prophets, but had refused to hear of him, had denied him and his judgments, but are now convinced by his presence. The seer would then be addressing the fallen in Israel alone, and the judgment would be a partial one, as it is in 90:26. Thus also it would be in perfect harmony with the conversion of the heathen nations to the Messianic kingdom described in chap. 57 and else-

14*

where. *In vain;* from the forensic character of the judgment
this must mean that nothing but justice shall here decide. —
4. Cf. Isa. xxi. 3; xxvi. 17; xxxvii. 3; Jer. iv. 31; xxii. 23;
xxx. 6; John xvi. 21; Homer, *Il.* 11, 269 sqq. — 5. *Son of
the woman,* found only here in all apocryphal writings. Hilgenfeld, p. 157, confidently claims this expression as a proof
of the Christian origin of the Parables, as the idea of a mysterious Messiah coming from on high and of a chosen man
born in the ordinary way could not have been combined until
the coming of Christ in the flesh. But we must remember
that the Messiah of the Parables is far from being a divine
being; and even if the name could not be based on a combination of Dan. vii. and Mic. v. 2 (as it may, however), the objection that is here raised against the human side of the Messiah
in his name as *Son of the woman* would be every bit as valid
against his name as *Son of man.* The name, however, was
easily suggested by the biblical *Son of man.* Furthermore,
as the translators of the Ethiopic Bible frequently introduced
New Testament expressions into the Old (cf. Herzog, *R. E.*
xii. p. 310) it is easily possible that the word *woman* was
introduced by the Christian translator for *man,* or by the
copyist, as *beezit* (woman) and *beeze* (man) are distinguished
by only one letter. — 6. *Rules,* from Dan. vii. 14. — 7, 8. *Was
hidden,* cf. 48 : 6, 7. The idea that this Messiah was hidden
is based on his sudden and mysterious appearance Dan. vii. 13.
The idea here could under no circumstances refer to the
dwelling of the Logos with God before Christ became man,
for here the Messiah is hidden until the day of judgment, and
then suddenly appears — a statement entirely strange to a
Christian, who knew the Messiah had appeared, but also that
the final judgment had not; whereas the appearance of the
Messiah on the final day only could easily have been developed from Old Testament premises by a one-sided exegesis.
Congregation of saints, cf. 38 : 1; 53 : 6. *Sown,* i.e. established; cf. 10 : 16. — 9. Now those who had denied him will

even petition the Messsiah for mercy. — 10, 11. But this will be in vain. *Shame and darkness*, cf. 46 : 6. *Angels of punishment*, cf. note on 53 : 3. — 12. *Spectacle*, cf. 27 : 3, 4 ; 48 : 9, 10. *Drunk*, cf. Isa. xxxiv. 5, 6. — 13. The punishment of the sinners after the sentence has been passed will take place where the just will not see them ; cf. note on 38 : 3. The act of judgment is the spectacle the just shall see, but the terrors of punishment they shall not behold. — 14. Cf. Isa. iv. 5, 6 ; lx. 17–22 ; Zeph. iii. 15–17 ; Zech. ii. 9, 15 ; ix. 7, 8 ; En. 38 : 1 ; 45 : 4 ; 105 : 2. Hoffmann strangely connects this passage with Matt. xxvi. 29. *To all eternity ;* the eternity of the Messianic kingdom is taught by many apocryphal writers ; cf. 3 Sibyl. 49–50, 766 ; Psalt. Salom. xvii. 4 (based on Jer. xxiv. 6 ; Ezek. xxxvii. 25 ; Joel iv. 20 ; Dan. vii. 27). — 15. *Will have risen* does not refer to the resurrection, but forms simply an antithesis to the second clause. *Garments of life*, cf. 10 : 17 ; 58 : 3, and note on 37 : 4. — 16. *Will not become old ;* as the garments of life are symbols of eternal life it is stated that they will not grow old ; cf. Deut. viii. 4 ; xxix. 5.

CHAP. 63, 1. Connecting with one of the most interesting statements in his account of the judgment, viz. the deliverance of the wicked into the hands of the angels of punishment, 62 : 11, the author relates what happens after these criminals have been removed from the presence of the just, 62 : 13. While the condemned are being led off to their punishment they petition their guards for rest, i.e. respite, until they can worship and petition the Lord of the spirits. It must be observed here that although their chief sin consisted in their relation to the Messiah and his kingdom, they desire still to petition *God* for mercy, again reminding us of the fact that the Messiah is only a deputy of God, and can act only in his name. — 2. Their prayer consists in acknowledging what they formerly denied. On the doxology cf. 22 : 14 ; 39 : 10 sqq. ; 61 : 11. — 3. Cf. 49 : 2. — 6. Cf. vs. 2 and note on 10 : 5. — 8. It is evidently a matter of importance for the author to inculcate the doctrine that after the appearance of the Messiah there will be no chance whatever of being delivered from the just punishment. — 10. Cf. chap. 53 and Ps. xlix. 7–12. *Hell;* the original has Sheol. That the punishment shall consist in burning is taught throughout the Parables; cf. 54 : 1, 2, 5, 6 ; 63 : 10 ; 48 : 9. — 11. Cf. vs. 11 and 12. — 12 is a formal conclusion, not to the third parable, but only to chap. 62 and 63.

CHAP. 64. But the Messianic kingdom is not yet completed. In 55 : 4 he had said that the Messiah should judge even the fallen angels, and now he records the fact that they were in reality judged. As however this judgment was of little importance for his object, he simply mentions it here in addition to the statements of 54 : 3 ; 55 : 3, 4; cf. 90 : 24. *Faces,* or forms, πρόσωπα ; cf. 17 : 1 and 40 : 2.

SECTION XI.

CHAP. 65. — And in those days Noah saw the earth that it was curved, and that its destruction was near. 2. And he lifted up his feet from there, and went to the ends of the earth, and called to his grandfather Enoch ; and Noah said with a bitter voice : " Hear me ! hear me ! hear me ! " three times. 3. And he said to him : " Tell me what is it that has been done on the earth, that the earth is so tired out and shaken ? May I not be destroyed with it ! " 4. And after this time there was a great trembling on the earth, and a voice was heard from heaven, and I fell on my face. 5. And Enoch, my grandfather, came and stood by me and said to me : " Why dost thou so bitterly and lamentingly cry to me ? 6. A command has come from before the presence of the Lord over all those who dwell on the earth, that their end is at hand, because they know all the secrets of the angels, and all the violence of the satans, and all the powers of secrecy, and all the powers of those who practice sorcery and the powers of fascination, and the powers of those who make metal images of the whole earth ; 7. and also how silver is produced from the dust of the earth, and how soft metal originates on the earth. 8. For lead and zinc are not produced like the former ; a fountain it is which produces them, and an angel who stands in it ; and that angel is excellent." 9. And after that my grandfather Enoch took hold of me with his hand, and raised me up, and said to me : " Go, for I have asked the Lord of the spirits concerning this shaking of the earth. 10. And he said to me : ' On account of their injustice their judgment is completed ; and will not be counted before me concerning the months which they have searched out, and *through which* they have learned that the earth will be destroyed and those who live thereon. 11. And for them there will be no place of refuge to eternity, because they have showed them that which was secret, and they will be judged ; but not thou, my son ; the Lord of the spirits knows that thou art clean and free of this blame concerning the secrets. 12. And he has strengthened thy name among the holy, and will preserve thee from those who dwell on the earth, and will strengthen thy seed in justice for kings and great honors ; and from thy seed will proceed the fountain of the just and the holy, without number, to eternity."

CHAP. 66. — And after that he showed me the angels of punishment, who are prepared to come in order to open all the powers of the water which is under the earth, that it may be a judgment and destruction over all those who live and dwell on the earth. 2. And the Lord of spirits commanded the angels who went forth, that they should not lift up *their* hands, but should wait; for these angels are over the power of the waters. 3. And I went away from the presence of Enoch.

CHAP. 67. — And in those days the voice of God was with me, and he said to me: "Noah, behold thy portion has ascended to me, a portion without blame, a portion of love and of rectitude. 2. And now the angels are making a wooden *building*, and when they are gone to that work, I will lift up my hands upon it and will preserve it; and out of it will be [i.e. come] the seed of life, and a change will come so that the earth does not remain empty. 3. And I will strengthen thy seed before me to all eternity, and will scatter those who dwell with thee over the face of the earth, and it [i.e. the seed] will be blessed and increased over the earth in the name of the Lord." 4. And they will enclose those angels who have showed injustice in that flaming valley which my grandfather Enoch showed to me before, in the west, in the mountains of gold and of silver and of iron and of soft metal and of zinc. 5. And I saw that valley, in which there was a great shaking and a shaking of the waters. 6. And as this took place there was produced from that flaming, flowing metal, and out of the shaking that shook them, at that place, an odor of sulphur, and it united with those waters; and that valley of the angels who had led astray burned under that earth. 7. And through the valley of that *earth* come rivers of fire, where those angels who had led astray those who dwell on the earth are condemned. 8. And those waters will be in those days for the kings and the powerful and exalted and those who dwell on the earth, a medicine of the soul and of the body, but for a judgment of the spirit, because their spirits are full of lust, that they be punished in their bodies, because they have denied the Lord of the spirits, and see their judgments daily, and still believe not in his name. 9. And as the burning of their bodies increases there will be a change in their spirit to all eternity; for no one will speak a vain word before the Lord of the spirits. 10. For the judgment comes over them, because they believe in the lust of their flesh, and deny the spirit of the Lord. 11. And those waters themselves, in those days, suffer a change, for when those angels shall be condemned on those days, the heat of those fountains of the waters changes, and when the angels ascend, this water of the fountains changes and becomes cold. 12. And I heard the holy Michael answering and saying: " This judgment wherewith the angels are condemned is a testimony for the kings and the powerful and for those who hold the earth. 13. For these waters of judgment are a healing of the angels, and a death to their bodies, but they will not see and will not believe that those waters change, and will become a fire, which burns to eternity."

CHAP. 68. — And after that my grandfather Enoch gave me the signs of all the secrets in a book, and the Parables which had been given to him, and he compiled them for me in the words of the book of the Parables. 2. And on that day the holy Michael answered, saying to Rufael: " The power of the spirit forces me and angers me, and on account of the severity of the judgment of the secrets, the judgment over the angels; who can endure the severity of the judgment which is passed and remains, and before which they melt away ?" 3. And the holy Michael answered again and said to

Rufael: " Who is he whose heart is not softened concerning it, and whose reins are not shaken by this
word ?   A judgment has come over them from [i.e. on
account of] those whom they have thus led out."   4.
And it came to pass as he stood before the Lord of the
spirits, the holy Michael spoke to Rufael: " And I will
not be for them under the eye of the Lord, for the Lord
of the spirits is angered at them, because they act as if
they were like gods.   5. Therefore judgment which is
hidden comes over them, to all eternity ; therefore,
neither angel nor man will receive his portion, but they
alone will receive their judgment to all eternity."

CHAP. 69. — And after this judgment they will terrify
and anger them, because they have showed this to those
who dwell on the earth.   2. And behold the names of
those angels ! and these are their names: the first of
them is Semjâzâ, the second Arestîqîfâ, the third Armên,
the fourth Kakabâêl, the fifth Turêl, the sixth, Rûmjâl,
the seventh Dânêl, the eighth Nûqaêl, the ninth Barâqêl,
the tenth Azâzêl, the eleventh Armers, the twelfth Ba-
tarjâl, the thirteenth Basasâêl, the fourteenth Anânêl,
the fifteenth Turjâl, the sixteenth Simâpîsîêl, the seventeenth Jetarêl, the eighteenth Tûmâêl, the nineteenth
Tarêl, the twentieth Rûmâêl, the twenty-first Izêzêêl.   3.
And these are the heads of the angels, and the names of
their chiefs over a hundred and the chiefs over fifty and the
chiefs over ten. 4. The name of the first Jeqûn ; he is the
one who has led astray all the children of the holy angels,
and has led them down on the earth, and has led them
astray through the daughters of men. 5. And the
second is called Asbeêl ; he is the one who has taught
the children of the holy angels the wicked device, and
has led them astray to destroy their bodies with the

daughters of men. 6. And the third is called Gâdreêl; he is the one who has taught the children of men all the blows of death, and led astray Eve, and showed to the children of men the instruments of death, the coat-of-mail and the shield and the sword for battle, and all the instruments of death to the sons of men. 7. And from his hand they have come over those who dwell on the earth, from that time to eternity. 8. And the fourth is called Pênêmû; he has taught the sons of men the bitter and the sweet, and taught them all the secrets of their wisdom. 9. He taught men writing with ink and paper (χάρτης), and thereby many sinned from eternity and to eternity and up to this day. 10. For men were not born to the purpose that they should thus strengthen their fidelity with a pen (κάλαμος) and with ink. 11. For man was not created otherwise than the angels, that they should remain just and pure, and death, which destroys all things, would not have touched them, but through this their knowledge they are destroyed, and through this power it devours me. 12. And the fifth is named Kasdejâ; he has taught the sons of men all the wicked beatings of the spirits and the demons, the beatings of the birth in the womb, that it [i.e. the birth] fall, and the beatings of the soul, the bites of the serpent, and the beatings which take place at noon, the son of the serpent whose name is Tabâ't. 13. And this is the number of Kesbeêl, who showed the head of the oath to the holy ones, when he dwelt high in glory; and his name is Bêqâ. 14. And this one said to the holy Michael that he should show them the secret name, that they might see that secret name, and that they might mention this name in the oath, and they may tremble before that name and the oath, those that

15

showed to the children of men all that is secret. 15. And this is the power of that oath, for it is powerful and strong, and he placed this oath Akâe' into the hands of the holy Michael. 16. And these are the secrets of this oath, and they were strengthened by his oath, and heaven was suspended before the earth was made, and to eternity. 17. And by it the earth was founded on the water, and from the secret places of the mountains come beautiful waters for the living, from the creation of the world to eternity. 18. And by that oath the sea was created, and as its foundation he placed for it sand for the time of rage, and it dare not pass over from the creation of the world and to eternity. 19. And by that oath the depths were strengthened and stand and do not move from their places, from eternity and to eternity. 20. And by that oath the sun and the moon complete their course and depart not from their commands from eternity and to eternity. 21. And by that oath the stars complete their courses, and he calls their names and they answer him from eternity and to eternity. 22. And also the spirits of the water and of the winds, and of all the zephyrs and their paths, according to all the unions of the spirits. 23. And in it are preserved the repositories of the voice of thunder and of the light of the lightning, and there are preserved the repositories of hail and of the hoar-frost, and the repositories of the fog, and the repositories of the rain and of the dew. 24. And all these believe in and render thanks before the Lord of the spirits, and praise him with all their power, and their food is all thanksgiving, and they thank and praise and exalt in the name of the Lord of the spirits to all eternity. 25. And over them this oath is strong, and they are preserved by it, and their paths are preserved, and the courses are not destroyed. 26., And there was great joy among them, and they blessed and honored and exalted, because the name of the Son of man had been revealed unto them. 27. And he sat upon the throne of his glory, and the sum of the judgment was given to him, the Son of man, and he causes to disappear and to be destroyed the sinners from the face of the earth, and also those who have led astray the earth. 28. They shall be bound with chains and shall be imprisoned in the assembling-place of destruction, and all their work shall disappear from the face of the earth. 29. And from that time on there will be nothing that will be destroyed, for he, the Son of man, has appeared, and sits on the throne of his glory, and all wickedness will disappear before his face and depart; but the word of that Son of man will be strong before the Lord of the spirits. This is the third Parable of Enoch.

CHAP. 65, 1. Now follows to 69 : 25 another Noachic interpolation. That it is such appears beyond a doubt from its contents. It has the peculiarities of chapter 60, and treats of the same subject, viz. revelation to Noah concerning the flood and attending circumstances. It is entirely of a fragmentary character, and certainly never existed as a tract of itself. In thought and expression it seeks to imitate the Parables. That Noah is here introduced as the seer alone stamps it as an addition foreign to the rest of the book. In 60 : 2 the vision was inaugurated with a motion of the heavens; here it is done by a curving of the earth. — 2. Enoch had ascended on high, 60 : 8, from the garden of Eden, therefore Noah goes to the ends of the earth to seek his explanation of what he had seen. — 3. The earth is here represented as weak and sickly, undoubtedly as a result of sin. — 4. Before an answer was

returned there was a violent shaking of the earth. *A voice,*
cf. vs. 6. — 6. *A command* was the voice heard in vs. 4.   The
destruction of the earth is at hand. *Secrets of the angels,* i.e.
of the fallen; cf. 7 : 1; 8 : 1 sqq. *Angels and satans;* a clear
proof that the fragmentist seeks to imitate the Parables, as the
satans are unknown to the first part; cf. note on 40 : 7. *Metal
images;* same as idolatry in chap. 7 and 8. — 7. *Out of the
dust,* cf. Job xxviii. 2. *Soft metal,* cf. 52 : 2, 5. — 8. This soft
metal is declared to be lead and zinc, whose origin the author,
after his peculiar manner (cf. 60 : 13–15, 16, 21, etc.), explains
in anything but a clear way.   That even this mysterious fountain has its angel agrees perfectly with 60 : 16 sqq. — 9.
Cf. vs. 4. — 10. Through their astrology (8 : 3) these sinners
had learned that a judgment would come at a certain time, but
on account of their sins God will not wait to the completion
of that time; cf. also Tertullian, *De Cultu Fem.* i. 10: Et
metallorum opera nudaverunt .... et incantationem vires pro-
mulgaverunt et omnem curiositatem usque ad stellarum inter-
pretationem designaverunt. — 11. Enoch here speaks to Noah.
Free, cf. Gen. vi. 9. — 12. Noah is to be the father of a generation of the righteous. *Fountain,* cf. Deut. xxxiii. 28; Ps.
lxviii. 26.

CHAP. 66. 1. *The angels of punishment,* found only in the
Parables (cf. notes on 53 : 3), are taken over from there, and
are here employed for a purpose entirely foreign to them.
Above they were employed in the final punishment, but here in
the first.   The object of the interpolator to connect his statements with the Parables is observed again here. — 2. There
is no difficulty in accepting *angels* here as referring to those
mentioned in the previous verses.   The angels of punishment
are, although enemies of God, nevertheless subordinate to his
will, like Satan in the Book of Job; cf. note on 40 : 7.

CHAP. 67, 1. The author's paraphrase on Gen. vi. 9. — 2.
As the ark is to be the means of saving the seed of life, angels
construct it.   That angels thus assist in forwarding God's

plans in this direct manner is not unknown to other writers: cf. 2 Macc. iii. 25 sq. with 4 Macc. § 4. The account by a different author, 89 : 1, is more biblical. *Lift up*, cf. Gen. vii. 16; En. 89 : 1. *To that work;* not to the building of the ark, but for the purpose of letting the waters loose; cf. chap. 66. — 3. Cf. 65 : 12. — 4. With this is connected the punishment of the angels also; and as they were the real cause of men's sin, their punishment shall be by a more terrible element — by fire. The portrait here given of this punishment, although based on the rest of the book, deviates in not a few particulars. *Showed me,* cf. chap. 52; 55. But what is stated above should take place in the final judgment the fragmentist boldly employs in the first. Notwithstanding the valley and the mountains are locally separated, 54 : 1, they are here placed together. *In the west;* taken from 52 : 1, and therefore does not require us to seek a place west of Palestine or Jerusalem; much less does it compel us to take a trip to Italy, and seek the burning valley near Vesuvius after the eruption, A.D. 79, as e.g. Hilgenfeld and Drummond want us to do. In the general indefinite character of the description here it is just as easy to understand by this valley Gehinnom, even if this was east and not west of Jerusalem. — 5. We see we are still in the time of the deluge. — 6—8. The picture drawn by the author is this: There is a valley in which is medicinal water, used for the purpose of health by the powerful of the earth. But this valley shall through eruptions become a river of fire, and with that the place where the fallen angels will be punished. For a subterranean fire in Gehenna cf. note on chap. 27. And as the water-place Dillmann refers to Kallirrhoe mentioned by Josephus, *Antiqq.* xvii. 6, 5; *Bel. Jud.* i. 33, 5. This is indeed open to the objection that Josephus in the last passage quoted expressly states that these waters were sweet enough for drinking purposes, hence were not sulphurous as stated in vs. 6. But not only was sulphur often found in Palestine, especially in the region from Jerusa-

lem to the Dead Sea (cf. Josephus, *Bel. Jud.* vii. 6, 3), but is
also in the Old Testament a standard medium of punishment
for the wicked (cf. Deut. xxix. 23; Job xviii. 15; Ezek
xxxviii. 22; Ps. xi. 6); and that an author like ours, so characterized by inaccuracy, should fail in his chemistry when the
failure was easily suggested by numerous Scripture passages
is not surprising.   Hilgenfeld and others have deemed it necessary to insist on the baths at Baiae and the eruption of
Vesuvius, A.D. 79, as the only legitimate explanation of this
passage.   Hence, too, at least the present compilation of the
Book of Enoch could not have taken place before that date.
But even if we must do what the author permits us nowhere
else, — go to the far west, and seek the baths of Baiae, — it is
therefore by no means necessary to think of the eruption of
Vesuvius.   As Holtzmann has already remarked (*Jahrbücher
für Deutsche Theol.*, vol. xii. p. 391), Mt. Epomeo on the
island of Ischia, much nearer Baiae than Vesuvius, suffered
eruptions in the years 46 and 35 B.C., and then not again
until 1301 A.D.   This explanation is also recommended by the
fact that Enoch pictures these phenomena as repeated.   In
verse 8 the so-called Trichotomy is distinctly taught. — 9.
Their spirits will change, will no longer remain so proud,
haughty, and God-denying; their pride will be broken. — 11.
But after the angels have been removed for their final punishment from this place of temporal punishment, then those
warm waters will grow cold.   This makes it clear that the
author imagined those springs heated by the fire underneath
where the fallen angels were enduring their temporal torture.
The author evidently does not trouble himself about the fact
that the first part plainly taught that the temporal punishment
consisted in being bound under the hills; cf. chap. 10. — 12.
The moral of his account is that this temporal torture of the
fallen angels in such a manner that its evidence is constantly
before the eyes of the rich who are luxuriating in the bathing-
places is a warning for them.   In making the powerful the

object of his warning he again connects with the Parables. — 13. The stress in *a* lies on *angels*; they were healed, i.e. as Dillmann remarks, probably repent; but it does not produce a similar effect on the rulers and powerful. Therefore, too, the second judgment shall be by a more terrible element — by fire; cf. Wisd. x. 7; Jude 7.

CHAP. 68, 1. Should there have been any doubt that the author of the Noachic fragments seeks to follow the Parables, this doubt will be removed here, where he expressly quotes them as the source of his information. As the Parables treat mainly of the second judgment it is probable that the fragmentist desires to do so too in the following. This probability is heightened by the fact that the judgment is *hidden*. The author stands at the time of the first judgment, but there is in reserve yet a hidden future judgment that seems almost too severe in the eyes of the angels. Then, too, the judgment, according to verse 5, is *to all eternity.* — 3. *By this word*, i.e. the word of God that declares this punishment. — 4. But before the throne of God Michael acknowledges the justice of the judgment, and suppresses the involuntary pity; cf. Isa. xiv. 11–13. — 5. This verse seems to say that the final punishment of the angels is so severe that none other will be like it.

CHAP. 69. After again dwelling briefly on the terrors of this punishment, the author gives a catalogue of the angels that fell, differing to some extent from the account in 6 : 7. Most of these names in both places are of doubtful etymology and of little importance, nothing but the invention of some ingenious speculator. — 4. This task is assigned to Semjaza in 6 : 3. — 9. The abuse of this art was sinful. The writers sin for such reasons as are assigned 99 : 2; 104 : 9, 10. — 10, 11. Writing is sinful, as it indicates a state of dishonesty; cf. Wisd. i. 13, 14; ii. 23, 24; Matt. v. 37. *It*, i.e. death. — 12. Cf. Ps. xci. 5, 6, 13, according to the old Jewish interpretation. *Beatings that take place at noon*, cf. Ps. xci. 6. — 13. The divine name used in swearing and witchcraft. — 17. Cf. Ps. xxiv. 2;

cxxxvi. 6. — 18. Cf. Jer. v. 22; Prov. viii.; Job xxxviii. —
19. Cf. Prov. viii. 28. — 21. *Calls their names,* cf. Isa. xl.
26; Ps. cxlvii. 4. — 24. Cf. En. 41 : 7. — 26. With this verse
we are, as the name *Son of man,* used of the Messiah, already
indicates, again in the Parables, and this is proved by the ending of vs. 29.   But whether these verses to 29 are a portion of
a chapter cut out by the interpolater to furnish room for his
remarks, or are to be connected with a certain part of the
third parable must remain doubtful.   They are, however, a
good summary and close of this parable.

SECTION XII.

CHAP. 70. — And it came to pass after this that his
name was elevated during his lifetime to that Son of
man, to the Lord of the spirits, away from those who
dwell on the earth.   2. And it was elevated on the
wagons of the spirit, and the name departed in their
midst.   3. And from that day I was not drawn in their
midst, and he set me between two winds, between the
north and the west, there where the angels took the cords
to measure for me the place for the chosen and for the
just.   4. And there I saw the first fathers and the just,
who dwell in this place from the beginning.

CHAP. 71. — And it came to pass after this that my
spirit was hidden, and it ascended into the heavens;
there I saw the sons of the angels stepping on a flame of
fire; their clothes were white and also their garments;
and the light of their faces was like crystal.   2. And I
saw two rivers of fire, and the light of that fire flamed
like hyacinth, and I fell on my face before the Lord of
the spirits.   3. And Michael, an angel from among the
chiefs of the angels, took me by the right hand and

lifted me up, and led me out to all the secrets of mercy and to the secrets of justice. 4. And he showed me all the secrets of the ends of heaven, and all the repositories of the stars and of the luminaries, and whence they proceed into the presence of the holy ones. 5. And the spirit moved Enoch into the heaven of heavens. And I saw there in the midst of the light how there was something which was built of crystal stone, and between these stones tongues of living fire. 6. And my spirit saw how a fire surrounded this house, on the four sides rivers full of living fire, and how they surrounded this house. 7. And around about were Seraphim and Cherubim and Ophanim; these are they who do not sleep, but guard the throne of his glory. 8. And I saw angels who could not be numbered, a thousand times thousand, and ten thousand times ten thousand, surrounded that house, and Michael and Rufael, Gabriel and Fanuel, and the holy angels who are in the high heavens enter and leave that house. 9. And Michael and Gabriel, Rufael and Fanuel, and many holy angels without number came out of that house; 10. and with them the Head of days, his head white and clean as wool, and his garments beyond description. 11. And I fell on my face, and all my flesh melted, and my spirit was changed; and I cried with a loud voice, with the spirit of power, and I blessed and honored and exalted. 12. And these blessings, which proceeded from my mouth, were pleasing before that Head of days. 13. And that Head of days came with Michael and Gabriel, Rufael and Fanuel, and with thousands and with ten thousand times thousand angels without number. 14. And that angel came to me and greeted me with his voice and said to me: "Thou art

a son of man who was born to justice, and justice
dwells over thee, and the justice of the Head of days
will not depart from thee." 15. And he said to me:
" He calls ' Peace ' unto thee in the name of the world
which is to come, for thence peace proceeds since the
creation of the world, and thus it will be to thee to eternity and from eternity to eternity. 16. And all who
will continue to walk in thy path (thou, whom justice
does not leave in eternity), their dwelling-places will be
with thee, and they will not be separated from thee in
eternity and from eternity to eternity. 17. And so
long life will be with that Son of man, and peace will
be to the just, and his right path to the just, in the
name of the Lord of the spirits to all eternity.

CHAP. 70. This chapter, containing an account of the translation of Enoch into Paradise, is an interruption of the sense.
This, together with internal evidences, mark it as an interpolation ; but by whom made cannot, on account of its brevity, be
decided. *Name,* vs. 1, often for *person.* Enoch's elevation
took place, like Elijah's, *on wagons ;* cf. 2 Kings ii. 11. The
pre-existence of the Son of man is, at least unconsciously, here
presupposed. *Their midst,* i.e. of men. *He set me ;* indefinite
expression for *I was set. North and west* is surprising, as according to the ancients the earthly paradise was in the north-
east; cf. En. 77 : 3 and chap. 33. — 4. The statement that the
first patriarchs were in the garden of justice is more in harmony with the method of thinking pursued by the Noachic
fragmentist than by the author of the Parables ; cf. note on
60 : 7, 8, and Sibyl. *Proœm.* ii. 48 ; but cf. 61 : 12 and 89 : 52.
From eternity modifies *fathers,* not *dwell.*

CHAP. 71. Enoch's spiritual translation into the congregation of the Messianic saints is a worthy conclusion of the
Parables as a whole; cf. 39 : 8 (37 : 4) ; 90 : 31. 1. *After*

that, i.e. probably after the vision recorded in chap. 62–64. *Sons of angels,* imitation of *sons of men,* as a designation for angels; cf. also 69 : 4, 5 ; 106 : 5. — 2. *Rivers of fire,* cf. Dan. vii. 10 and En. 72 : 6, 14, 19. — 3. Unlike in the Noachic fragments, 60 : 4, Michael himself raises the seer ; cf. Dan. x. 13 ; xii. 1. *Secrets of mercy and justice,* referring to the Messianic judgment. — 5. *Secrets of the ends of heaven,* i.e. the secrets of the physical world; cf. chap. 14. — 7. Cf. 39 : 13 ; 61 : 10, 12. — 8. But cf. 14 : 21, 22, thus showing another difference between the two main parts of the book; cf. 1 : 9. — 9. Cf. Dan. vii. 9 ; En. 46 : 1. — 11. *Spirit of power,* cf. 61 : 11. — 14. *That angel,* i.e. undoubtedly Michael, vs. 3. — 15. *The world which is to come,* the Messianic kingdom, the הבא עולם. —17. With the Old Testament blessing of long life, i.e. eternal life, the Parables characteristically close.

SECTION XIII.

CHAP. 72. — The book of the courses of the luminaries of heaven, how it is with each one of them, as to their classes, their governments, and their times, as to their names and origin, and as to their months, which their leader Uriêl, a holy angel who was with me, showed to me, and their whole description as it is he showed to me, and how it is with respect to all the years of the world and to eternity, till a new creation is made which will continue to eternity. 2. And this is the first law of the luminaries: the luminary sun has its ascent in the portals of the heavens which are towards the east, and his descent in the western portals of heaven. 3. And I saw six portals, out of which the sun ascends, and six portals into which the sun descends; the moon also rises and sets in these portals,

and the leaders of the stars and those led by them ; six
in the east and six in the west, and all, each after the
other, aright ; also many windows to the right and to
the left of these portals. 4. And first comes forth the
great luminary called the sun ; and his circuit is like the
circuit of the heavens, and he is entirely filled with
flaming and heating fire. 5. The wagons on which he
ascends are driven by the wind, and the sun descending
disappears from the heavens and returns through the
north in order to reach the east, and is led that he
comes to that portal and shines on the surface of
heaven. 6. And thus he comes forth, in the first
month, in the great portal, and he comes forth from the
fourth of these six portals towards the east. 7. And in
that fourth portal, from which the sun comes forth in
the first month, there are twelve window openings, from
which a flame proceeds when they are opened in their
time. 8. When the sun rises from the heavens he
comes out of that fourth portal thirty mornings, and
descends directly into the fourth western portal of
heaven. 9. And in those days the day is daily lengthened, and the nights nightly shortened to the thirtieth
morning. 10. And in that day the day is two parts
longer than the night, and the day is exactly ten parts
and the night eight parts. 11. And the sun comes
forth from this fourth portal and sets in the fourth and
returns to the fifth portal of the east thirty mornings,
and comes forth from it and descends into the fifth portal. 12. From then on the day is lengthened two parts,
and the day is eleven parts, and the night is shortened
and is seven parts. 13. And the sun returns to the
east and goes into the sixth portal, and comes forth and
descends into the sixth portal, thirty-one mornings on

account of its sign. 14. And on that day the day is longer than the night, and the day will be double the night, and the day is twelve parts, and the night is shorter and is six parts. 15. And the sun is raised so that the day is shortened and the night is lengthened, and the sun returns to the east and enters the sixth portal and rises from it and sets thirty mornings. 16. And when the thirty mornings are completed the day diminishes by exactly ONE part, and the day is eleven parts and the night seven parts. 17. And the sun comes forth from this sixth portal in the west and goes to the east and rises in the fifth portal thirty mornings and sets in the west again in the fifth portal. 18. On that day the day diminishes two parts, and the day will be ten parts and the night eight parts. 19. And the sun comes forth from that fifth portal and descends into the fifth portal of the west and rises in the fourth portal, on account of its sign, thirty-one mornings and descends in the west. 20. On that day the day is equal to the night and becomes equal, and the night is nine parts and the day nine parts. 21. And the sun comes forth from that portal and sets in the west and returns to the east and comes forth from the third portal thirty mornings and sets in the west in the third portal. 22. And on that day the night is longer than the day to the thirtieth morning, and the day becomes shorter daily to the thirtieth morning, and the night is exactly ten parts and the day eight parts. 23. And the sun comes forth from that third portal and sets in the third portal in the west and returns to the east, and the sun goes into the second portal of the east thirty mornings, and in like manner into the second portal in the west of the heavens. 24. And on that day the night is eleven parts and the

16

day seven parts.   25. And the sun comes forth on that
day from the second portal and descends in the west
into the second portal and returns to the east in the
first portal thirty-one mornings and descends into the
west into the first portal.   26. And on that day the night
will be so long that it will be the double of the day, and
the night is exactly twelve parts and the day six parts.
27. And with that the sun has completed his stations,
and he again returns to his station and enters in this
portal thirty mornings; he rises and sets opposite it in
the west.   28. And on that day the night diminishes
in length by ONE part, and is eleven parts and the day
seven parts.   29. And the sun returns and goes into
the second portal of the east and returns to his course
thirty mornings, rising and setting.   30. And on that
day the night diminishes in length, and the night is ten
parts and the day eight parts.   31. And on that day
the sun comes forth from the second portal and descends
in the west and returns to the east and rises in the
third portal thirty-one mornings and sets in the west of
the heavens.   32. And on that day the night is shortened and is nine parts, and the day is nine parts, and
the night is equal with the day, and the year has exactly
three hundred and sixty-four days.   33. And the length
of the day and of the night, and the shortness of the day
and of the night — by the course of the sun they are
made separated.   34. On that account the day-course
becomes longer daily and the night-course shorter
nightly.   35. And this is the law and the course of the
sun and his return when he returns; sixty times he returns and comes out, that is the great, eternal luminary
which is called the sun to all eternity.   36. And that
which thus ascends is the great luminary, as it is called

on account of its appearance, according to the command
of the Lord. 37. And thus he ascends and descends,
and is not diminished, and does not rest, but runs day
and night in his chariot, and his light shines seven
times stronger than that of the moon; but as regards
size they are both equal.

CHAP. 72, 1. From here on till chapter 105 we have again
the author of chapters 1–37; cf. Introd. The part here introduced with the special title of book of the courses of the luminaries, or the astronomical book, extends to chap. 82, but with
the peculiarity of chap. 1–37, that with the discussion of the
luminaries is also connected an account of the winds and other
physical secrets. It may be regarded as an attempt to systematize the biblical accounts on these topics, but scarcely with
any polemical intentions. *Classes*, literally *families* or *clans*.
These are sun, moon, and stars, with the subdivisions of the
last, 82 : 4 sqq. *Government*, cf. 82 : 4–20; 75 : 3. *Names*,
cf. 78 : 1, 2. *Origin*, literally *places of birth*, i.e. of their
rising. *Uriel*, cf. 21 : 5 ; 33 : 3 ; an evidence that we are
again having the author of the first part, as this name is not
mentioned in the Parables, at least not expressly ; cf. note on
40 : 2. Yet these arrangements are not permanent, but will
give way to new and better ones; cf. Isa. lxv. 17 ; lxvi. 22 ;
2 Pet. iii. 13 ; Apoc. xxi. 1 ; En. 91 : 15, 16. — 2. With a
special superscription an account of the sun's course is opened,
and extends to verse 37. *Portals ;* with this the author refers
to his own theory, developed in 33–36. — 3. Cf. 75 : 1–3 ;
80 : 6 ; 82 : 4–20. *Windows*, explained vs. 7 and 75 : 7. *Right
and left*, i.e. north and south. — 4. Cf. 41 : 5–7. The composition of the sun is pure fire. — 5. The movements of the
heavenly bodies are on wagons, cf. 73 : 2 ; 75 : 3, 8, driven by
the wind, 18 : 4 ; 73 : 2. Why the plural is used is uncertain. *Returns through the north*, cf. 41 : 5. The sun's punc-
tual return is secured by his being *led* back to the right portal

of the east, possibly by an angel, 43 : 2. — 6. *Great portal*, in contradistinction from the small windows vs. 7. He commences his account with the first Hebrew month, *Abib*, the time of the vernal equinoxes (Josephus, *Antiqq.* iii. 10, 5), hence about our April. In the olden times it was called *Abib*, i.e. grain month, Ex. xiii. 4; xxiii. 15; Deut. xvi. 1; but after the exile it is called *Nisan;* Neh. ii. 1; Esther iii. 7. It was the month of the Paschal festival. He does not begin with the first portal, at the time when the day is shortest and the night longest, but with the fourth, when the day has been already lengthening, in order to accommodate his system to the Jewish almanac. Of this verse probably Anatolius, bishop of Laodicea, made use, as recorded in Euseb. *H. E.* 7, 32 as τὰ ἐν τῷ Ἐνὼχ μαθήματα. — 7. *Twelve window-openings;* the number determined by his general system of twelve, and presupposed at the other portals; cf. 72 : 3; 75 : 7. *Flame* probably is heat; cf. 75 : 7. — 8. With this verse the course of the sun is commenced. The author's system is briefly this: There are twelve portals, six in the east, and six in the west. The sun ascends and descends from the time of the shortest day in the year in the first portal to the time of the longest day in the sixth portal, in each one of them one month; all the time the days increase. Returning, he begins his course in the sixth, and returns by monthly changing his portal, and daily decreasing the length of the day, to the first portal. Thus the sun ascends in one portal, and descends in the corresponding opposite one for two months every year. Therefore, too, each portal in the east and its corresponding one in the west represent two signs of the zodiac. From the first to the sixth they are respectively Capricornus, Aquarius, Pisces, Aries, Taurus, and Gemini; and returning from the sixth to the first, respectively Cancer, Leo, Virgo, Libra, Scorpio, and Sagittarius. The months are nominally thirty days; but in order to at least approach a solar year, the author makes the third, sixth, ninth, and

twelfth, or the months of the vernal and autumnal equinoxes, and of the summer and winter solstices, have thirty-one
days "on account of its sign," vs. 13, 19 ; but cf. 25 : 31. The
author's division of the νυχθήμερον into eighteen parts and
their increase and decrease is of course simply a production of
his desire to systematize, without any scientific value whatever.
Much less could it be cited as proof that the author did not
write in Palestine, as Laurence asserted. — 9. *Mornings*, as
the chief part of the day for day itself in Job vii. 18 ; Ps.
lxxiii. 14 ; Lam. iii. 23. — 13. *Its*, referring to *portal*, being
the point of solstice. — 15. *Is raised*, i.e. probably removed
further from the earth, to explain the decreasing of the days.
Dillmann translates, *raises himself*, i.e. starts on his trip anew,
like a traveller. — 35. *Sixty times*, because the sun is two
months in the same portal. The author here disregards the
extra day in the third, sixth, ninth, and twelfth portals. *Eternal*, cf. Ps. lxxii. 5, 17 ; lxxxix. 37. — 37. In size sun and
moon are equal, but not in light; cf. 78 : 3 and Isa. xxx. 26.

SECTION XIV.

CHAP. 73. — And after this law I saw another law
with reference to the smaller luminary whose name is
moon. 2. And her circuit is like the circuit of the
heavens, and her chariot in which she rides is driven by
the wind, and in a measure light is given to her. 3.
Every month her ascent and her descent is changed ;
her days are like the days of the sun, and when her
light is equal [full] her light is the seventh part of the
light of the sun. 4. And thus she rises. And her
beginning in the east comes forth on the thirtieth morning, and on that day she becomes visible and is for you
the beginning of the moon, on the thirtieth morning,

together with the sun in the portal whence the sun proceeds. 5. And the one half is prominent by the seventh part, and her whole circuit is empty, and there is no light with the exception of the one seventh part of the fourteen parts of light. 6. And on that day when she takes up the seventh part and the half of her light, her light contains one seventh and one seventh part and the half of it. She sets with the sun. 7. And when the sun rises the moon also rises with him and takes a half portion of light, and in that night in the beginning of her morning on her first day the moon sets with the sun, and is darkened in that night, with the seventh and the seventh portions and the half of one. 8. And she will rise on that day with exactly the seventh part, and will come out and become smaller from the rising of the sun and shine the rest of her days, with the seventh and the seventh part.

CHAP. 74. — And I saw another course and law for her, making her monthly course according to that law. 2. And Uriel, the holy angel, who is the leader of them all, showed me all things, and I wrote down all their positions as he showed them to me, and I wrote down their months as they were and the appearance of their lights till fifteen days are completed. 3. And in seven single parts she completes all her light in the east, and in seven single parts she completes all her darkness in the west. 4. And in certain months she changes her settings, and in certain months she goes her peculiar course. 5. And in two the moon sets with the sun, in those two portals which are in the middle, in the third and in the fourth portal. 6. She comes forth seven days, and turns and returns again by that portal through which the sun comes; and in that she completes all her light and recedes from the sun; and enters in eight days into the sixth portal, through which the sun comes forth. 7. And when the sun comes out of the fourth portal she comes out seven days, so that she comes out of the fifth, and returns again in seven days into the fourth portal and completes all her light, and recedes and enters the first portal in eight days. 8. And she returns again in seven days to the fourth portal, through which the sun comes forth. 9. Thus I saw their places, the sun rising and setting according to the order of their months. 10. And in those days, if five years are taken together, the sun has thirty superabundant days; and all the days which belong to him for one of these five years, when they are full, are three hundred and sixty-four days. 11. And the superabundance of the sun and of the stars is six days; of five years, each at six, are thirty days, and the moon recedes from the sun and the stars thirty days. 12. And the moon brings in all the years exact, so that their place neither precedes nor recedes ONE day, but she changes the years with exact justice in three hundred and sixty-four days. 13. Three years have one thousand and ninety-two days; and five years, eighteen hundred and twenty days; so that there will be in eight years two thousand nine hundred and twelve days. 14. To the moon alone belongs for three years one thousand and sixty-two days, and for five years she recedes fifty days, viz. to the sum of these are added sixty-two days. 15. And thus in five years there will be seventeen hundred and seventy days, so that the days of the moon for eight years will be two thousand eight hundred and thirty-two days. 16. For her receding in eight years is eighty days, and all the days she remains behind in eight years are eighty days.

17. And the year is justly finished, in accordance with their stations and the stations of the sun, rising through their portals, through which they rise and set thirty days.

CHAP. 75. — And the leaders of the heads of the thousands, who are over all creation and over all the stars, are also with the four intercalary days, which cannot be separated from their places, according to the whole reckoning of the years, and these serve the four days which are not counted in the reckoning of the years. 2. And on their account men make a mistake in them, for these luminaries serve in reality on the stations of the world, one in the first portal and one in the third portal and one in the fourth portal and one in the sixth portal; and the harmony of the course of the world is brought about by its separate three hundred and sixty-four stations. 3. For the signs and the times and the years and the days, these the angel Uriel showed to me, he whom the eternal Lord of glory had placed over all the luminaries of heaven in the heavens and in the world, that they should rule on the surface of the heavens, and be seen on the earth, and be leaders for the day and for the night, viz. the sun and the moon and the stars and all the serving *creatures* who keep their course in all the chariots of heaven. 4. The angel Uriel showed me also twelve openings in the circuit of the chariot of the sun from which the feet [i.e. the rays] of the sun come forth; and from them comes the warmth over the earth, when they are opened at times destined for them. 5. There are also some for the winds and for the spirit of the dew, when they are opened at times, standing open in the heavens at the ends. 6. Twelve doors I saw in the heavens, in the ends of the earth, out of which come forth the sun and the moon and the stars and all the deeds of heaven, from the east and from the west. 7. And many window-openings are to the left and to the right thereof, and ONE window in its time produces warmth, like those portals from which the stars come forth as he has commanded them, and in which they set according to their number. 8. And I saw chariots in heaven, running in the world, above and below these portals, in which the stars that never set turn. 9. And one is greater than all, and this one courses through the whole world.

CHAP. 73, 1. This and the following chapter treats of the course of the moon. — 2. Cf. 72 : 4, 5. *In a measure*, cf. 72 : 37, and vs. 3, and 74 : 3 ; 78 : 4, 6, 7. — 4. *Beginning*, i.e. her reappearance, or new moon. *Thirtieth morning*, with reference to the course of the sun. The periods of the moon are from twenty-nine to thirty days; and on the twenty-ninth she is in conjunction, and again appears on the thirtieth. At conjunction sun and moon are in the same portal. — 5. From new moon to full moon is fourteen (or fifteen) days, and the same number from full moon to new moon again. For this period she has fourteen portions of light, and consequently changes during the lunar month of thirty days, each day one half of one of these fourteen parts. In a month in which there are fifteen days to full moon the first day shows a light that is one of the seven parts attributed to the one half of the moon. — 6. But when there are fourteen days to full moon, then on the first day she takes one fourteenth and one twenty-eighth, equal to three twenty-eighths of light. — 7. But this becomes visible only when the moon has assumed yet one fourteenth of light additionally. *In the beginning of the morning she sets*, as the day for the moon begins in the evening. — 8. Thus the moon

increases day by day, by one seventh of one half, or one fourteenth of light; cf. 78 : 6 sqq.

CHAP. 74, 1. The above was the special law on the motions
of the moon in a month; now follows the more general law
on her motions during a series of months and the year. — 2.
Uriel, cf. 72 : 1. *Of them all*, i.e. either of all the luminaries
or of all the phases of the moon. *Appearance of light*, i.e.
how much light appeared. — 3. Cf. chap. 73 and 78. — 4. The
position of the moon with reference to the sun. *Peculiar*, i.e.
independent of the course of the sun. — 5. In two months her
course is not peculiar, but is with the sun, viz. when she is in
the third and in the fourth portal, the former corresponding to
the sign of Libra and Pisces, the latter Aries and Virgo.
When the sun is in Aries and Libra the new and full moon
are in the same portals. — 6. Refers to the third portal, as the
next verse shows. For seven days she goes through the portals from the first, until she reaches the third, in which the sun
is, and her light is then full; and then continues for eight days
to the sixth portal. — 7, 8. The fourth portal, in which is new
moon. In returning to it in fourteen days there is in it full
moon; then goes to the first portal, and returns to the fourth
in fifteen days. — 10. He now enters on the difference between a solar and lunar year. According to 78 : 15, 16 there
are six months with thirty and six months with twenty-nine
days, i.e. three hundred and fifty-four days in a lunar year.
But the year has three hundred and sixty by counting twelve
months at thirty days, to which are added four intercalary days
in the equinoxes and solstices. Accordingly the difference
between the solar and lunar year is six days without, and ten
days with, these additional days. Thus without intercalary
days the sun gains on the moon in five years thirty days,
although when full the sun really has every year three hundred and sixty-four days, and not three hundred and sixty, as
he counts to get the thirty days in five years. — 11. Repeats
this more plainly. — 12. As the author stands, or wants to

stand, on biblical ground, and is conservative over against all innovations, he defends the lunar year as the best, as the Israelites followed that alone before the exile; cf. De Wette, *Archäologie*, 4 ed., p. 236, and Winer, *R. W.* sub voc. *Jahr. Three hundred and sixty-five days*, i.e. with the intercalary days. — 14. In three years the difference between the solar and lunar years at ten days (cf. vs. 8) will be exactly one month. In five years the difference is fifty days, which sum is reached by *adding to these*, i.e. to the thirty days in three years the intercalary days intervening between the 1092 days of the three years, and the 1820 of the five years. — 16. Accordingly, too, in eight years she recedes eighty days. — 17. Conclusion, cf. vs. 12 and 75 : 2.

CHAP. 75, 1. This treats of the intercalary days, the stars, and the sun. The importance of the four intercalary days was noticed in 74 : 10, and is repeated here in the statement that the guardians of the other days were also over these four. Who these leaders are is uncertain; not angels, but probably higher stars, for they are called luminaries in verse 2; cf. 72 : 3; 80 : 6. *These*, i.e. the heads of the thousands, the chiliarchs. — 2. Most men, not knowing the mystery of the intercalary days, make mistakes accordingly; cf. 80 : 7; 82 : 4, 5, 6. — 3. But notwithstanding this ignorance it is the absolute truth that there are such days, because the angel Uriel, who is over all these phenomena, 72 : 1, showed them to Enoch. *Rule*, cf. Gen. i. 15–18. *Chariots*, cf. 72 : 5. — 4. In the chariot of the sun — for the chariot from the appearance is considered a circuit, i.e. round, 72 : 5, — there are twelve openings, from which heat descends when these are opened. In this manner he explains how the sun does not give an equal amount of heat at all times, as at different times a greater or less number of these openings are closed. — 5. *Some*, i.e. openings; but these are in the ends of heaven, entirely distinct from those just mentioned; cf. chap. 76 and 34–36. This verse is probably the work of an interpolator, as it entirely interrupts the sense, but was easily suggested by the context. — 6, 7. Besides the well-known twelve portals there are many window-openings, on which see 72 : 3, 7. — 8, 9. Different from the stars just mentioned, that rise and set, are the never-setting stars, those continually on the horizon at nights. What the special one is cannot be decided, since it is not even certain whether he refers to one of the setting, or of the never-setting stars. In the first case Dillmann thinks of the morning star, and of the Great Bear in the second. Did not the connection occasion some difficulty Hoffmann's idea that the sun alone can here be meant would be very probable.

SECTION XV.

CHAP. 76. — And on the ends of the earth I saw for all the winds twelve portals opened, from which the winds come and blow over the earth. 2. Three of them are open on the face [i.e. the east] of the heavens, and three in the west, and three on the right [i.e. south] of heaven, and three on the left [i.e. north]. 3. And the first three are those towards the east, and three towards the north, and three behind those which are on the left, towards the south, and three in the west. 4. Through four of these come winds of blessing and of peace, and through those eight come winds of injury : when they are sent they bring destruction to all the earth and to the water on it and to all those who dwell on it and to everything that is in the water and on the land. 5. And the first wind from these portals, which is called the eastern, comes forth from the first portal which is towards the east, inclining towards the south ; out of it comes destruction, dryness and heat and death. 6. And through the second middle portal comes forth the right *mixture*; there come forth rain and fruitfulness and peace and dew. And through the third portal, which is towards the north, come forth coldness and dryness. 7. And after these the winds towards the south come forth through three portals; firstly through the first portal of them, which inclines towards the east, there comes forth the wind of heat. 8. And from the middle portal, which is beside that one, there come forth a sweet incense and dew and rain and peace and life. 9. And through the third portal, which is towards the west, there come forth dew and rain and grasshoppers and destruction. 10. And after these northerly winds from the seventh portal, which is towards the east, inclining to the south, there come forth dew and rain, grasshoppers and destruction. 11. And out of the middle portal direct there come forth rain and dew and life and peace, and through the third portal, which is towards the west, which inclines towards the north, there come forth fog and hoar-frost and snow and rain and dew and grasshoppers. 12. And after these the winds which are towards the west: through the first portal, which inclines towards the north, there come forth dew and rain and grasshoppers and coldness and snow and frost. 13. And from the middle portal there come forth dew and rain, peace and blessing, and through the last portal, which is towards the south, there come forth dryness and destruction, burning and death. 14. Thereby the twelve portals of the four portals [directions] of the heaven are completed, and all their laws and all their destructions and their virtues I have showed to you, my son Methuselah.

CHAP. 77.—They call the first wind the eastern, because it is the first, and they call the second the

southern because the Most High descends there, and
especially does the Blessed One in eternity descend
there.   2. And the name of the west wind is the diminishing, because there the luminaries of the heavens
diminish and go down.   3. And the fourth wind, called
the north, is divided into three parts, one of them is *for*
the dwelling of men, the second for the seas of water
and for the valleys and for the woods and for the streams
and for the darkness and for the fog; and the third
part with the garden of justice.   4. I saw seven high
mountains, which were higher than all the mountains
which are on the earth, and from them there comes
hoar-frost; and days and times and years cease and depart.   5. I saw seven rivers on the earth, larger than
all the rivers; one of them coming from the west
empties its water into the great sea.   6. And two of
them come from the north to the sea, and empty their
water into the Erythræan sea in the east.   7. But the
other four come from the side of the north over to the
sea, *two of them* to the Erythræan sea, and two empty in
the great sea; according to others, in the desert.   8.
I saw seven great islands in the sea and on the land:
two on the land and five in the great sea.

CHAP. 78.—The names of the sun are these: the
first Orjârês, the second Tômâs.   2. And the moon has
four names: first Asônjâ, the second Eblâ, the third
Benâsê, the fourth Êrae.   3. These are the two large
luminaries; their circuit is like the circuit of heaven,
and in size both are equal.   4. And in the circuit of
the sun there is a seventh portion of light from which
some is given to the moon, and according to a measure
it is added till the seventh portion of the sun is ended.
5. And they set and enter the portals of the west, and

go around by the north, and come out of the portals of the east on to the surface of the heavens. 6. And when the moon is raised she is seen in the heavens, having in herself the half of the seventh part of the light, and in fourteen *days* her light is completed. 7. Also three times five portions of light are put into her, so that on the fifteenth day her light is completed, according to the sign of the year, and it becomes three times five portions, and the moon becomes so by the half of the seventh part. 8. And in her decrease on the first day she decreases to fourteen parts of her light, and on the second she decreases to thirteen parts, and on the third she decreases to twelve parts, and on the fourth she decreases to eleven parts, and on the fifth she decreases to ten parts, and on the sixth she decreases to nine parts, and on the seventh she decreases to eight parts, and on the eighth she decreases to seven parts, and on the ninth she decreases to six parts, and on the tenth she decreases to five parts, and on the eleventh she decreases to four parts, and on the twelfth she decreases to three parts, and on the thirteenth she decreases to two parts, an on the fourteenth she decreases to the half of the seventh part, and her light which was left of the whole disappears altogether on the fifteenth day. 9. And in certain months the moon has each time twenty-nine days, and once twenty-eight. 10. And Uriel showed me another law, when the light is added to the moon, and from which side of the sun it is added. 11. All the time in which the moon continues in her light she increases opposite the sun, till on the fourteenth day her light is completed in heaven; and when she shines in full her light is completed in the heavens. 12. And on the first day she is called the new moon, for on that

day the light is raised upon her. 13. And she is completed exactly on the day the sun descends in the west
and when at night she ascends from the east and shines
all night till the sun rises opposite her and the moon is
seen opposite the sun. 14. Whence the light of the
moon comes, there again she decreases till all her light
disappears, and the days of the moon cease, and her
circuit remains empty without light. 15. And three
months she makes thirty days in her time, and three
months she makes each time twenty-nine days, in which
she makes her decrease, in the first time and in the
first portal for one hundred and seventy-seven days.
16. And in the time of her departure she is seen each
time thirty days during three months, and each time
twenty-nine days during three months. 17. At night
she appears each time as a man twenty times, and during the day like the heavens, for there is nothing in her
except her light.

CHAP. 79. — And now, my son Methuselah, I have
showed you all things, and the whole law of the stars is
completed. 2. And he showed me all their laws for
every day and for every time and for every government
and for every year, and her departure, according to her
order in each month and in every week ; 3. and the decrease of the moon, which takes place in the sixth
portal, for in that sixth portal her light is completed,
and from then there is the beginning of the month ;
4. also the decrease which takes place in the first portal,
in its time, till one hundred and seventy-seven days are
completed ; in the law of weeks, twenty-five weeks and
two days ; 5. and how she tarries behind the sun and
according to the law of the stars five days in one time
exactly ; and when this place which thou dost see is

completed. 6. This is the picture and the portrait of each luminary which the great angel Uriel, who is their leader, showed to me.

CHAP. 80. — And in those days Uriel answered and said to me : " Behold, I have showed thee all things, O Enoch, and have revealed to thee that thou shouldst see this sun and this moon, and those who lead the stars of heaven and all those that revolve, their deeds and their times and their departures. 2. And in the days of the sinners the years will be shortened, and their seed will be tardy on their lands and on their meadows, and everything on the earth will change and will not appear in its time ; the rain will be prevented, and the heavens will retain *it*. 3. And in those times the fruit of the earth will be tardy and will not grow in its time ; and the fruit of the trees will be prevented in its time. 4. And the moon will change her order and will not appear in her time. 5. And in those days it will be seen on the heavens that a great unfruitfulness will come on the outermost chariot in the west; and she will shine more brightly than according to the order of light. 6. And many of the leaders of the stars of command will err, and they will change their paths and deeds, and those subject to them will not appear in their time. 7. And the whole order of the stars will be kept from the sinners, and the thoughts of those who dwell on the earth will err concerning them, and they will be turned from all their ways, and will err and consider them gods. 8. And evil will increase over them, and punishment will come upon them to destroy them all."

CHAP. 81. — And he said to me : " O Enoch, contemplate the writing of the tablets of heaven, and read what

17*

is written thereon, and learn each one." 2. And I
contemplated everything on these tablets of heaven, and
read everything that was written, and learned everything and read the book and everything that was written
in it, all the deeds of men and all the children of flesh
who *will be* on the earth to the generation of eternity.
3. And then I immediately blessed the Lord and the
everlasting King of glory, that he had made all the
things of the earth, and I blessed the Lord on account
of his patience, and blessed *him* on account of the children of the world. 4. And at that time I said:
" Happy the man who dies as a just and good one, concerning whom there is no book of iniquity written, and
against whom no blame is found." 5. And those three
holy ones brought me and placed me on the earth before the door of my house and said to me : " Announce
everything to thy son Methulselah, and show to all thy
children that no flesh is just before the Lord, for he has
created them. 6. One year we will leave thee with thy
children, till thou art again strengthened, that thou
mayest teach thy children and write for them, and
mayest testify before them all, thy children ; and in the
second year they will lift thee up out of their midst. 7.
Let thy heart be strong, for the good will announce
justice to the good, the just will rejoice with the just
and will congratulate themselves among themselves.
8. But the sinner will die with the sinner, and the
renegade sink down with the renegade. 9. And those
who do justice will die on account of the deeds of men,
and will be gathered in on account of the deeds of the
impious." 10. And in those days they completed conversing with me, and I went to my people blessing the
Lord of the worlds.

CHAP. 82. — And now my son, Methuselah, all these things I relate to thee and write for thee, and I have revealed to thee everything, and have given thee books concerning them all: preserve, my son, Methuselah, the books from the hand of thy father, and give them to the generations of the world. 2. Wisdom I have given thee and thy children and those who will be thy children, that they give it to their children, the generations to eternity, namely this wisdom above their thoughts. 3. And those who understand it will not sleep, but will hear with their ears, that they may learn this wisdom, and it will please those who eat of it more than good food. 4. Happy are all the just, happy all those who walk in the paths of justice and have no sin like the sinners, in the counting of all their days, in which the sun goes through the heavens, entering and departing from the gates, each time thirty times, together with the heads of the thousands of this order of the stars, together with the four that are added and separate between the four portions of the year, which they lead and enter with them four days. 5. And on their account men will be at fault, and will not count them in the reckoning of the whole world; but men will be mistaken and will not know them exactly. 6. For they belong to the reckoning of the year and are exactly marked forever, one in the first portal and one in the third and one in the fourth and one in the sixth, and the year is completed in three hundred and sixty-four days. 7. And the account of it is true, and the marked reckoning exact; for the luminaries and the months and the festivals and the years have been shown and given to me by Uriel, to whom the Lord of all creation had given command, in reference to me, of the host of the heavens. 8. And he has power over night and day in the heavens, that he may show light over men; the sun and the moon and the stars and all the powers of heaven which turn in their circuit. 9. And this is the order of the stars that set in their places and in their times and in their festivals and in their months. 10. And these are the names of those who lead them, who watch that they enter in their times and in their order and in their occasions and in their months and in their powers and in their positions. 11. Their four leaders who divide the four portions of the year enter first; after them the twelve leaders of the orders, who separate the months and the year into three hundred and sixty-four days, together with the heads of the thousands who divide the days; for the four intercalary days these are the leaders who separate the four parts of the year. 12. And of those heads of the thousands, one is placed between the leader and the led, back of the position, but their leader divides. 13. And these are the names of the leaders who separate the four parts of the year which are ordained: Melkeêl and Helemmêlêch, and Mêlêjal and Nârêl. 14. And the names of those they lead: Adnârêl and Ijasusâêl and Ijelumîêl, these three follow after the leaders of the orders, and one follows after the three leaders of the orders, who follow after those leaders of positions who separate the four portions of the year. 15. In the commencement of the year Melkejâl rises first and rules, he who is called Tamaânî and sun, and all the days of his government that he rules are ninety-one days. 16. And these are the signs of the days which are seen on the earth in the days of his government: sweat and heat and anxiety, and all the trees producing fruit, and the leaves appearing on all the trees, and the harvest of wheat, and the blooming of roses, and all the flowers blooming in the fields, but the trees of winter become withered. 17. And these are the names of the leaders who are under them : Berkeêl, Zalbesâêl, and one other who is added, a head of a thousand, called Hêlojâsêph ; and ended are the days of the power of this one. 18. The other leader, who is after them, is Helemmêlêk, whom they call the shining sun, and all the days of his light are ninety-one days. 19. And these are the signs of the days of the earth : burning heat, dryness, and the trees bringing their fruit to ripeness and completion, and the sheep mate and become pregnant ; and all the fruit of the earth is gathered in, and everything that is in the fields ; and the making of wine ; this takes place in the days of his power. 20. These are the names and the orders and the subordinate leaders of those heads of the thousands : Gêdâêl and Kêêl and Hêêl, and the name of the head of a thousand, which is added to them, Asfâêl ; and completed are the days of his power.

CHAP. 76. This and the following chapter treat of the winds and speak of some geographical matters, and may be regarded as a continuation of chap. 34–36, as the twelve portals for the winds there spoken of are here treated in detail. — 2. The points of the compass here given are taken from the position of a man standing with his face to the east, although the writer says *west*, or literally *the descent*, instead of *back*. This method of designating the four directions is frequently found in the Old Testament. — 3. *The first three*, beginning in counting them from the east, the place where the sun rises; cf. vs. 4, 7, etc. — 4. Through four of these portals, i.e. through the middle one of the three in each direction, come winds of

blessing, while the outer two in each group produce winds
of injury. — 5. The first wind described comes from the portal
in the south-east, i.e. the south-east wind.   Its character is destructive. — 6. Like all those winds from the middle portal of
a group, the east wind has the right mixture, i.e. is neither too
warm nor too cold, too wet nor too dry. *Peace ;* Dillmann, *Wohl-
sein* ; Hoffmann, *Heil.*   The north-east wind brings coldness and
dryness. — 7. The south-east-south wind produces heat. — 8.
But from the middle portal of this group comes a good wind,
and brings with it proofs of the sweet vegetation in the south ;
cf. chap. 24 and 25. — 9, 10. South-west-south and north-east-
north winds.   After *northerly* the translator adds *whose name
is the sea.*   The Palestine writer had northerly winds ; but to
him the Mediterranean Sea was in the west, while it was in the
north for the Ethiopian. — 11. The symmetry of his description demands that even the north wind should be a good one ;
but the north-west-north wind is again injurious.   On the *rains*
cf. Prov. xxv. 23. — 12. The western group, and first the north-
west wind. — 13. The west and the south-west winds. — 14.
Methuselah.   It is a peculiarity of these parts that they are entrusted to Enoch's son Methuselah ; cf. 79 : 1 ; 82 : 1.   It is
manifestly the object of the writer to explain how these mysteries, already made known by Enoch, were preserved so many
years.   This is especially shown by 82 : 1.

CHAP. 77. This presents a clear proof that the author wrote
Hebrew or Aramaic.   The first wind is called eastern, i.e. קֶדֶם
east because it is the first, i.e. קַדְמוֹנִי. — The second is the southern, the νότος or דָּרוֹם or דְּרוֹמִי, because either the Holy One
descends there, ירד, רָם, or because he abides there הָד רָם ; cf.
25 : 3. — 2. The west wind is the diminishing.   The Hebrew
probably had אַחֲרוֹן and the Greek ὕστερος, hence ὑστερέω. — 4.
Of course these seven hills are not those of 18 : 6 ; 24 : 2 ;
32 : 1.   The use of the word *seven* is based on its sacred
character. — 5. *Great sea* is the Mediterranean Sea ; cf.
Num. xxxiv. 6, 7.   *West*, probably a corruption for south ;

cf. Dillmann on Ethiop. Ex. xxiv. 20. The river here meant is the Nile. — 6. These two rivers are the Tigris and the Euphrates. — 7. The first two are the Indus and Ganges, and the last two possibly the Oxus and Jaxartes. The author evidently pictured the Mediterranean, Black, and Caspian seas as one. But others, says the translator (not the author, for these words are evidently interpolated), claim that these last two empty into the desert. — 8. What islands he means must remain uncertain.

CHAP. 78. Names of the sun. To give these was suggested by his giving the names of the winds above. Orjares is אוּרִי חֶרֶס, the latter word being used for sun already, Judg. viii. 13, 14, 18. *Tomas* is probably חַמָּה used of the sun, Isa. xxiv. 23. He has thus the three names used for the sun in the Old Testament שֶׁמֶשׁ, חֶרֶס, and חַמָּה. — 2. Names of the moon. *Asonja* is uncertain. Dillmann thinks it contains a remnant of הַסָּהֲרָא known as the name of the moon (in Heb. Aram). *Ebla* may be corrupted from Lebna, i.e. לְבָנָה; Eccl. vi. 10; Isa. xxx. 26. *Benaze* is explained by Hoffmann as בֶּן־חַצִי, i.e. son of the half, i.e. the half moon; but Dillmann thinks of כְּסָא. *Erae* is the ordinary יְרֵחַ. — 4. Cf. 72 : 37 ; 73 : 3. This portion of light the moon receives gradually. — 5. Cf. 72 : 5. — 6. On the topic commenced here and continued to verse 17, cf. 73 : 4–74 : 2. On the first day the moon receives the one half of the one seventh part of the light of the sun. — 7. But it happens that it takes the moon fifteen days to become full, and in this case she receives three times five portions, i.e. fifteen fourteenths, of light. — 8. In this case, in the decrease she decreases on the first day from fifteen portions to fourteen, etc. — 9. Evidently flatly contradicts plain statements made elsewhere. The verse is probably an interpolation. — 10. This second, or other, law refers to the relative positions of sun and moon. — 11. The full moon. — 12. The new moon. — 15, 16. Length of the months.

CHAP. 79. *Methuselah*; cf. 76 : 14. — 2. *For every time*; cf.

78 : 15, 16. *Every government*, i.e. of the leaders of the stars; cf. chap. 82. — 3, 4 are both objects of *he showed me*, vs. 2. — 5. Cf. 74 : 10–17.

CHAP. 80. But all these laws, now so firm and fixed, shall be set entirely aside on account of the sinners. The revolution in the laws of nature is recognized by other writers also as the sign of the last times; cf. 3 Sibyl. 795–807 ; 2 Macc. v. 2, 3 ; 4 Ezra v. 1–13 ; vi. 7–28 ; viii. 63–ix. 6 ; xiv. 15–17. *Those that revolve*, either winds, 72 : 5 ; 73 : 2, or stars. — 2. In 72 : 1 it has been stated that these laws should continue to the time of a new creation. But, on account of their sins, men have occasioned a change in these laws. As a punishment from God these laws are changed ; cf. Jer. v. 22–25 Cf. Book of Jubilees, chap. 23. This verse is probably the basis of *Barnabae Epistola*, iv. 3. — 5. 4 Ezra says that in the last times the sun will shine at night and the moon by day.—7. The effect of this change in the laws of nature will, instead of bringing about the sinners' return to God, only cause them to sin more, by learning to worship them as stars ; cf. similar sentiment in Sibyl. *Prooem.* i. 25. — 8. Then after these certain signs of the approaching evil the judgment will come ; cf. on the whole Matt. xxiv. 29 ; Luke xxi. 25, 26.

CHAP. 81. An account of the end of his trip. First, however, he is allowed to see the tablets of heaven. *Tablets ;* cf. 93 : 2 ; 103 : 2 ; 106 : 19 (107 : 1 ; 108 : 7) ; mentioned frequently in the Book of the Jubilees, are the πλάκες τοῦ οὐρανοῦ of the *Test.* XII. *Patriarcharum.* Synonymes are *writing, book,* and *books,* 81 : 1, 2 ; 93 : 1, 3 ; 103 : 2, 3 ; 108 : 7 ; cf. 104 : 1. The idea from passages like Ex. xxv. and xxvi.; xxxii. 32 ; Ps. lxix. 28 ; cxxxix. 16 ; Dan. xii. 1 ; cf. Harnack on Past. Her. *Vis.* 1, 3, 2. — 2. Not only the deeds of men, but even their names — for this is meant by *and all the children* — are recorded ; cf. 82 : 1 ; 83 : 10 — 3. Cf. note on 22 : 14 and *Apoc. Bar.* xxiv. 2. *Patience*, that notwithstanding the record of men's sin in heaven God was so slow in his judgment. — 4.

Yet the judgment shall come, and therefore he is to be esteemed happy whose name is not recorded in the book of iniquity. It should be noticed here that the author teaches a retribution after death; cf. 22 : 12, 13. — 5. From 87 : 2, 3 ; 90 : 31 we learn that the expression *the other three angels* is used to distinguish three archangels from Michael as the head and chief. If the author of the Parables had written this we could know the names of these three (cf. chap. 40), but our author nowhere states that there were but four archangels. The passage is a strange one, and points to an omission in the previous verses. Compared with the justice of God no flesh is just before him ; cf. Job iv. 17. The creature is nothing compared with the Creator. *Methuselah*, cf. 76 : 14. — 6. *Strengthened*, i.e. rested from the effects of thy travels ; cf. Dan. viii. 16–19. But this year shall be devoted to instructing his children in the important secrets he has received. — 7. Although there is so much wickedness, as the records in heaven show, yet the generation of the just will not die out, and in the Messianic times after the period of the sinners, the just will rejoice together. —8. As he is speaking of the final judgment, this sinking refers to their sinking in the valley of Hinnom ; cf. chap. 26 and 27. — 9. Death, indeed, comes to the just also on account of the sinners ; but there is a retribution after death, vs. 4, and these just shall rise again, 22 : 12, 13. *Gathered*, cf. Isa. lvii. 1 and 2 Kings xxii. 20 ; Job iii. 13 ; Wisd. iv. 7–14. *Lord of the world*, cf. note on 1 : 3.

CHAP. 82. Address of Enoch himself. — 2. *Wisdom*, cf. note on 37 : 1 ; cf. Ps. lxxviii. 5, 6. *Above thought*, i.e. that could not have been developed by human thought. — 3. And those who understand this wisdom will be so interested in it and desirous of it that they will forget sleep. *Good food*, cf. Ps. xix. 10 ; cxix. 103 ; Prov. xvi. 24 ; xxiv. 13, 14 ; Sir. xxiv. 26 sqq. Tertullian also considers Methuselah as the recipient and transmissor of Enoch's revelation ; cf. *De Cultu Fem.* i. 3. " Enoch filio suo Matusalae nihil aliud mandaverit quam ut notitiam

18

eorum posteris suis traderet." — 4. As he is treating specially of the luminaries in this book, from chapter 72 to here, he speaks of the true reckoning of the year. The four days, i.e. the intercalary days, are introduced by four leaders; cf. 75 : 1, 2 ; 82 : 11.— 5. Cf. 75 : 2 ; 80 : 6. — 6. *They,* i.e. the intercalary days. *Portal,* cf. chap. 75. — 7. *Uriel* had been commissioned by God to give these instructions to Enoch. — 9. With the exception of a few casual remarks, nothing has been said of the stars. Hence his account here. — 11. These four leaders are named in verse 14 ; cf. 75 : 1 sqq. ; 82 : 4. — 12. Chiliarchs. — 13. *Melkeel,* vs. 15, *Melkejal,* i.e. מלכיאל ; *Helemmelek,* i.e. חיל־מלך ; *Melejal,* i.e. מלאיאל ; *Narel,* נ־אל. — 14. A verse defying all attempt at explanation. — 15. *In the commencement,* i.e. in the time from spring to summer. — 16. *Roses,* unknown in the Old Testament; but cf. Sir. xxiv. 14 ; Wisd. ii. 8 ; En. 106 : 2. — 17. The subordinate leaders, those in each one of the three months of which he is here treating. — 18. The hot time from summer to autumn. The names are all Semitic, but mostly of uncertain etymology.

SECTION XVI.

CHAP. 83. — And now, my son Methuselah, I will show thee all the visions that I have seen, relating them before thee. 2. Two visions I saw before I took a wife, and the one of them was not similar to the other ; the first time, when I was learning to write, the second time, before I took thy mother I saw an awful vision ; and on their account I petitioned to the Lord. 3. As I was reposing in the house of Malâlêl, my grandfather, I saw there in a vision that the heavens were lowered and disappeared and fell on the earth. 4. And as it fell on the earth I saw the earth that it was devoured in a great abyss, and mountains descended on mountains, and hills sank upon hills, and high trees were torn from the trunks, and fell down and sank into the abyss. 5. And on account of this a speech fell into my mouth, and I began to cry and to say: " The earth is destroyed!" 6. And Malâlêl, my grandfather, aroused me, as I was reposing near him, and said to me: " Why dost thou cry so, my son, and why dost thou lament so?" 7. And I related to him the whole vision which I had seen, and he said to me: " A terrible thing thou hast seen, my son, and the power of the vision of thy dream is concerning the secrets of all the sins of the earth; it will be about to descend into the abyss and be destroyed terribly. 8. And now, my son, arise and petition the Lord of glory — since thou art a believer — that a remnant may remain on the earth and all the earth be not destroyed. 9. My son, from heaven all this will come on the earth, and over the earth there will be a great destruction." 10. After that I arose and prayed and petitioned, and wrote down my prayer for the generations of the world, and I will show thee everything, my son, Methuselah. 11. And as I went out below, and looked at the heavens and the sun rising in the east, and the moon descending in the west, and some few stars, and everything as he had known it from the first, I blessed the Lord of the judgment, and to him I gave greatness, because he led forth the sun from the windows of the east, and he ascends and rises on the surface of the heavens, and elevates himself, and goes the path which is shown to him.

CHAP. 84. — And I raised my hands in justice, and blessed the Holy and the Great One, and I spoke with the breath of my mouth and with the tongue of flesh, which God has made for the children of men, that they should speak with it, and gave them breath and the tongue and the mouth, that they might speak therewith: 2. " Blessed art thou, O Lord, King both great and powerful in thy greatness, the Lord of all the creation of heaven, King of kings, and God of all the world, thy Godship and thy kingdom and thy greatness will remain in eternity, and to all eternity, and to all the generations thy power, and all the heavens are thy throne in eternity, and all the earth thy footstool in eternity and to all eternity.   3. For thou hast made and dost govern all things, and nothing is too difficult for thee, and no wisdom escapes thee ; she does not turn away from her throne, thy throne, and not from thy face, and thou dost know and see and hear all things, and there is nothing that is hidden before thee, for thou dost see all things. 4. And now the angels of thy heavens do sin, and thy wrath is over the flesh of men to the day of the great judgment.   5. And now, God and Lord and great King, I petition and ask that thou wouldst establish my prayer for me, that there remain to me a posterity on earth, and that thou wouldst not annihilate all the flesh of men, and not make empty the whole earth, and there be an everlasting destruction.   8. And now, my Lord, annihilate from the earth the flesh which has angered thee, but the flesh of justice and of rectitude establish as a plant of the seed to eternity, and do not hide thy face from the prayer of thy servant, O Lord ! "

CHAP. 83. Tideman, following the example of Seiffert, has declared chapters 83–91 a production of a new Essenic writer, but without good reason.   There is no interruption of the connection here, for the fact that he does not deal minutely with the contents of the tablets of heaven until 92, after having mentioned

them in 81, has its parallels throughout the book, where certain
subjects are mentioned, and then treated *in extenso* in later
chapters. In fact, these dream visions-form a necessary part
of the book. The author had announced the coming judgment, but had given no answer to the all-important *when*. To
determine this is the object of 83–91. And as he always associates the two judgments, the first of the deluge and the final,
it is but natural that he should mention both here. That the
revelation is given to Enoch through a dream is no argument
whatever for attributing these chapters to a different author,
for, then, 13 : 8 would fall under the same condemnation. In
fact, it was necessary to state that these revelations were received through dreams, and not through immediate association
with the angels and a trip through the upper regions, in which
manner the other revelations were usually received, not only on
account of the nature of the contents, but mainly because they
were received in his younger days, before the privilege of
moving in super-terrestrial worlds was accorded him. And
as the contents fully harmonize with the rest of the book, it is
difficult to see why we should here claim a different author.
1. states expressly that the following revelations had been received in visions, and not in the manner usually observed in
the preceding chapters. — 2. *Learning to write*, easily understood from 12 : 3. *Before I took*, i.e. before he was sixty-five
years old ; cf. Gen v. 21. *Mother ;* according to 85 : 3, her
name was *Edna ;* according to the Book of the Jubilees, chap.
4, p. 18, *Edna* or *Adna*. The second vision was *awful*, because
more important for the contemporaries of the true author. —
3. *The heavens were lowered* shows that the first vision refers to
the deluge. — 5. *Fell*, to designate the sudden and spontaneous
character of the speech. — 7. The experienced Mahalaleel
immediately explains this dream as portending the coming
destruction of the earth on account of its sins. This destruction is, however, yet a secret. — 8. *Lord of glory*, cf. note on
22 : 14. Being one of the few that are still faithful he could

expect God to hear his petition. — 9. *From heaven*, i.e. from God. — 11. Ewald, on the basis of Joseph. *Bel. Jud.* ii. 5, 8, and 9, finds here a trace of Essenism. But why an ordinary Jew could not utter this prayer without being an Essene is certainly a mystery. Enoch had just heard, vs. 9, that this destruction should come from heaven, and thus it is natural that he should address his prayer for deliverance to heaven. This God, who in his greatness could lead forth the mighty sun, could grant his petition. Interpreting this prayer to the God of judgment, 22 : 14; 90 : 40, in any other manner robs it of all sense in this connection.

CHAP. 84. *Holy and Great*, cf. note on 1 : 3. *Tongue of flesh*, cf. note on 14 : 2. — 2. Cf. 9 : 4 sqq.; Isa. lxvi. 1. — 3. God's throne is also wisdom's throne; the latter is here personified; cf. on 42, 1. — 4. The author refers to his own statements, chap. 6 sqq. Were these words from a new author he would undoubtedly have said more concerning the fall of the angels. *Flesh of man*, cf. Job xii. 10. — 5. *Empty, denudes*; cf. 9 : 2. — 6. *Plant*, cf. 10 : 16.

SECTION XVII.

CHAP. 85. — And after this I saw another dream, and I will show thee all, my son. 2. And Enoch began, and said to his son Methuselah: "To thee, my son, I will speak; hear my words, and lend thy ear to the vision of the dream of thy father. 3. Before I took thy mother Ednâ, I saw in a vision on my couch, and behold, a bullock came out of the earth, and this bullock was white; and after him there came a female of the same species, and together with this one came other cattle, one of them was black and one red. 4. And that black one horned the red one, and followed it over the earth ; and then I could no longer see that red one. 5. And that black one grew, and a cow came with it, and I saw that many cattle, like it and following it, came from it. 6. And that cow, the first one, came from the presence of that first bullock, seeking that red one, and did not find it, and then raised a great cry, and hunted it. 7. And I looked until that first bullock came to her and quieted her ; and from that time she did not cry aloud. 8. And after that she brought forth another white bullock, and after that she brought forth many bullocks and black cows. 9. And I saw in my sleep that white bullock grow and become a large white bullock, and from him came many white bullocks, and they were similar to him. 10. And they commenced to beget many white bullocks, and these were similar to them, and one followed the other.

CHAP. 86. — And again I saw with my eyes, while I was sleeping, and I saw the heavens above, and behold one star fell from heaven, and arose and ate and pastured among those bullocks. 2. And after that I saw the large and the black bullocks, and behold all changed their stalls and their pastures and their cattle, and began to lament one with the other. 3. And again I saw in the vision, and looked at the heavens, and behold I saw many stars ; and they fell from heaven, and were thrown from heaven near that first star, and among those cattle and bullocks ; there they were with them, pasturing among them. 4. And I looked at them, and behold they all let out their sexual members, like horses, and began to mount the cows of the bullocks ; and these all became pregnant, and brought forth elephants and camels and asses. 5. And all the bullocks feared them, and were affrighted at them; and they commenced to bite with their teeth, and to devour, and to push with their horns. 6. And they then began to devour those bullocks, and behold all the children of the earth began to tremble, and to shake before them, and fled.

CHAP. 87.—And again I saw them as they began to horn each other, and to devour each other, and the earth began to cry aloud. 2. And I again raised my eyes to heaven, and saw in the vision, and behold there came from heaven those who were like white men: one came out from that place, and three with him. 3. And those three who came out last took me by the hand, and bore me away from the generations of the earth, and elevated me to a large place, and showed me a tower higher than the earth, and all the hills were lower. 4. And they said to me: "Remain here until thou seest everything that comes over those elephants and camels and asses, and over the stars, and over all the bullocks."

CHAP. 88.—And I saw one of those four who had come out before, and he took that star which had first fallen from heaven, and bound it hand and foot, and put it in an abyss; and this abyss was narrow and deep and terrible and dark. 2. And one of them drew his sword, and gave it to those elephants and camels and asses; and they began to beat one another, and the whole earth shook on their account. 3. And as I saw in the vision, behold then one of those four who had descended threw from heaven, and gathered and took all the great stars, whose sexual members were like the sexual members of horses, and bound them all hand and foot, and put them in an abyss of the earth.

CHAP. 89.—And one of those four went to that white bullock, and taught him a mystery while he was trem-

bling; he was born a bullock, and became a man, and
he made for himself a large vessel, and lived in it; and
three bullocks lived with him in that vessel, and it was
covered over above them. 2. And I again raised my
eyes towards heaven, and saw a high roof and seven
sluices to it; and those sluices emptied much water into
a yard. 3. And I saw again, and behold fountains
were opened on the earth, in that great yard; and that
water began to swell, and to be lifted above the land,
and caused that yard to disappear, until all the land
was covered with water. 4. And the water and the
darkness and the fog increased over it; and as I looked
at the height of this water, this water was elevated over
that yard, and emptied over the yard, and stood on the
earth. 5. And all the bullocks which were in the yard
were collected, so that I immediately saw how they sank
down and came to naught, and were destroyed in that
water. 6. But that vessel swam on the water, and all
the bullocks and elephants and camels and asses on the
earth sank down, and all the animals; and I was not
able to see them, and they were unable to come out,
but were destroyed, and sank down into the abyss. 7.
And again I saw in the vision till those sluices were put
away from that high roof, and the fountains of the earth
dried up, and other abysses were opened. 8. Then
the water began to run into these till the earth became uncovered; but that vessel reached the earth, and
the darkness retreated, and it became light. 9. But
that white bullock, which had become a man, came out
of that vessel, and the three bullocks with him; and
one of the three bullocks was white, similar to that
[first] bullock, and one of them was red like blood, and
one black; and that one, the white bullock, went away

from them. 10. And they began to bring forth animals of the desert and birds, so that there arose out of them a varied diversity of kinds: lions and panthers and dogs and wolves and hyenas and wild boars and foxes and squirrels and hogs and falcons and vultures and buzzards and eagles and crows; and among them was born a white bullock. 11. And they began to bite one another; but that white bullock which was born among them begat a wild ass and a white bullock with it; and the wild ass increased. 12. But that bull which was born from him begat a black wild boar and a white sheep; and this wild boar begat many boars, but that sheep produced twelve sheep. 13. And when these twelve sheep had grown, they gave one of them to the asses, and these asses then gave that sheep to the wolves, and that sheep grew up among the wolves. 14. And the Lord brought the eleven sheep to live with it, and to pasture with it among the wolves; and they increased, and became many herds of sheep. 15. And the wolves began to fear, and oppressed them till they [the wolves] finally destroyed their [i.e. the sheep's] young, and threw their young into a stream of much water; but those sheep began to cry aloud, on account of their young, before the Lord. 16. And a sheep which had been saved from the wolves fled, and escaped to the wild asses; and I saw the sheep as they lamented and cried and asked their Lord with all their power, till that Lord of the sheep descended at the voice of the sheep from his high abode, and came and looked after them. 17. And he called to that sheep which had escaped from the wolves, and spoke with it concerning the wolves, that it should counsel them not to touch the sheep. 18. And that sheep went to the wolves by the voice of the Lord;

and another sheep met that sheep, and went with it, and these two came together to the abode of those wolves, and spoke with them, and admonished them that henceforth they should not touch the sheep. 19. And then I saw the wolves, and how they exceedingly oppressed the sheep with all their power; and the sheep cried aloud. 20. And their Lord came to the sheep, and began to beat those wolves, and the wolves began to lament; but the sheep became quiet, and from then on did not cry. 21. And I saw the sheep till they had gone away from the wolves, and the wolves were blinded as to their eyes, and those wolves went out that they might follow the sheep with all their power. 22. And the Lord of the sheep went with them, leading them, and all the sheep followed him; and his face was shining, and his appearance terrible and sublime. 23. But the wolves commenced to follow those sheep till they reached them in a sea of water. 24. And this sea of water was divided, and the water stood from this side and from that before their faces; and their Lord leading them stood also between them and the wolves. 25. And as those wolves did not yet see the sheep, they went into the middle of the sea of water; and the wolves followed the sheep, and ran after them into the sea of water. 26. And when they saw the Lord of the sheep they turned that they might flee from before his face; but this sea of water gathered itself together, suddenly took again its own character, and the water swelled and rose till it covered those wolves. 27. And I saw till all the wolves which had followed those sheep were destroyed, and sank down. 28. But the sheep escaped from that water, and went into the desert, where there was no water and no grass; and they began to open their eyes and to see; and I saw the Lord of the sheep pasturing them and giving them water and grass, and that [former] sheep going and leading them. 29. And this sheep ascended to the height of a high rock, and the Lord of the sheep sent it to them. 30. And after that I saw the Lord of the sheep as he stood before them; and his appearance was terrible and powerful, and all those sheep saw him, and were afraid before his face. 31. And they were all afraid, and trembled before him, and cried after that sheep which was with him to the other sheep which was among them: " We are not able to exist before our Lord, or to look at him." 32. And that sheep which led them returned, and ascended to the height of that rock; but the sheep began to be blinded as to their eyes, and erred from the path which it had showed to them; but this sheep did not know it. 33. And the Lord of the sheep was enraged over them greatly; and that sheep discovered it, and descended from the height of the rock, and came to the sheep, and found the greater part of them blinded as to their eyes, and erring from his path. 34. And as they saw it they feared and trembled before its face, and desired to return to their folds. 35. And that sheep took other sheep with it, and came to those erring sheep; and then it began to kill them, and the sheep feared its countenance; and thus that sheep brought back those erring sheep, and they returned to their folds. 36. And I saw there in the vision till that sheep became a man, and built the Lord of the sheep a house, and placed all the sheep in that house. 37. And I saw till that sheep that had met the sheep which led the sheep reposed [in death]; and I saw till all the large sheep were destroyed, and small ones arose in their places; and they came to a pasture, and approached a stream of water. 38. And this sheep which led them, and which became a man, was separated from them, and reposed [in death]; and all the sheep sought it, and cried over it exceedingly. 39. And I saw till they became quiet from their crying over this sheep, and they crossed that stream of water; and there always arose other sheep that led them in the place of those which had departed, and led them. 40. And I saw the sheep until they came into a good place, and into a pleasant and glorious land; and I saw these sheep till they were satisfied; but the house stood among them in the beautiful land. 41. And sometimes their eyes were opened, and sometimes they were blinded, till another sheep arose, and led them, and conducted them all back, and their eyes were opened. 42. And the dogs and the foxes and the wild boars began to devour those sheep till another sheep arose, a buck, in their midst, which led them. 43. And this buck began to butt those dogs and those foxes and those wild boars from both sides, till he had destroyed them all. 44. And that sheep had its eyes opened, and saw this buck which was among the sheep departing from his honor, and beginning to butt those sheep, and to tramp on them, and to walk unseemly. 45. And the Lord of the sheep sent that sheep to another sheep, and exalted it to become a buck, and to lead the sheep in the place of that sheep which had deserted his honor. 46. And it went to it, and spoke to it alone, and elevated it to become a buck, and made it the prince and leader of the sheep; but during all that time those dogs oppressed the sheep. 47. And the first buck pursued the second buck, and the second buck arose, and fled before its face; and I

saw till those dogs cast down the first buck. 48. And
that second buck arose, and led the smaller sheep, and
this buck begat many sheep, and reposed [in death] ;
and a small sheep became the buck in its place, and was
the prince and leader of those sheep. 49. And those
sheep grew and increased ; and the dogs and the foxes
and the wild boars were afraid, and fled before it ; and
that buck butted and killed all the wild beasts, and
those wild beasts had no more power among the sheep,
and never robbed them of anything. 50. And that
house became great and broad, and a large tower was
built on that house of the Lord of the sheep for those
sheep ; and the house was low, but the tower was high
and broad ; and the Lord of the sheep stood on that
tower, and they placed a full table before him. 51. And
I again saw those sheep that they again erred, and
went many ways, and left their house ; and the Lord of
the sheep called some from among them, and sent
them to the sheep, but the sheep began to kill them.
52. And one of them was saved, and was not killed, but
escaped, and cried over the sheep ; and they wanted to
kill it, but the Lord of the sheep saved it out of the
hands of the sheep, and brought it up to me, and caused
it to dwell there. 53. And he sent many other sheep
to those sheep to admonish them, and to lament over
them. 54. And after that I saw, as they left the house
of the Lord of the sheep and his tower, they departed
entirely, and their eyes were blinded ; and I saw the
Lord of the sheep that he caused much death among
them in each one of their herds, till these sheep *even*
called for this death, and they betrayed his place. 55.
And he left them in the hand of the lions and tigers and
wolves and jackals, and in the hand of foxes and all the

wild beasts, and these wild beasts began to tear those sheep to pieces. 56. And I saw that he left that house of theirs and their tower and gave them all into the hand of lions that they should tear and devour them, into the hand of all the wild beasts. 57. And I began to cry aloud with all my power, and called upon the Lord of the sheep and showed him this in reference to the sheep, that they were being devoured by all the wild beasts. 58. But he remained silent, seeing it, and rejoiced that they were devoured and swallowed and robbed, and left them in the hand of all the wild beasts as food. 59. And he called seventy shepherds and put away those sheep, in order that they should pasture them, and he spoke to the shepherds and to their companions: ' Each single one of you shall now pasture the sheep, and everything I command you, do ! 60. And I deliver them over to you according to number, and will tell you which of them shall be destroyed ; those kill ! '' 61. And he gave those sheep over to them. And to another he called and said to him : " Watch, and see everything that the shepherds do concerning these sheep ; for they will destroy more of them than I have commanded. 62. And each superabundance and the destruction which the shepherds do to these write down, how many they destroy by my command, and how many they destroy by their own will, and write down separately each destruction by each shepherd. 63. And according to the number recite before me how many they have destroyed of their own account and how many were given them for destruction, that this may be a testimony for me against them, that I may know every deed of the shepherds to give them over, and may see what they do, whether they do my commands which I have commanded them or not.

64. And they shall not know, and thou shalt not let them know nor admonish them, but write down all the destruction of the shepherds, each one in its time, and lay everything before me." 65. And I saw till those shepherds pastured in their times and began to kill and to destroy more than was commanded them, and left those sheep in the hands of the lions. 66. And the lions and the tigers devoured and swallowed the greater part of those sheep, and the wild boars devoured with them; and they burned that tower and demolished that house. 67. And I mourned a great deal over that tower because that house of the sheep was demolished; and after that I could no longer see those sheep whether they entered that house. 68. And the shepherds and their companions delivered over those sheep to all the wild beasts to devour them, and each one of them received in his time a *certain* number, and of each one the other wrote down in a book how many he destroyed. 69. And each one killed and destroyed more than was ordered him; and I began to cry and to lament exceedingly concerning those sheep. 70. And in the vision I saw that scribe as he wrote each one that was destroyed by those shepherds on each day and brought up and opened and showed this whole book to the Lord of the sheep, everything that they had done and every one that each single one had removed and every one that they had handed over for destruction. 71. And the book was read before the Lord of the sheep, and he took the book in his hand, and read it and sealed it and laid it down. 72. And after that I saw that shepherds pastured twelve hours, and behold, three of those sheep turned around and came and entered and began to build everything that was demolished of the house, but

the wild boars attempted to hinder them, and they could not. 73. And they again began to build, as before, and put up that tower, and it was called "the high tower"; and they again began to place a table before that tower, and all the bread on it was unclean and not pure. 74. And concerning all this the sheep were blinded as to their eyes, and did not see, and their shepherds likewise; and a great many were delivered to their shepherds for destruction, and they trod on the sheep with their feet and devoured them. 75. And the Lord of the sheep remained quiet till all the sheep were scattered in the field and mixed themselves with them and did not save them from the hands of the wild beasts. 76. And he who wrote the book brought it to the houses of the Lord of the sheep, and showed it and read it and petitioned him on their account and asked him, while showing him all the deeds of their shepherds and testifying before him against all the shepherds. 77. And he took the book and laid it beside him, and departed.

CHAP. 90. — And I saw to the time when thirty-six shepherds thus pastured, and each one completed his time like the first; and others received them in their hands to pasture them in their time, each shepherd in his own time. 2. And after that I saw in the vision all the birds of heaven coming: the eagles and the vultures and the buzzards and the crows; but the eagles led all the birds; and they began to devour those sheep and to pick out their eyes and to devour their flesh. 3. And the sheep cried out because their flesh was being devoured by the birds. And I cried and lamented in my sleep over that shepherd who was pasturing the sheep. 4. And I saw until those sheep were devoured by the dogs and the eagles and the buzzards, and they did not leave on them meat or skin or muscles till the skeletons stood there alone, and the skeletons fell to the ground also, and the sheep became less. 5. And I saw to the time when twenty-three shepherds pastured, and they completed, each in his time, fifty-eight times. 6. But small lambs were born from those white sheep, and they began to open their eyes and to see and to cry to the sheep. 7. But the sheep did not cry to them and did not hear what they said to them, but were exceedingly deaf, and their eyes exceedingly and powerfully blinded. 8. And I saw in the vision that the crows flew on to those lambs and took one of those lambs, but broke the sheep and devoured them. 9. And I saw till horns came to those lambs and the crows threw down those horns; and I saw till ONE great horn came forth, ONE of those sheep, and their eyes were opened. 10. And it looked at them, and their eyes were opened, and it cried to the sheep, and the bucks saw it, and all ran to it. 11. And with all that those eagles and vultures and crows and buzzards to that time were tearing those sheep to pieces, and flew down on them and devoured them; but the sheep remained quiet, and the bucks lamented and cried out. 12. And those crows fought and battled with it and sought to remove that horn, but had no power over it. 13. And I saw them till the shepherds and the eagles and those vultures and buzzards came, and they cried to those crows that they should break that horn of the buck; and they fought and battled with it, and it fought with them and cried that its help might come to it. 14. And I saw till that man who had written down the names of the shepherds and brought them up to the Lord of the sheep came, and he helped that buck and showed it everything, that its help had come

down. 15. And I saw till that Lord of the sheep came
to them in anger, and all who saw him fled, and all fell
into his shadow before his face. 16. All the eagles and
vultures and crows and buzzards assembled and brought
with them all the sheep of the desert, and they all came
together and assisted one another in order to break that
horn of the buck. 17. And I saw that man who had
written the book by the voice of God till he opened that
book of destruction which those last twelve shepherds
had practised, and showed that they had destroyed more
than those before them, before the Lord of the sheep.
18. And I saw till the Lord of the sheep came to them
and took the rod of anger in his hand, and struck the
earth so that the earth was rent apart, and all the beasts
and the birds of heaven fell away from those sheep,
and sank down into the earth, and it was covered over
them. 19. And I saw till a great sword was given to the
sheep; and the sheep came to those wild beasts to kill
them, and all the beasts and the birds of heaven fled from
their face. 20. And I saw till a throne was built on the
earth in the pleasant land, and the Lord of the sheep sat
upon it, and he took all the sealed books and opened those
books before the Lord of the sheep. 21. And the Lord
called to those first six white ones, and commanded that
they should bring to him, from the first star on, which
had come forth, all the stars whose sexual members had
been similar to the sexual members of horses, and also
the first star that had first fallen ; and they brought all
before him. 22. And he said to that man who wrote before him, who was one of the six white ones, and said
to him : "Take those seventy shepherds to whom I have
delivered the sheep, and taking them, they of their own
account killed more than I had commanded them."

23. And behold I saw them all bound, and all stood before him. 24. And the judgment was first over the stars, and they were judged and were *found to be* sinners, and went to the place of judgment and were thrown into an abyss filled with fire and burning and filled with pillars of fire. 25. And those seventy shepherds were judged and were *found to be* sinners, and THEY were thrown into this abyss of fire. 26. And I saw at that time that an abyss like it was opened in the middle of the earth, which was full of fire, and they brought those blinded sheep, and they all were judged and were *found to be* sinners, and were thrown into this abyss of fire and burned; and this abyss was to the right of that house. 27. And I saw those sheep burning, and their bones burned. 28. And I stood looking till he enveloped that old house, and they took out all the pillars, and all the planks and the ornaments of that house were wrapped in with it, and they brought it out and put it in one place, on the right [i.e. south] of the earth. 29. And I saw the Lord of the sheep till he produced a new house, larger and higher than that first, and put it in the place of the first, which had been enveloped, and all its pillars were new, and the ornaments new and larger than of the first old one, which he had removed, and all the sheep were in its middle. 30. And I saw all the sheep that had been left and all the animals on the earth and all the birds of the heavens, falling down and worshipping those sheep and petitioning and obeying them in every word. 31. And after that those three who were dressed in white, who had led me up before, took me by the hand, and the hand of that buck taking hold of me, they raised me, and put me down in the midst of those sheep before the judgment took place. 32. But those

sheep were all white, and their wool large and clean. 33. And all that were destroyed and scattered, and all the wild beasts and all the birds of heaven were collected in that house, and the Lord of the sheep rejoiced greatly, for they were all good and had returned to his house. 34. And I saw till they laid down that sword which had been given to the sheep, and returned it to his house; and it was sealed before the face of the Lord, and all the sheep were closed up in that house, but it could not contain them. 35. And the eyes of all of them were opened, and they saw the good, and there was not ONE among them that did not see. 36. And I saw that that house was large and broad and exceedingly full. 37. And I saw that a white bullock was born, and his horns were large, and all the wild beasts and all the birds of heaven feared him and petitioned him at all times. 38. And I saw till all their generations were changed, and they all became white bullocks, and the first one of them [was the word, and that word] was a great animal, and had on its head large and black horns; and the Lord of the sheep rejoiced over them and over all the bullocks. 39. And I reposed in their midst, and I awoke and saw everything. 40. And this is the vision that I saw as I was asleep; and I awoke and blessed the Lord of justice and gave him glory. 41. And then I cried greatly, and my tears did not stand still till I was not able to endure it; when I looked they flowed on account of that which I saw, because everything will come and be fulfilled; and all the deeds of men in their order appeared to me. 42. And in that night I remembered my first dream, and on its account I cried and trembled, because I had seen that vision.

CHAP. 85. The second vision, which reaches to chapter 90, gives a history of the world from the beginning to the completion in the Messianic times. As in Daniel, the men of Israel and of other neighbors are given under the symbolism of animals. The representatives of the "plant of righteousness" are pictured as tame animals, the patriarchs are bullocks, and in later times the faithful are sheep; names suggested by the gradual decrease of faith and fidelity in Israel. Those not of the people of God and the enemies of Israel are symbolized as wild beasts and vultures. Single persons are individuals of the species to which they belong, the nations are herds, their leaders are especially prominent members of such herds. The account itself is based chiefly on the Old Testament record.—1. *Another*, cf. 83 : 2. — 2. Cf. Prov. v. 1. — 3. *Edna*, cf. note on 83 : 2. This bullock is Adam. *White* is the color of the theocratic line of descent, 85 : 3; 87 : 2; 90 : 6, 21, 31–37, symbolizing moral purity; cf. Isa. i. 18; Ps. li. 10; Dan. vii. 9; Cant. iv. 2. *A female* etc., designating Eve as a virgin; after verse 6 she is called a *cow*. Cain is black, the emblematic color of sin; Abel is red, a color in token of his martyrdom; cf. 22 : 7 and Num. xix. — 4. Death of Abel. — 5. *A cow* is Cain's wife, according to Jewish tradition, his sister. — 6. Eve seeking Abel. The Book of the Jubilees, chap. 4, relates that Adam and Eve lamented over Abel "four times seven years." — 8. *White bull*, i.e. Seth. The cows are called black to explain how afterwards the daughters of men were so easily enticed by the fallen angels. Dillmann thinks *black* should stand before *bullocks*; cf. Gen. v. 4. — 9. Origin of the Sethites, opposed to the Cainites.

CHAP. 86. As 88 : 1 shows, this fallen star is Azazel. *Bullocks*, both Sethites and Cainites. — 2. The result was tumult and confusion among mankind. *The large* are probably the Sethites, the *black* certainly the Cainites. — 3. *Fall of the rest of the angels.* The three kind of giants; cf. note on 7 : 2. — 6. *Children of the earth*; the angels being children of heaven; cf. 6 : 2.

CHAP. 87. The contest between the bullocks and the giants; the former horn the latter, the latter devour the former; cf. 7 : 4. — 2. *Like white men*, i.e. angels. Throughout the whole tableau angels are always dignified as men. They are *white* because holy and pure; cf. 85 : 3. The four are probably Michael and three other archangels; cf. note on 81 : 5. — 3, 4. This removal of Enoch is explained by the prominent part he takes in the punishment of the angels; cf. chap. 12 sqq. On this tower he remains also till the Messianic judgment, 89 : 52; 90 : 31. Where that tower was is uncertain.

CHAP. 88. Rufael binds Azazel, 10 : 4–8. — 2. The work of Gabriel described in chap. 10 : 9, 10. — 3. Michael, according to 10 : 11–14.

CHAP. 89. *These four*, i.e. the four archangels. Mentioning Noah as *that* white bullock, as if he had been spoken of before, is surprising. The author knew he would be immediately recognized by the context. But as a bullock cannot build a vessel, i.e. an ark, Noah becomes a man. The three that lived with him are his sons. *Covered*, cf. Gen. vii. 16 and En. 67 : 2. — 2. As men are symbolized as animals, the earth is consistently called a *yard*, and the heavens above, *a high roof*. *Seven*, cf. 77 : 4. — 4. The deluge. — 6. *And all the animals*, i.e. all the *real* animals. — 7. *Other abysses were opened*, to receive the mass of water, as verse 8 shows. — 8. *Darkness*, cf. verse 4. — 9. The white bullock is, as is interpolated in one MS. Shem, the patriarch of the Israelites as a link in the theocratic chain. The red one is Japheth, the black one Ham. The white bullock went away, i.e. Shem became isolated as the bearer of the theocratic idea. — 10. The origin of the different anti-theocratic nations from the three sons of Noah. The white bullock that was born is Abraham. — 11. The first clause is unintelligible, but may refer to Gen. xiv. 1 sqq. The *wild ass* is Ishmael, the white bullock, Isaac. In the following verses, 13 and 16, the Arabs, the descendants of Ishmael, are called wild asses; cf. Gen. xvi. 12. — 12. The *black wild boar* is Esau, the *white sheep* is Jacob.—The name sheep for Jacob can scarcely indicate a decrease in faith towards Jehovah, but was probably suggested by his profession. — 13. *One of them*, i.e. Joseph. *Asses*, i.e. the Midianites, one of the tribes of Arabia. *Wolves* is the constant name for the Egyptians. — 15. The oppression of the Israelites in Egypt. — 16. Moses. — 18. *Another sheep*, i.e. Aaron. — 20. *Beat* refers to the plagues. — 22. *His face was shining* refers to the cloud of fire. — 28. *Commenced to see* must, according to the *usus loquendi* in this and the next chapter, be interpreted according to Ex. xiv. 31; Hos. ii. 15; Jer. ii. 2. — 29. *Sinai*, cf. Ex. xix. — 30. *Powerful* is about ἰσχυρός. — 31. With reference to Ex. xx. 18 sqq.; Deut. v. 19 sqq. *That sheep* is Moses, the *other sheep* is Aaron. — 32. Ex. xxiv. 12 sqq. and xxxii. sqq. and *Book of the Jubilees*, chap. i. — 34. *It*, i.e. Moses. — 35. Cf. Ex. xxxii. 26–29. — 36. This sheep, i.e. Moses, becomes a man for the same reason that Noah did, vs. 1 and 9, for he here builds the tabernacle, which became the centre of Israel's worship. — 37. The death of Aaron (the phrase from verse 18) and of the older generations in the desert. The stream of water is the Jordan. — 38. Cf. Deut. xxxiv. — 39. Crossing the Jordan, and the rule of the judges. — 40. Palestine; cf. also 26 : 1. *Satisfied*, cf. Deut. xxxii. 14, 15. — 41. Their religious condition during the period of the judges to the time of Samuel. — 42. *The dogs* are the Philistines (cf. vs. 46 and 47), the *wild boars* are the Edomites (cf. vs. 12), the *foxes*, probably the Amalekites. The lately discovered Greek fragment of verses 42–49 has 42ᵃ as two clauses as follows: καὶ οἱ κύνες ἤρξαντο κατεσθίειν τὰ πρόβατα καὶ οἱ ὗες καὶ οἱ ἀλώπεκες κατήσθιον αὐτά. The Ethiopian translator, by uniting the subjects, makes the sentence smoother and avoids the unnecessary repetition of κατεσθίειν, and, besides that, is more definite in its *harânja hakel*, i.e. wild boars, than the Greek with its indefinite ὗες. According to most MSS. 42ᵇ would read : till another sheep was raised to the Lord of the sheep. This senseless statement is fully cleared

up by the better Greek text, which reads: μέχρι οὗ ἤγειρεν ὁ
κύριος τῶν προβάτων κριὸν ἕνα, — 43. Wars of Saul against his
enemies. The Ethiopic is somewhat abbreviated, but it is
questionable whether the *many* of the Greek is, in view of
verse 49, and that the Hebrew frequently uses *all* for many,
e.g. Gen. xli. 57, a better reading than the *all* of the Ethiopic. — 44. There is no reason to think that the Greek reading which says that the eyes of the sheep were opened, and
not the eyes of Samuel, is better than the Ethiopic. Although
the expression is generally used of a return to God and his
covenant, it is manifestly used here in the modified sense of
learning the true character of Saul. Samuel, too, had been de-
ceived in Saul, hence his eyes were opened. And, besides,
we have no evidence whatever that Israel became more faithful and theocratic after discovering Saul's wickedness. In fact,
Samuel suits better as subject, as it is to furnish a motive for
his mission described in the following. — 45. Samuel anoints
David. In this and the two next verses the Greek and Ethiopic are virtually the same. — 48, 49. *Small sheep*, i.e. Solomon.
The account in vs. 49 is, beyond all doubt, a description of
the reign of David, and not of Solomon. Hoffmann therefore
proposes to change the place of this verse. The Greek solves
the enigma, as there vs. 49 is immediately joined to 48ª. —
50. The tower is, beyond all doubt, the temple; but what is
the house? It might seem from vs. 36 and 40 that it is the
tabernacle, but if we notice that in vs. 66 sq. and 72 sq. this
house is mentioned as still existing, even after the Exile, when
there was neither temple nor tabernacle, and that vs. 72 speaks
of the *rebuilding* of the house, there can scarcely be any doubt
but that Jerusalem, as the central point of Israel's worship, is
intended to be understood. And thus, too, from a religious point
of view the house was by no means as important as the tower,
for God dwells in his temple. This interpretation proposed
by Dillmann, p. 262, and accepted by Vernes, p. 89, is certainly
correct. With this cf. *Test. Levi.* x. ὁ γὰρ οἶκος ὃν ἂν ἐκλέξηται

κύριος, Ἰερουσαλὴμ κληθήσεται, καθὼς περιέχει βίβλος Ἐνὼχ τοῦ δικαίου. *Table*, i.e. offerings. — 51. The religious fall of the Israelites and the fate of the prophets. — 52. The escape and translation of Elijah. That Enoch should especially note this is natural, since he and Elijah were the only persons who escaped death; cf. 93:8. — 53, 54. The fruitless labors of the prophets to the time of the Exile. *In each one of their herds*, i.e. in each tribe of Israel. *Till*, etc. refers to the calling in of foreign heathen nations to their support, thereby hastening their own destruction. By allowing strange nations to influence the fate of Israel they virtually betrayed "his place." — Verses 55–58, evidently refer to unfortunate wars of the Israelites immediately before and at the Exile; but just what nations are symbolized by the animals here mentioned can scarcely be determined with any degree of confidence. *Devoured*, vs. 57; cf. Jer xii. 9; Ezek. xxxiv. 5, 8; Isa. lvi. 9. Vs. 56 is almost literally quoted in *Barnabae Epist.* xvi. 5. — 59. *Seventy shepherds*, a first class *crux interpretum*. It almost seems as if the different interpreters vied with each other in misunderstanding the object and character of these shepherds. Accepting as self-evident that *shepherds* must mean men, and in this connection rulers, the commentators have sought high and low, in Israel and out of Israel, in Egypt, Chaldea, Babylonia, Greece, and other countries for seventy shepherds who superintended the oppression of the chosen people. Others, again, have thought of seventy periods of time or periods of government, and, based on their respective suggestions, have placed the origin of the book at all times from the period of Judas Maccabi to the revolution of Bar-chochbas. It is impossible to mention all the various theories circulating on these seventy shepherds, for that would require too much space; it is also unnecessary to do so and to refute them, for this has been done to the satisfaction of all candid seekers of truth by Gebhardt in *Merx's Archiv*, ii. 2, p. 163–246, who has made these seventy shepherds a special topic of inquiry, and has conclusively shown the utter impossibility of accepting any of the explanations that make them leaders or rulers of heathen nations. We therefore turn immediately to the only true, legitimate, and satisfactory explanation. This was first mentioned by Hofmann (*Schriftbeweis*, I. p. 422), accepted and strengthened by Schürer, p. 531, and lately adopted by Drummond, p. 40. According to them these shepherds are not men, not rulers of heathen nations, but they are *angels*. There can be no doubt whatever of the truth of this interpretation, for the following reasons: 1. Throughout all this symbolism men are always represented as animals, and the heathen nations as wild beasts or birds of prey. That Noah and Moses are pictured as men in 89 : 1, 9, 36 finds its explanation in the peculiar object in which they are engaged. Besides, it is expressly stated that they *became* men ; cf. notes. Now, in contradistinction from men symbolized by animals, angels are symbolized by men, as 87 : 2 ; 90 : 14 clearly demonstrate. Angels alone are dignified as men ; and what possible reason could there be for calling the leaders of the wild beasts and of the birds men, and thus giving them a name even more dignified than the names given to the Israelites? 2. Before they go out to pasture they all appear *contemporaneously* before the Lord, 89 : 59, and how could that suit *successive* rulers? Schürer ironically asks if these rulers were to be regarded as pre-existing? 3. In the last judgment they are associated with the fallen *angels*, 90 : 20 sqq. 4. The *angel* who keeps the record of the deeds of the shepherds is simply called *another*, 89 : 61, thus signifying their oneness of being with him. 5. The shepherds are appointed, according to 89 : 75, to *protect* the sheep from the wild animals, i.e. from the heathen nations. Interpreting the shepherds as heathen rulers would give the senseless sentence that the heathen rulers were to protect the Israelites *from themselves*, i.e. from these rulers! The author's idea is simple and plain. During the time that Israel, by the will of God, was to be oppressed and overcome

by the nations around her, he had placed them in the hands
of seventy shepherds, as guardians, who should watch that
Israel should not suffer and endure more than was God's will.
This the shepherds neglect to do, and deliver to the wild beasts
and birds of prey more than they should have done; hence
these shepherds shall be punished, and be cast with the fallen
angels, who had also proved faithless, into the fiery abyss. The
idea that Israel suffered more than her sins deserved is not
strange or unexpected. It is the author's exegesis of passages
like Isa. xl. 2^b (according to the true interpretation of the Targumim, Luther, Authorized Version, Delitzsch, and others),
Isa. lxi. 7 and Jer. xvi. 18, where it is stated that Israel has
received double for all her sins. The choice of the mystical
and sacred number *seventy* can be no surprise to the student
of the Old Testament. Although all these shepherds appear
contemporaneously before the Lord when they receive the
commission, they shall not pasture together, but one after the
other. That God speaks here directly to the shepherds, and not
through the medium of angels, as we should expect from the
analogy of the rest of the book and from the example of the
Old Testament if they were men, and especially heathen rulers,
shows conclusively that the shepherds were beings enjoying
intimate communication with God, in other words, were angels.
An author who but once (14 : 24) permits even the sacred
person of Enoch to go into the presence of God, could under
no circumstances have imagined heathen rulers, the oppressors
of God's children, as standing before him, and receiving their
orders from his own mouth. — 60. *According to number*, i.e.
a certain number. These shepherds were not to act inde-
pendently, but, like the angels in the Old Testament and in
Enoch, were simply executors of God's will and command.
These are functions that a Jew, writing not in the time of the
return from the Exile when the heathen Cyrus had appeared
as the instrument in God's hand for the benefit of his people,
but in a time when experience had exhibited the surrounding

heathen nations as the most bitter haters and revilers of Israel's
God and persecutors and tormentors of the people, in the time
when the cruel scenes inaugurated by Antiochus Epiphanes
were still vivid before the author — these are functions, we
say, that a Jew at that time could never have ascribed to Gentile rulers. — 61. God calls another shepherd, i.e. angel, to keep
record of the deeds of these seventy shepherds. The "other
one" is clearly and evidently an angel, as is seen from 90:22
and 14, probably the archangel Michael, the patron angel of
Israel; cf. Dan. x. 4 sqq. — 62. *Superabundance*, πλησμονή,
Uebermass, the number slain above those intended by God.
These shall be written down that the shepherds may be judged
accordingly. — 63. *Give them over*, i.e. to punishment. — 64.
These shepherds knowing God's will that only a certain number should be destroyed are not to be disturbed or advised in
their labor. But how could we suppose that, e.g. Antiochus
Epiphanes should have a knowledge of the fact that he was to
be an instrument to punish Israel, and should also be able to
determine how far the divine will would allow him to go? For
this knowledge, presupposed here as the basis of the just judgment of God over the shepherds for the transgression of God's
law, is clearly in possession of these shepherds, according to
vs. 59 and 60. — 65. Shows that the killing of the sheep consisted in giving them over into the hands of the wild beasts,
as also that the shepherds were beings entirely different from
the lions. Did the ridiculous incongruity of calling princes
and leaders of *wild beasts* "*shepherds*" never strike the advocates of the heathen potentate theory? As the *lions* are in all
probability the Assyrians, the author evidently places the beginning of the reign of the shepherds in the time of the struggle of the northern kingdom with Assyria. — 66. The fall of
the two kingdoms is summed up in the attack of the lions and
the tigers, the latter being the Chaldeans. The wild boars are
the Edomites (cf. vs. 12), who also took part in the destruction of Jerusalem; cf. Obad. 10–12; Lam. iv. 21; Ezek. xxv.

20*

12 sqq.; xxxv. 12 sqq.; Isa. xxxiv. 35; lxiii. 1–4; Ps. cxxxvii. 7. — 67, 68. *Could no longer see*, i.e. the Israelites were led into captivity. This being a break in the history of Israel, he remarks that the sins of the shepherds in this first period of Israel's humiliation and the partly undeserved sufferings are recorded by the other angel; cf. vs. 61. Cf. also Jer. xii. 9; Ezek. xxxiv. 5, 8; Isa. lvi. 9. — 71. With the sealing of the book the first scene is closed. How many shepherds pastured, and how long each one pastured, in the period just closed is not mentioned. — 72. Embraces the whole period of the captivity, which is stated in round numbers to have been twelve hours. That these twelve hours are to designate the time of the captivity alone is as clear as daylight from the *after that*, i.e. after the events to the destruction of Jerusalem, just mentioned, had transpired, *then* a certain number of shepherds pastured *till* the time when three sheep returned. How Dillmann can say that these hours embrace the time from Jojaqim to Cyrus is incomprehensible. Cyrus is certainly the *terminus ad quem*, but that Jojaqim is not the *terminus a quo* is equally certain. *Three* returned; Dillmann thinks this a corruption for *two*, i.e. Zerubabel and Joshua. If the word *three* is a change made by the Ethiopic translator, he probably means by this third one not Nehemiah or Ezra, but Jeremiah. The Ethiopic church has in many of her biblical codices a unique Book of Baruch, that claims inspiration and was extensively used in Ethiopia; in which book it is expressly stated that Jeremiah returned to Jerusalem, and a record is made of his labors and death there. (Cf. Dillmann *Chrest. Aethiop.*, pp. 1–15, or my translation of it in Lutheran Quarterly, July 1878, pp. 333–352.) The rebuilding of Jerusalem and the interruption as recorded Ezra iv.–vi. — 73. The building of the temple. *Table and bread*, i.e. offerings; cf. vs. 50. The contempt here expressed for the second temple is no indication that the author was an Essene, as Tideman asserts, as others could have felt the same contempt. The expression here is not any stronger

than we find in Mal. i. and ii. ; nay, the very words here seem to be taken from Mal. i. 7. — 74. The reason why this second temple was unclean was because even after the captivity the Israelites were still blinded, i.e. had not returned to God. Passing over the efforts of Ezra for the strengthening of the law shows that our author was certainly no Pharisee. It is the author's view of the religious condition and fate of Israel in the Persian period. — 75. In addition to internal sinfulness, Israel forgot that it was the people of God, and sinned by mixing themselves with the wild beasts of the field, i.e. with the nations of the world. The author here refers to the beginning of the diaspora. With this another period closes.

CHAP. 90. Critics are unanimous that the thirty-six, or as some MSS. have it thirty-seven, is an error for thirty-five. That this correction is not only legitimate, but is demanded by the account that follows will be seen presently. The seer sums up his vision in the words that so far thirty-five shepherds, including those that had ruled twelve hours, 89:72, had governed. *Like the first*; as those governing twelve hours completed their times, thus did also the rest of the thirty-five. — 2. Introduces a new period and new enemies. They are pictured as birds of prey to show that they are distinct from the previously mentioned enemies, from an altogether different stock or family. It is the period of the invasion of the Greeks and their allies. The *eagles* leading the rest are naturally the Greeks, or, more specifically, the Macedonians. The *crows*, according to vs. 8, 9, and 12, are the Syrians. Who the *vultures* and *buzzards* are does not appear ; most probably these are general terms to designate the other nations allied with the Greeks, so that the author did not intend to designate any particular nations with these names. *Pick out the eyes and devour their flesh*, because they were *birds*. The statements of the author are so broad that it is impossible to fix them to any particular historical events, except in general that the fate of the people under Alexander the Great and his successors are portrayed. — 4. Who the *dogs* are cannot be determined; but cf. Tideman, p. 281. Above, 89:46, 47, they were the Philistines, who cannot, even with Sir. l. 26 on hand, be meant here. He mentions the dogs, a domestic animal, hence belonging to a class of enemies of the period preceding the Grecian, since the period of the birds of prey and the eagles designate the enemies of the period just under consideration, to show that at the end of the Greek period Israel had to suffer from both their former and their present enemies, an idea well suiting the struggles between the various successors of Alexander the Great in the East and in the West; cf. Mic. iii. 2, 3. — 5. This Greek period was superintended by twenty-three shepherds, and thus all from the beginning, the thirty-five of vs. 1 and the twenty-three here, had completed fifty-eight times. Here we see the necessity of correcting the thirty-six or thirty-seven of vs. 1 into thirty-five. Thus, then, each shepherd completes one time, and in 89:72, then, there must have been twelve shepherds for the twelve hours. With this another period closes. It is interesting to see what martyrdom history must suffer to furnish the advocates of the heathen rulers theory with kings enough to satisfy the demands of this verse. — 6. The last period of heathen rule. This epoch is marked by the birth of small lambs, or, more literally, small male lambs, who began to open their eyes, i.e. began to return to the God of Israel. He designates by this name those in Israel who, about this time, especially in the days of Antiochus Epiphanes, when the leaders of the people and the sheep themselves began to adopt Greek ideas and manners (cf. 1 Macc. i. 11–15), took a firm position for the religion and law of their fathers. In short, they are the well-known חֲסִידִים, 1 Macc. vii. 13; 2 Macc. xiv. 6, the pious. They are called *small* on account of their small number, and *lambs* because they were the generation of the future, destined to grow and increase. They cried to the *sheep,* i.e. to the renegade Israelites; warned them, and appealed to them for help. — 7. But this cry was in vain, the Greek party would not depart

from its erring ways or assist the faithful. — 8. *The crows*, i.e.
the Syrians, attack these lambs and kill one. Who this one
is will be seen in verse 9. But they alone are not the suffer-
ers, the sheep too, the other unfaithful Israelites, are "broken."
In this verse he pictures the beginning of the struggle of the
faithful under Mattathias and his sons. — 9. The preceding
has brought us to the beginning of the struggle between the
Chasidim and the Greek party. Naturally we should then
expect that the *great horn* would be no one else but the great
Judas Maccabi. To this, however, Ewald, Dillmann, and
nearly all other investigators object, and find this horn in
John Hyrcanus. The only reason for doing so is acknowledged to be the fact that the time from Antiochus Epiphanes,
with whom this last period commences, to Judas is too short
a period for either twelve foreign, heathen kings, or for the
rule of twelve angel shepherds (Schürer). This objection is,
however, not valid, for it should be especially noted — what has
been so far overlooked entirely — that the writer does not consider the period of the last twelve shepherds *closed* with the
coming of the great horn, but only by the inauguration of the
Messianic kingdom. The great horn, and with it the writer,
is in the middle and midst of this last epoch, the rule of the
last shepherds. Just how many of these had governed before
the rise of the horn, and how many were to arise yet until the
new kingdom was established, is nowhere stated. The horn
itself is historically not the *terminus ad quem* for this rule, but
only an important factor in the events of this rule. We are,
then, not even allowed to seek twelve periods from Antiochus
Epiphanes to the great horn, but must place the horn rather
early in this last period, as great struggles are still expected
before the ungodly rule of the shepherds will end. The
period will be short, for only twelve shall rule, and the character of this period is reflected in the words "that these last
shepherds had slain more than the rest," and thus certainly
points to the eventful days of Judas Maccabi, and not to the

comparatively peaceful days of John Hyrcanus. Then the
specific number *twelve*, further than indicating a short period,
should have little weight in determining who the great horn
was, as this *twelve* is simply the completion of the author's
arbitrary and unhistorical system of the rule of the shepherds
in Israel, enigmatically dividing them into four periods of $12 +$
$23 + 23 + 12$ shepherds. Other reasons, too, point to Judas,
and not to John Hyrcanus. 1. It is impossible that an author
like ours, reciting the weal and woe of the faithful, should have
passed over in silence, or in insignificant words, the events of
the Maccabean period, which was so important just for him, the
establishment of religious and political freedom, purification of
the temple, the power of the Chasidim in the days of John Hyrcanus. 2. If the one slain in the previous verse is Jonathan
(Dillmann), how can it be said that *after* that period horns grew
for the lambs? Did political enthusiasm and success not take
place until after the death of Jonathan? Besides it was
only a *lamb*, i.e. a man of lesser importance who was slain, —
in all probability the High Priest Onias III., one of the faithful, murdered 171 B.C.; cf. 2 Macc. iv. 33–35. 3. The spirit
of the book points to the tumultuous days of Judas, and not
to the quiet times of Hyrcanus; cf. Special Introd. § 4. —
10. Appeal of Judas to the Jews. *All*, not in an absolute
sense, but rather *many*, a fact proved by the victories of
Judas. — 11–15. Struggle between the horn and its enemies.
This appears here as a struggle for the very existence of that
horn, and hence cannot find an explanation in the rather insig·
nificant two wars of John Hyrcanus against Antiochus Sidetes
and Antiochus Cyzicenus, especially as the latter was an
aggressive measure of John Hyrcanus in which he was not
even present, — something that is demanded by the context.
The words can be properly understood and appreciated only
by referring them to the ever-memorable events in the times
of Judas Maccabi, and regarding them as a reflex of those
bloody, but glorious days. Dillmann himself admits that in

this manner vs. 13 could aptly find its explanation in 1 Macc. iii. 7; vi. 53; v.; then 2 Macc. vi. 8 sqq., 13, 14; 1 Macc. vii. 41, 42; and in 2 Macc. xv. 8 sqq. In this struggle against so many foes Judas is represented as being assisted by the man, i.e. angel, who wrote the names of the unfaithful shepherds. — 15. In the midst of this contest the Lord himself comes to take part in the struggle. With this the author goes from an historical basis into a prophetic vision of the future, and what follows cannot be regarded as historical, but only as showing how the writer thought, from the present state of affairs, the future would shape itself. We see, then, the author stands in the midst of the Maccabean struggle. The horn Judas has already conquered in battle; his enemies are preparing to crush him. So far the author's knowledge goes. Of the death of Judas he knows nothing. The expected assistance from God himself, together with what follows, is the prophetic picture he draws of the future fate of this great horn. — 16. The last attack of the enemies, a feature frequently found in Messianic portions of apocryphal writers. And in this contest the sheep of the desert, i.e. the renegades in Israel, shall side with the open enemies of the faithful. The attack is still against that *horn*, showing that this horn existed even after the author had to leave the past and go to the future. — 17. During this time, from vs. 6, twelve shepherds had ruled. The terrible sufferings of Israel during that short period find expression in the words, that in spite of so short a period of time more had been destroyed than ever before. These twelve added to the fifty-eight of vs. 5 give us the whole sum of seventy shepherds. Now their times are completed, they can be judged and the Messianic kingdom inaugurated. — 18. The Lord himself destroys these last enemies of Israel. The picture is taken from the destruction of Korah and his adherents, Num. xvi. 31 sqq. — 19. With this the Messianic times commence. The first thing is the subjection of the old enemies by the sheep, mentioned also 91 : 12. Temporally the hopes expected here

are certainly to be fulfilled before those of the previous verse.—
20. Then follows the judgment, according to the books that
were sealed (cf. Dan. vii. 10) at different periods, and deposited
with God. This judgment takes place in a *pleasant land*, in
Palestine, 89 : 40. This involves no contradiction with 1 : 4,
as it is not stated there that God will judge from Mount Sinai.
Unlike the Parables the Messiah has nothing to do here with
the judgment.— 21. *Six white ones* are archangels, in vs. 31
those three white ones. Whether we are to read six or seven
here cannot be determined from the MSS. Were chap. 20 an
authentic part of the book, six would be preferred, but from
Tob. xii. 15 seven is to be preferred. But if, as Dillmann
supposes, reference is here made to Ezek. ix. 2 sqq., then six
is the number. *Star*, cf. chap. 86–88. — 22. Before these are
judged the seventy shepherds are associated with them, thus
showing that they were beings of the same kind. — 23. Cf.
53 : 5; 54 : 1, 2. — 24. Cf. 55 : 4. *Abyss of fire*, cf. 18 : 11;
19 : 1–3; 21 : 7–10. — 25. The shepherds are cast into the
same place of punishment. According to chap. 18 and 21, the
angels have also their own place of punishment, different from
the account in the Parables, 54 : 1, 2. — 26. Now follows the
punishment of the renegades in Israel, but in a different place,
in the midst of the earth (cf. 26 : 1), i.e. in the valley of Hinnom; cf. chap. 27. *To the right of the house*, i.e. south of
Jerusalem, 89 : 50. The judgment here is partial and not
universal; cf. chap. 51. — 28, 29. Removal of the old and
building of the new Jerusalem; cf. 61 : 1 sqq.; Ezek. xl.–
xlviii.; Isa. liv. 11 sqq.; lx.; Hag. ii. 7–9; Zech. ii. 6–17;
xiv. 6–9; and passages like Isa. iv. 5, 6; Zech. ix. 8. *Planks*,
Dillmann in his translation has *Balken*, but in *Lex.* col. 505
gives the meaning as *paxillus*, πάσσαλος, i.e. a small stake or
post. A new Jerusalem belongs to apocryphal visions of the
Messianic times; cf. 4 Ezra ix. 23–x. 55; cf. Drummond, p. 337
sqq. — 30. But the animals themselves that did the wicked
deeds shall not be judged, but will take part in the Messianic

kingdom; cf. (Mic. vii. 16, 17); Isa. xiv. 2 (xlix. 22, 23; lv. 5; lx. 4–16; lxii. 5 sqq.); lxi. 12, 19–21; Zech. viii. 20–28.— 31. *That buck* is probably Elijah, 89 : 52. *Those three in white,* cf. 81 : 5. They brought him to Palestine, where the judgment takes place. To explain how he knew of this judgment just mentioned he says that this transportation took place *before* the judgment, i.e. the statement here temporally precedes the facts recorded in the verses from vs. 16 on.— 32. Those who are to enjoy the Messianic kingdom are white, i.e. are pure and holy; cf. 85 : 3. Cf. Isa. i. 26; iv. 3; xi. 9; lx. 18, 21, etc. *Their wool is large,* i e. their deeds of righteousness and their virtues are many.— 33. *Those destroyed,* i.e. those that had been slain in the persecutions, shall rise again; cf. notes on 22 : 12, 13; and those in the diaspora shall again be assembled; cf. Mic. iv. 6, 7. The seat of this new government shall be in the new Jerusalem. Then the Lord will rejoice; cf. vs. 38; Zeph. iii. 17; Isa. lxii. 3–5; lxv. 19; and also 10 : 21.— 34. End of the period of the sword, vs. 19. This sword being no longer required is sealed up. The Messianic kingdom will not be disturbed in its tranquillity. The number of the saints is so large that Jerusalem cannot contain them; cf. Isa. xlix. 19–21; liv. 2, 3; Zech. ii. 8 sqq.— 35. This multitude has not one that does not see, that is spiritually blind.— 37. The appearance of the Messiah. In the Parables the Messiah appears before the judgment and conducts it; in chap. 1–37 and 72–105, God conducts the judgment, and the Messiah does not appear until the Messianic kingdom has been established in all its glory. He is here a product of the kingdom, while in the Parables the kingdom proceeds from him. He is born as a bullock to show his superiority over the sheep and the lambs, and this puts him on an equal footing with the patriarchs; cf. above. *His horns were large,* an indication of his power. — 38. In its perfection the members of the congregation become, like the Messiah, white bullocks. But the Messiah, too, increases, and becomes a certain large animal with

21

large, black horns, i.e. with increased power; cf. Zech. xii. 8. The words in brackets cause some difficulty. They are not a Christian interpolation with reference to the Logos, as the classical term for λόγος is not *nager*, which we have here, but *qâl*, while *nagar* is ῥῆμα, although it sometimes translates λόγοι. Most probably the text read רְאֵם, the name of the mysterious animal in the Old Testament, usually, after the LXX, rendered *unicorn*. The Greek translator, knowing no word equivalent to רְאֵם, simply transcribed it ῥημ, which the Ethiopian took for ῥῆμα = word. The original then read: "and the first of these was a רְאֵם, and this," etc.; cf. Hommel, *Physiologus*, p. xx. and chap. 22. *Over them*, i.e. over the sheep that had become bullocks. — 39. During his sleep he had been among these saints, and awakening he finds himself in their midst. — 40. In a sleep; cf. 85 : 1. — 41, 42. The threatenings of God had not been in vain, and the present condition of the author's contemporaries causes tears to flow for their fate.

SECTION XVIII.

CHAP. 91. — And now, my son Methuselah, call to me all thy brothers, and assemble to me all the children of thy mother, for the word calls me, and the spirit is poured out over me, that I show you all that will happen to you to eternity. 2. And then Methuselah went and called all his brothers to him and assembled his relatives. 3. And he conversed with all his children *concerning* justice, and said: "Hear, my children, all the words of your father, and listen properly to the voice of my mouth, for I admonish you and tell you, my beloved, love rectitude and walk in it. 4. And do not approach rectitude with a double heart, and do not associate with those of a double heart, but walk in justice, my children, and she will lead you in the good path, and justice will be your companion. 5. For I know that a condition of oppression will grow strong on the earth, and great punishment will be completed over the earth, and all injustice will be completed and be cut off by the roots, and its whole habitation destroyed. 6. And again injustice will be repeated, and all the deeds of injustice and the deeds of oppression and of sin will be renewed on the earth. 7. And when injustice and sin and reviling and oppression and all the deeds will increase, and falling-off and reviling and uncleanness will increase; there will be a great punishment from heaven upon them all, and the holy Lord will come forth in anger, and with punishment, that he may pass judgment on the earth. 8. And in those days oppression will be cut off from its roots, and the roots of injustice together with deception, and they will be destroyed from under heaven. 9. And all the pictures of the heathens will be given away; the towers will be burned by fire, and they will be removed from the whole earth, and will be thrown into a condemnation of fire, and will be destroyed in anger, and in a strong judgment which will be to eternity. 10. And the just one will arise from sleep, and wisdom will arise and will be given to them. 11. And then the roots of injustice will be cut off, and the sinners will be destroyed with the sword, and the roots of the revilers will be cut off in every place, and those who contemplate oppression and revile will be destroyed by the edge of the sword. — 12. And after that there will be another week, the eighth, that of justice, and the sword will be given to it, that it may pass judgment and justice on those who practise injustice, and the sinners will be delivered into the hands of the just. 13. And in the end of it they will acquire houses through their justice, and they will build a house to the Great King as an honor to eternity. 14. And after that, in the ninth week, the judgment of justice will be revealed to all the world, and all the doings of the impious will depart from the world, and the world will be written out for destruction, and all men will look for the path of rectitude. 15. And after this, in the tenth week, in the seventh part, there will be the judgment to eternity, which is held over the watchers and the great heavens of eternity which will spring forth from the midst of the angels. 16. And the first heaven will pass away and cease, and a new heaven will appear, and all the powers of heaven will shine to eternity seven fold. 17. And after that there will be many weeks, without number, to eternity, in goodness and in justice, and sin will not be mentioned from that time on to eternity. — 18. And now I tell you, my children, and show you the paths of justice and the paths of oppression, and I will show them to you again that ye may know what will come. 19. And now hear, my children, and walk in the paths of justice, and do not walk in the paths of oppression, for they will be destroyed in eternity who walk in the paths of injustice.

CHAP. 91. Having given his children an account of the events to come, Enoch proceeds to instruct them as to their conduct in preparation for that event. The parenetic words that now follow are thus intimately connected with the two visions. He tells Methuselah to call together his family to instruct them, 81 : 6. *Word*, the ῥῆμα spiritually discerned; cf. 14:24. — 3. *He*, i.e. Enoch. *Properly*, literally, in rectitude, in a right manner. *Love*, cf. 94 : 1. — 4. Double heart, cf. Ps.

xii. 2. *Associate*, 94 : 2, 3 ; 104 : 6. *Companion*, cf. Prov. vii. 4. — 5. This conduct is necessary, because injustice will at last be cut off, vs. 8 and 11, and completed, i.e. will have to end. The reference is here to the first judgment, the deluge. — 6. The period after the deluge. *Come forth*, 1 : 3. — 8. Final judgment. *Roots*, vs. 11. *Deception,* chosen with reference to the *double heart*, vs. 4 ; cf. Past. Her. *Vis.* ii. 2, 4 ; *Barn.* xix. 5. — 9. *Pictures*, i.e. idols. *Towers*, i.e. temples. The author has not forgotten the symbolism of his two visions. Idolatry is abhorred in 80 : 7 ; 99 : 7–9, 14. *They,* i.e. who ? the unconverted heathen, as Dillmann supposes, or those that fell off and reviled, vs. 7, and consequently worshipped in these temples ? — 10. *Just one*, collectively used. *Will rise*, cf. notes on 51 : 1, 2. *Wisdom will arise*, easily understood from chap. 42 ; cf. 5 : 8 ; 48 : 1. — 11. *Sword*, cf. 90 : 19 ; 91 : 12. — 12–17. will be treated after 93 : 14, where they undoubtedly belong. — 18. Good continuation of vs. 11. *Again,* i.e. in the following. — 19. Cf. vs. 5 and 7–11.

SECTION XIX.

CHAP. 92. — Written by Enoch, the scribe, all this doctrine of wisdom, praiseworthy to all men, and a judge of all the earth, to all my children who will dwell on the earth, and to the future generations who will practise rectitude and peace. 2. Let not your spirits be sorrowful on account of the times, for the Great Holy One has given days for everything. 3. And the just one will arise from sleep, will arise and walk in the paths of justice, and all his paths and ways will be in everlasting goodness and grace. 4. He will be gracious to the just one, and will give him everlasting rectitude and will give power, and will be in goodness and justice, and he will walk in the everlasting light. 5. But sin will be destroyed in darkness to eternity, and will not be seen from that day on to eternity.

CHAP. 93. — And after that Enoch commenced to relate out of the books. 2. And Enoch said : " Concerning the children of justice and concerning the chosen of the world and concerning the plant of justice and of rectitude, of these I will speak to you and announce to you, my children, I, Enoch, as it has appeared to me in a vision from heaven, and what I learned through the voice of the holy angels and understood from the tablets of heaven." 3. And Enoch commenced to relate from the books, and said : " I was born the seventh in the first week, while judgment and justice were yet retarded. 4. And there will arise after me in the second week great evil, and destruction will spring up ; and in it there will be the first end ; and in it a man will be saved ; and after it is finished injustice will grow, and he will make a law for the sinners. 5. And after that, in the third week, in the end thereof, a man will be chosen as the plant of the judgment of justice, and after him the plant of justice will come forever. 6. And after that, in the fourth week, in the end thereof, visions of the holy and the just will be seen, and a law for all generations, and a court will be made for them. 7. And after that, in the fifth week, in the end thereof, a house of glory and of supremacy will be built to eternity. 8. And after that, in the sixth week, those who will exist in it will all be blinded, and their hearts will all forget wisdom, and in it a man will ascend ; and in the end thereof the house of supremacy will burn with fire, and the whole race of the chosen root will be cut off. 9. And after that, in the seventh week, a rebellious generation will arise, and many will be their deeds, and all their deeds will be rebellious. 10. And in the end thereof the chosen just of the everlasting plant of justice will be rewarded; seven portions of learning are given to them concerning all his creatures. 11. And who is there of all the children of men that is able to hear the voice of the Holy One, and does not tremble, and who is able to think his thoughts, and who that is able to see all the works of heaven? 12. And how could one know the deeds of heaven and be able to see his breath and his spirit, and be able to relate *it*, or ascend and see all their ends, and think them or act like them? 13. And who is the man that is able to know what the breadth and the length of the earth is, and to whom has the measure of them all been shown? 14. Or is there any man who is able to know the length of heaven, and what is its height, and upon what it is established, and what is the measure as regards the number of the stars, and where all the luminaries rest?

CHAP. 94.—And now I say to you, my children, love justice and walk in it, for the paths of justice are worthy that they be accepted; and the paths of injustice are destroyed suddenly and cease. 2. And to certain men of *a future* generation the paths of violence and of death will be revealed, and they will retreat from them, and will not follow them. 3. And now I say to you, the just: Do not walk in the wicked path and in violence, and not in the paths of death, and do not approach them, that ye be not destroyed. 4. But love and choose for yourselves justice and a pleasing life, and walk in the paths of peace, that ye may live and have joy. 5. And hold in the thoughts of your hearts, and let not my words be eradicated from your hearts, for I know that the sinners will deceive men to make wisdom wicked, and it [i.e. wisdom] will not find a place, and all kinds of temptations will not cease. 6. Woe to those who build injustice and violence, and found deception, for they will be rooted out suddenly, and will have no peace. 7. Woe to those who build their houses in sin, for they will be rooted out from their foundation, and will fall by the sword; and they who acquire gold and silver will be destroyed by sudden judgment. 8. Woe to you rich, for ye have trusted in your riches, but ye will come away from your riches, because ye have not remembered the Most High in the days of your riches. 9. Ye have done reviling and injustice, and were prepared for the day of bloodshed, and for the day of darkness, and for the day of the great judgment. 10. Thus I speak to you, and announce to you that he who has created you will destroy you from the foundation, and over your fall there will be no pity, and your Creator will rejoice in your destruction. 11. And your just in those days will be a disgrace to sinners and the impious.

CHAP. 95. — Oh that my eyes were clouds of water, and I could weep over you, and pour out my tears like a cloud of water, and I could rest from the sorrow of my heart. 2. Who has empowered you to practise hate and wickedness? May the judgment reach you, the sinners! 3. Fear not the sinners, ye just, for God will give them into your hands again, that ye may pass judgment over them, as ye desire. 4. Woe to you who pronounce curses that they be not loosened, and healing will be far from you on account of your sins! 5. Woe to you who repay evil to your neighbor, for ye will be repaid according to your deeds! 6. Woe to you, the witnesses of untruth, and to those who weigh injustice, for ye will be destroyed suddenly. 7. Woe to you sinners, for ye pursue the just; for ye will be given over and pursued, ye men of injustice, and heavy will be their yokes upon you.

CHAP. 96. — Hope, ye just, for the sinners will be destroyed suddenly before you, and the power over them will be to you as ye desire. 2. And in the day of the trouble of the sinners your children will mount and rise like eagles, and your nest will be higher than the hawk, and ye will ascend and go like the squirrels into the recesses of the earth, and into the clefts of the rock to eternity, before the unjust; but they will lament over you, and cry like satyrs. 3. But fear not, ye who suffer, for a healing will be to you, and a brilliant light will shine for you, and ye will hear the voice of rest from heaven. 4. Woe to you, sinners, for your riches make you appear like the just, but your hearts prove to you that you are sinners; and this word will be a testimony against you, as a remembrance of wicked deeds. 5. Woe to you who devour the marrow of the wheat, and drink the power of the root of the fountain, and trod down the lowly by your power. 6. Woe to you who drink water at all times, for ye will be repaid suddenly, and will dry up and wither, because ye have left the fountain of life. 7. Woe to you who practise injustice and destruction and reviling; there will be a remembrance against you for evil. 8. Woe to you powerful, who throw down with power the just ones, for the day of your destruction will come. In those days many and good days will come to the just, on the day of your judgment.

CHAP. 97. — Believe, ye just, for the sinners will come to shame, and will be destroyed on the day of injustice. 2. It will be known to you that the Most High is mindful of your destruction, and the angels rejoice over your destruction. 3. What will ye do, ye sinners, and whither will ye flee, on that day of judgment, when ye will hear the voice of the prayer of the just? 4. Ye will not be like those, ye against whom this word will be a testimony: "Ye have been companions of the sinners." 5. And in those days, the prayer of the just will reach the Lord, and the days of your judgment will come to you. 6. And all the words of your injustice will be recited before the Great and Holy One; and your faces will be filled with shame, and each work that is founded on injustice will be cast off. 7. Woe to you sinners, in the midst of the ocean and over the land whose remembrance of you is evil! 8. Woe to you who acquire silver and gold without justice, and say: "We have become rich, and have treasures, and possess everything we desire; 9. And now we will do what we contemplate, for we have gathered together silver, and our treasuries are filled, and as water so many are the workmen of our houses." 10. And like water your lies will float away, for wealth will not remain for you, but will ascend suddenly from you, for ye have acquired it all in injustice, and ye will be given over to a great condemnation.

CHAP. 98. — And now I swear to you, the wise and the foolish; for ye will see much on this earth. 2. For ye, men, will put on more ornaments than the women, and colored stuffs more than the virgin; in royalty, and in greatness, and in power, and in silver, and in gold, and purple and honor, and in food, they will float away like water. 3. And therefore they will have no knowledge and no wisdom, and thereby they are destroyed together with their treasures, and with all their glory and their honor, and in shame and in murder and in great poverty their spirits will be cast into an oven of fire. 4. I swear to you sinners: as a mountain has not and will not become a slave, nor a hill the maid of a woman, thus too has sin not been sent on the earth, but man of himself has created it, and it will be for a great curse to those who do it. 5. And barrenness has not been given to a woman, but on account of the deeds of her hands she dies without children. 6. I swear to you sinners, by the Holy and the Just One, that all your wicked deeds are revealed in the heavens, and none of your deeds of violence are covered or hidden. 7. And do not think in your souls, and do not say in your hearts, that ye do not know and do not see that every sin is daily being written down in heaven before the Most High. 8. And from now ye know that all your violence which ye commit is written down on each day to the day of your judgment. 9. Woe to you fools, for ye will be destroyed by your foolishness; and ye do not listen to the wise, and will not attain anything good! 10. And now know that ye are prepared for the day of destruction, and do not hope that ye will live, ye sinners, but ye shall depart and die, for ye do not know a ransom; for ye are prepared for the day of the great judgment, and for the day of trouble and of great disgrace to your souls. 11. Woe to you hardened of heart, who do evil and devour blood; whence have ye good eating and drinking and satisfaction? from all the good which our Lord the Most High has spread in abundance over the earth; and ye will have no peace. 12. Woe to you who love the deeds of in-justice; why do ye hope for goodness to yourselves?

Know that ye shall be given into the hands of the just; they will cut off your necks and slay you, and will not pity you. 13. Woe to you who rejoice in the trouble of the just, for a grave will not be dug for you. 14. Woe to you who make the words of the just in vain, for the hope of life will not be to you. 15. Woe to you who write down words of untruth and words of the impious; for they write down their lies that they be heard, and do not forget their foolishness; and there will be no peace to them, but they will die a sudden death!

CHAP. 99. — Woe to those who act impiously, and glory in the words of untruth, and honor them; ye will be destroyed, and will have no good life. 2. Woe to you who change the words of rectitude, and who transgress the law of eternity, and make themselves that which they are not, namely, sinners; they will be trod down on the earth. 3. And in those days prepare yourselves, ye just, to raise your prayers of remembrance, and ye will place them as a testimony before the angels, that they may lay the sins of the sinners before the Most High as a remembrance. 4. In those days the nations will be disturbed, and the generations of the nations will arise on the day of destruction. 5. And in those days the fruit of the womb will miscarry, and they will mangle their own children; and they will cast their children from them, and miscarriages will pass from them; they will cast sucklings from them, and will not return to them, and will not pity their beloved. 6. Again I swear to you sinners, that sin has been prepared for a day of blood which does not end. 7. And they will worship stones; and others will make images of gold and of silver and of wood and of clay, and others will worship unclean spirits and demons and all kinds of idols, even in the idol temples; but no help will be found in them. 8. And they will become impious in the foolishness of their hearts, and their eyes will be blinded through fear in their hearts and through a vision of their dreams. 9. Through them they will be impious and will fear, because they do all their deeds in untruth, and worship stones; but they will be destroyed in an instant. 10. But in those days blessed are all they who receive the words of wisdom and know them, and do the paths of the Most High, and walk in the path of justice, and do not act impiously with those who act impiously; for they will be saved. 11. Woe to you who spread evil among your neighbors, for ye will be killed in hell. 12. Woe to you who make a foundation for sin and deception, and who cause bitterness on the earth, for thereby they will reach an end. 13. Woe to you who build your houses by the labor of another, and whose building material is nothing but the bricks and stones of sin. I tell you ye will have no peace. 14. Woe to those who cast away the measure and the inheritance of their fathers, which is forever, and cause their souls to follow after idols; no rest will be to them. 15. Woe to those who practise injustice and aid oppression, and kill their neighbors, to the day of the great judgment! 16. For he will cast down your glory, and put the wickedness to your hearts, and will raise the spirit of his anger, and will destroy you all with the sword; and all the the just and holy will remember your sins.

CHAP. 100. — And in those days the fathers will be slain in one place with their sons, and brothers with the others will fall in death, till it flows like a stream from their blood. 2. For a man will not in mercy draw his hand from his sons, and from his sons' sons, to kill them; and the sinner will not draw his hand from his honored brother; from the dawn to the setting sun they will kill each other. 3. And a horse will walk up to his breast in the blood of the sinners, and a wagon will sink in to its height. 4. And in those days the angels will come into the secret places, and will collect in one place all those who aided sin; and the Most High will arise on that day to pass a great judgment over all the sinners. 5. But over all the just and holy he will place holy angels as watchmen to watch them like the apple of an eye, till an end has been made to evil and to all sin; and even if the holy sleep a long sleep there is nothing to fear. 6. And the wise among men will see the truth, and the children of the earth will understand all the words of this book, and know that their riches will not be able to save them in the overthrow of their sins. 7. Woe to you sinners, if ye trouble the just, on the day of great pain, and burn them with fire; ye will be repaid according to your work. 8. Woe to the hardened of heart, who watch to contrive wickedness: fear will be about to come over you, and there will be none to save you. 9. Woe to you sinners, for on account of the words of your mouth, and on account of the deeds of your hands, which ye have done, ye who act impiously will burn in a pool of flaming fire. 10. And now know that the angels will seek out your deeds in heaven from the sun and the moon and the stars in reference to your sins, because ye pass judgment on the earth on the just. 11. And he will call to testify over you each cloud and fog and dew and rain, for they all will be kept back from you that they do not descend upon you; and shall they not think of your sins? 12. And now give presents to the rain that it may not be kept back from descending upon you, or the dew when it has received gold or silver from you. 13. When hoar-frost and snow and their coldness descend upon you, and all the winds of the snow and all their plagues, in those days ye will not be able to stand before them.

CHAP. 101. — Notice the heavens, all ye children of heaven, and all the doings of the Most High, and have fear of him, and do no evil before him. 2. When he locks the windows of heaven, and prevents the rain and the dew from descending upon the earth on your account, what will ye do then? 3. And when he sends his anger over you and over all your deeds, ye cannot petition him, because ye have spoken concerning his justice proudly and boldly, and ye shall have no peace. 4. And do ye not see the kings of the ships, how their ships are chased about by the waves, and tremble before the winds, and are troubled? 5. And therefore they fear, because all their good treasures go into the sea with them, and they are troubled in their hearts that the sea might swallow them and they perish in it. 6. Is not all the sea and all its waters and all its movements a work of the Most High, and has he not sealed all its doings, and bound it all in the sand? 7. It dries up at his threats, and is afraid, and all its fish die, and all that is in it; and ye sinners who are on the earth do not fear him. 8. Has he not made heaven and earth, and all that is in them? And who has given understanding and wisdom to all who move on the earth, and to those on the sea? 9. Do not the kings of the ships fear the sea? but the sinners do not fear the Most High.

CHAP. 102.—And in those days when he brings a painful fire upon you, whither will ye flee, and where will ye save yourselves? and when he brings his word upon you, will ye then not be aghast and fear? 2. And all the luminaries will tremble in great fear, and all the earth will be aghast, and will tremble and quake. 3. And all the angels will fulfil their commands, and will desire to hide themselves from before him, great in glory, and the children of the earth will tremble and shake; and ye, sinners, are cursed to eternity, and will have no peace. 4. Fear not, ye souls of the just, and hope for the day of your death in justice. 5. And be not sorrowful that your souls descend into Sheol, in great trouble and lamentation and sorrow, and in grief, and that your bodies have not found it in your life as your goodness deserved, but rather on a day on which ye were like the sinners, and on the day of the curse and the punishment. 6. And when ye die the sinners speak over you: "As we die the just die, and what benefit have they in their deeds? 7. Behold, as we, they have died in anxiety and in darkness, and what advantage have they over us? from now on we are equal. 8. And what will they receive, and what will they see to eternity? For behold they too have died, and from now on to eternity they do not see the light." 9. I tell you sinners: it is sufficient for you to eat and to drink and to make a man naked, and to rob and to sin, and to acquire wealth, and to see good days. 10. Have ye seen the just, how their end was peace, because no oppression was found in them to the day of their death? 11. "And they were destroyed, and became as if they had not been, and the souls descended into Sheol in trouble."

CHAP. 103. — And now I swear to you the just, by his great glory and his honor, and by his glorious kingdom and by his greatness I swear to you: 2. I know this mystery, and have read it in the tablets of heaven, and have seen the book of the holy ones, and have found written in it and inscribed on their account, 3. that all goodness and joy and honor are prepared for them, and are written down for the spirits of those who have died in justice, and that much good is given to you as a reward for your labor, and that your portion is better than the portion of the living. 4. And your souls will live, ye who have died in justice, and your spirits will rejoice and be glad, and their remembrance will be before the face of the Great One to all the generations of eternity. And now do not fear their shame. 5. Woe to you, sinners, if ye die in your sins, and those who are like you say concerning you: "Blessed are they, the sinners, they have seen all their days; 6. and now they have died in good fortune and in wealth, and have not seen trouble or murder in their life; in glory they have died, and judgment has not been passed over them in their life." 7. Do ye know that their souls will be caused to descend into Sheol, and it will be ill with them, and their trouble great? 8. And in darkness and in toils and in a burning flame their spirits will burn at the great judgment; and a great judgment will be for all generations to eternity. Woe to you, for ye will have no peace! 9. Say not to the just and good who are in life: " In the days of our need we have endured labor, and have seen all need, and have met much evil, and have been injured and diminished, and our spirit has become small. 10. We have been destroyed, and there was none to help us; with word and deed we were incapable, and attained to nothing whatever; we were tortured and destroyed, and did not hope to see life, day by day. 11. We hoped to be the head, and were the tail; we labored exceedingly, and did not gain by our labor; we became food for sinners, and the unjust laid their yoke heavily upon us. 12. Those who hated and those who beat us became our rulers; and we bent our neck to our haters, and they did not pity us. 13. And we desired to go from them in order to flee and to rest, but we did not find whither to flee and to save ourselves from them. 14. We complained to the rulers in our trouble and in our pain over those who devoured us; but they did not attend to our cry, and did not wish to hear our voice. 15. And they helped those who robbed and devoured us, and those who diminished us, and they made secret their oppression, so that they did not remove their yoke from us, but devoured us and scattered us and murdered us; and they kept secret our murder, and did not think of it that they had lifted up their hands against us."

CHAP. 104. — I swear to you, just ones, that in heaven the angels will have a remembrance concerning you for good before the glory of the Great One. Your names will be written before the glory of the Great One. 2. Hope, for at first ye were disgraced in evil and need, but now ye will shine like the luminaries of heaven, and will be seen, and the portals of heaven will be opened to you. 3. And continue your cry for a judgment; it will appear to you, for all your trouble will be avenged on the rulers, and on all those who help those who oppressed you. 4. Hope, and do not cease your hope, for ye will have great joy, like the angels in heaven. 5. Since such will be yours, ye will not hide on the day of the great judgment, and ye will not be found as sinners, and the everlasting judgment will be *far* from you for all the generations of the world. 6. And now, fear not, ye just, when ye see the sinners strengthening and rejoicing in their desires, and be not associates with them, but keep far from their oppression, for ye shall be companions of the hosts of heaven. 7. Ye sinners, although ye say: "Ye cannot search it out, and all our sins are not written down"; still they will continually write down your sins every day. 8. And now I show it to you, that light and darkness, day and night, see all your sins. 9. Be not impious in your hearts, and do not lie, and do not change the words of rectitude, and do not call a lie the words of the Holy and Great One, and do not glorify your idols; for all your untruths and all your impiety will not be to you for a justification, but for a great sin. 10. And now, I know this mystery that the words of rectitude will be changed, and many sinners will rebel, and will speak wicked words, and will lie and make great works, and write books concerning their words. 11. But when they write all my words in rectitude in their languages, and do not change or abridge anything of my words, but write all in rectitude, all that I have first testified on their account, 12. then I know another mystery, that books will be given to the just and to the wise for joy and for rectitude and for much wisdom. 13. And the books will be given to them, and they will believe in them and will rejoice in them; and then all the just, who have learned all the paths of rectitude out of them, will be rewarded.

CHAP. 105. — "And in those days," says the Lord, "they will call and testify over the sons of the earth concerning their wisdom: show it to them, for ye are their leaders, and the rewards over all the earth. 2. For I

and my son will join with them to eternity in the paths
of rectitude in their lives. And peace will be to you;
rejoice, ye children of rectitude, in truth!"

CHAP. 92. With this the practical part proper begins, and
goes to chap. 105. The revelations Enoch had received and
had promulgated were not without a purpose, but were intended for the instruction of mankind. He therefore applies
what he has taught, admonishes, warns, upbraids, and instructs
his contemporaries as to the way they should go. Of this
parenetic part proper chap. 92 is the special introduction,
which has some similarity with the introductions to the three
Parables, chap. 38, 45, and 58. *Scribe*, cf. 12 : 4. *Doctrine
of wisdom*, 37 : 1, in contradistinction from visions of wisdom.
It is his object here to *teach* practical wisdom, hence the stress
lies on *doctrine.* — 2. The days of sin shall pass away, the day
of judgment will come, the העולם הזה will give way to the
העולם הבא; therefore the faithful should remain firm, and be
in joyful hope. — 3. *Just one*, collectively used, like 91 : 10,
and cf. notes. — 4. *He*, i.e. God. *Power*, cf. 90 : 19, 30; 96 :
1; 98 : 12. *Light*, cf. note on 38 : 2. — 5. Cf. 10 : 16, 20;
41 : 2; 69 : 29; 91 : 11, etc.

CHAP. 93. But before proceeding to his admonitions the
author gives a brief survey of the development of the world's
history in ten world-weeks, each consisting of seven parts. We
have then again the mysterious number seventy. Of these ten
weeks seven belong to history, and three to the future. *Out
of the books;* Enoch, the scribe, writes down his revelations,
and reads them to his children; probably the books written
during his tour by himself or the angel; cf. 33 : 3, 4; 74 : 2;
81 : 1 sqq. (Parables 40 : 8). — 2. The sources of his knowledge, as written in these books, were visions, angels, and tablets
of heaven, 81 : 1; cf. 103 : 2 (106 : 19; 107 : 1; 108 : 7).
Plant, cf. 10 : 16. — 3. The first week goes from the creation
to Enoch's time. *Seventh*, not like Jude 14, but with Dill-

mann and Ewald, in the seventh part of the first week, counting seven generations for this week. *Retarded*, i.e. the period
closed before the deluge. — 4. The second week goes to the
deluge and the covenant with Noah, Gen. viii. 21–ix. 17. — 5.
The third week ends with the call to Abraham. *Plant of the
judgment of justice*, i.e. the people among whom God will hold
his judgment. — 6. The fourth week ends with the giving of
the law on Mount Sinai. *Visions*, etc., i.e. revelations will be
made to the holy and just, referring κατ' ἐξοχήν to the revelation of the Torah. *Court*, scarcely Palestine, 89 : 2, because
the giving of the law was already *in the end thereof*, but rather
a central place of worship, the tabernacle, 89 : 34, 35. — 7.
The fifth week ends with the building of Solomon's temple.
Supremacy, referring to the temple ; cf. next verse ; i.e. of religious supremacy, as the temple is the house of the Great King,
91 : 13. *To eternity*, for in the Messianic times it shall be re-
built. — 8. The sixth week ends with the burning of the temple and the Captivity. It is the period of religious degenera-
tion, 89 : 51 sqq. *A man shall ascend*, i.e. Elijah ; cf. 89 : 52.
Forgetting true wisdom is synonymous with departure from
God. — 9. The seventh is the week in which the author lived,
and hence he characterizes it more minutely ; it is a rebellious
age, i.e. rebellious not politically, but against God and his laws ;
cf. 89 : 73–75. — 10. As according to the whole spirit and letter of the book the condition of the just shall not be ameliorated
until *after* the judgment and the condemnation of the sinners,
the reward here spoken of, and the seven portions of learning
must refer to something given them during the Messianic reign.
It is in all probability the much-lauded wisdom that is to form
one of the blessings of this reign, e.g. 91 : 10 ; 92 : 1, and often.
To see in vs. 11–14 an epexegesis of this verse, so that the
sevenfold learning consists in the instruction on the physical
world (Dillmann), or that this learning should refer to the book
of Enoch itself, is certainly a mistake. Even if our author is
not overburdened with modesty, he would scarcely dare to put

a sevenfold higher estimate on his instructions than on the biblical. Besides, the author has been treating the history of his people solely and alone from a purely *religious* stand-point, and now to sum up all wisdom and warning in the strange, and by no means genial statements of the next verses is not only an improbability, but an impossibility. If these words are from the author of the previous parts, they certainly do not belong here; but it is more probable that they are the product of some imaginative interpolator. The attempts made to determine from the known lengths of the first six weeks the unknown length of the seventh, either by counting the years, or by reckoning, after the biblical manner, by generations have all proved mere guesswork, and have only the merit of ingenious and interesting hypotheses. — 11. *Voice of the Holy One,* i.e. thunder; cf. Job xxxvii. 4, 5; Ps. xxix.; xlvi. 7; lxxvii. 17, 18. The incomprehensibility of God's thoughts, Job xxxviii. 33; Ps. xl. 5; xcii. 5, 6. — 12. Cf. Isa. xl. 13; Prov. xxx. 4; Eccles. xi. 5. *Ascend,* Job xxxviii. 22; Prov. xxx. 4. *Their ends,* probably ends of heaven so frequently spoken of above. — 13. Job xxxviii. 5, 18. — 14. *Heaven,* Job xi. 8; Isa. xl. 12; Jer. xxxi. 37. *Established,* 18:2, 3 (69:16). Now follow the other weeks in 91:12–17. The eighth week, the first one of the Messianic period, is that of justice, the time of the sword, 90: 19 (cf. vs. 34); 91:11. *Into the hands of the just,* 38:5; 92: 4; 95:7; 96:1; 98:12. The end of this period will be marked by the rebuilding of Jerusalem and of the temple; cf. in general Ex. i. 21; 2 Sam. vii. 11; Isa. lx. 21, 22; lxv. 20– 23. *Great King,* 84:5. — 14. The ninth week is the week of the judgment, however not of the final one. Dillmann explains it from 50:2–5; 90:30, 33, 35, as referring to the time when the true religion will proceed from Jerusalem to the so far neutral heathen nations to teach them to acknowledge the true God, and this certainly best harmonizes with the last clause. *Will depart,* 10:16, 20, 21; 92:5; cf. Ps. cii. 26, sq.; Isa. lxv. 17; lxvi. 22. — 15. The tenth week ends with the final judgment. *Watchmen,* of course the fallen angels. Even with this difference that the judgment over these watchmen is elsewhere placed in the beginning of the Messianic times, 90 : 21 sqq., 10 : 12 ; and 16 : 1, the lengthy exposition of the future times occasions a doubt as to the authenticity of these verses. That they are an interpolation is almost a certainty, from the fact that the future here is pictured without any mention of the Messiah whatever being made ; cf. Introd. — 16. *Powers,* 82 : 8. *Sevenfold,* Isa. xxx. 26 ; lx. 19, 20 ; Zech. xiv. 6, 7. — 17. *Mentioned,* Isa. lxv. 17

CHAP. 94. The parenetic part proper, commencing here, continues to chap. 105, the end of the original book. This verse has much similarity with 91 : 3. Enoch's exhortations are intended principally for the faithful. *Cease,* cf. Ps. i. 6. The suddenness of the sinner's destruction is noted also in vs. 6 and 96 : 1 and 97 : 10. — 2. It will easily be possible for his children to discover these paths of justice, for they will be revealed through Moses and the prophets. *Paths of death,* Prov. xiv. 12 (xvi. 25) ; Jer. xxi. 8. — 3. Having revealed the source of this justice, he reiterates his exhortation. *Approach,* 91 : 4 ; 104 : 6. — 4. *Pleasing,* i.e. in the sight of God. *Paths of peace,* as the opposite of the *paths of death.* — 5. This warning is of special importance, because in future times this justice, as taught by the sages of the Old Testament, will be changed and transformed and opposed by a false wisdom. With these words the true author gives us a view of his times when the lovers of Hellenistic language, ideas, and manners had become so numerous among the Israelites. Against these innovations he warns, and lauds the justice taught by the prophets. *Will not find,* 42 : 1 sqq. — 6. Cf. Isa. v. 8, 11, 18, 20, 22. But those who have already made " wisdom wicked " will be punished. *Build,* 91 : 5, to designate their intention of making these innovations permanent. — 7. *In sin,* Jer. xxii. 13. *Rooted out,* as the last clause shows, refers to men, vs. 10, not to houses. Not so much the acquisition of wealth, as the relying on wealth, is, as many other passages show, the cause of this " Woe." — 8. Ps. lii. 7; xlix. 6; Prov. xi. 28; Jer. ix. 22; and En. 46: 7; 63 : 10; 96 : 4–6; 97 : 7–9. — 9. As a consequence of their relying on wealth, they have reviled God and done injustice, and shall be destroyed in the manner described vs. 7. — 10. *From the foundation.* vs. 7. God will rejoice over this destruction, 89 : 58; 97 : 2, is unbiblical; cf. Ezek. xviii. 23, 32, 33; xxxiii. 11, although the different kinds of destruction here mentioned are all found in the Old Testament. — 11. *Your*, referring to his children.

CHAP. 95. Lamentation over the sufferings of the just. The address is to the wicked. Imitation of Jer. 9 : 1. — 3. Address to the just. In the Messianic times *ye* will have the power, explanation of 94 : 6 and 10; cf. notes on 91 : 12. — 4. The author evidently refers to those of his times who made a practice of magic and incantation. They shall not be healed, i.e. delivered from their punishment. — 6. *Weigh out*, as judges or witnesses. — 7. Ye who have pursued the just will experience the same fate at their hands; cf. note on vs. 3.

CHAP. 96. *Hope*. even although ye are persecuted, for a change in the Messianic times is sure to come. *Power will be to you*; cf. 91 : 12; and especially 92 : 4. — 2. In *the day of the trouble* that comes over the sinners this change will take place. *Like eagles*, Isa. xl. 31. *Higher than hawks*, Jer. xlix. 16. *Recesses and clefts*, cf. on the idea Isa. ii. 10, 19, 22; Judg. vi. 2; 1 Sam. xiii. 6; xiv. 11. He here shows the wonderful protection which the just shall enjoy on that terrible day. But different will be the fate of the sinners; they shall cry like satyrs; cf. LXX of Isa. xiii. 21. — 3. *Healing*, cf. 95 : 4. *Light*, cf. note on 38 : 2. — 4. *Riches make you appear;* in the Old Testament God promises the goods of this world to the faithful, hence those wealthy sinners used this retribution doctrine as a proof of their membership among the faithful. If they were not such, how could God give them wealth? This they claim, although in their hearts they know their true condition. *This word* (cf. 97 : 4), i.e. the words "that ye are sinners." *Remembrance*, cf. vs. 7. — 5. *Marrow of the wheat*, Deut. xxxii. 14 ; Ps. lxxxi. 16 ; cxlvii. 14. *Power of the root*, i.e. the best water. — 6. *Water* is here used as opposite of *fountain of life*, and symbolizes the abundance of the good things of this world. The wealthy have always sought them and cared for them alone, but have neglected to drink from the fountain of life ; cf. Ps. xxxvi. 9 ; Isa. ii. 13 ; xvii. 13. — 7. Cf. 91 : 7, 8 ; 94 : 6, 9. *Remembrance*, cf. vs. 4.

CHAP. 97. *Believe*, i.e. in the sure fulfilment of these promises. *On the day of injustice*, i.e. on the day when injustice will be avenged, the same as *the day of trouble*, 96 : 2. — 2. Address to the sinners. Above, 94 : 10, God rejoices over this destruction, here the angels, different from Luke xv. 10. — 3. Cf. 38 : 1 sqq. ; 102 : 1. *Prayer of the just*, vs. 5. — 4. *Those*, i.e. the just, for the simple words " Ye have been," etc. will be enough to condemn you ; cf. 96 : 4. — 5. *Reach*, i.e. will be heard ; cf. 47 : 1–4 ; 99 : 3, 16 ; 104 : 3. — 6. *Recited*, i.e. out of the books in which they are recorded ; cf. 81 : 4 ; 90 : 20 ; 98 : 7, 8 ; 104 : 7. *Great and Holy One*, cf. note on 1 : 3. *Shame*, 46 : 6 ; 62 : 10 ; 63 : 11. — 7. *Ocean and land*, i.e. everywhere. *Remembrance*, cf. 100 : 10, 11 ; 104 : 8. — 8. Cf. 94 : 7, 8 ; Sir. xi. 19 ; Luke xii. 19, and, in general, Isa. v. 8, 9 ; Micah ii. 2. — 9. *Workmen*, i.e. servants. — 10. The sinners had boasted, vs. 9, that they had treasures as abundant as water. " Yes," says the author, " like water your words will prove false, and like water your wealth will evaporate " ; cf. the figure in Isa. viii. 6 sqq.

CHAP. 98. *Swear you*, for the first time here, but frequently used in the following. — 2. Addressing the foolish. *Men*, i.e. although being men. *They will float*, i.e. men ; change from second to third person ; cf. note on 1 : 2. — 3. *In murder*, i.e. they will die the everlasting death ; cf. note on 22 : 12, 13. *Poverty*, as the opposite of their wealth in this world. *Fiery oven*, i.e. hell, same as fiery pool, 10 : 6, etc., or fiery abyss,

10 : 13, etc.   The use of the word *spirit* in this connection, 103 : 8 ; 108 : 3, does not presuppose that they had no bodies, but rather that they had such. — 4. Sin is man's work, hence he is the author of his own destruction.   *Hill*, i.e. גִּבְעָה a *feminine* noun, therefore *maid* is used.   As certain as these things cannot occur, so sure is it also that sin has not originated in God. — 5. As a consequence of this sinfulness evils have come on the earth ; they are punishments for this sin.   *Barrenness* is simply a type of evils in general ; cf. Gen. xx. 18 ; xxix. 31 ; Hos. ix. 14. — 6. These sins too are known in heaven ; cf. 97 : 6.   It will not do to deny stoically that God takes no account of the doings in this world, Job xxii. 13, 14 ; Ps. lxxiii. 11 ; xciv. 4–7, but they all lie open before him ; cf. also 100 : 10 ; 104 : 7, 8. — 7. They need not deny their knowledge of this fact, because it has been revealed by God. — 8. *From now*, i.e. since ye have heard my words. — 9. Therefore, woe to those fools, vs. 1, who in spite of this knowledge still deny. *Fools*, in the sense of Ps. xiv. 1 and liii. 1. — 10. *Prepared*, 94 : 9.   They cannot hope like the just, 96 : 1.   *Die*, as the opposite of live, implies not only eternal death, but also the loss of eternal life ; cf. vs. 3.   *No ransom*, Ps. xlix. 7, 8 ; Matt. xvi. 26.   *Great judgment*, 19 : 1 ; 22 : 4 ; 25 : 4 ; 94 : 9 ; 99 : 15 ; 100 : 4 ; 103 : 8, a name not found in the Parables. — 11. *Devour blood*, a heinous offence against the Mosaic law ; cf. Book of the Jubilees, chap. vii.   In addition to having all the good things of this world the renegades in Israel even sinned against the Levitical ordinances. — 12. They do these deeds because they *love* them, not because they are forced to them by persecution.   *Into the hands*, cf. 95 : 3, 7. — 13. Cf. Isa. xiv. 19, 20 ; Jer. viii. 2 ; xxii. 19. — 14. *In vain*, declare vain by word and deed the admonitions of the just.   *Hope*, 96 : 1. — 15. But more, they even write books, 104 : 10, inculcating their false wisdom, and opposing the true wisdom of the prophets, and of such as the author of Enoch ; cf. Isa. x. 1. *Sudden*, 94 : 1, 6, 7 ; 95 : 6 ; 96 : 1, 6.

CHAP. 99. Woe to those also who applaud these wicked writings; cf. especially 98 : 15; also 94 : 5; 104 : 10; 108 : 5. — 2. *Law of eternity*, or eternal law, i.e. the Mosaic law; while *words of rectitude*, mean the Old Testament revelation in general. They being members of the chosen people of God originally, go into the sphere of the sinners, i.e. of the heathens, to which they do not belong. — 3 Cf. 97 : 5. Angels assist in prayer, 9 : 2; 15 : 2; 104 : 1; cf. Tob. xii. 12. And also in the punishment of the wicked, 1 : 9; 10 : 4 sqq.; 90 : 21; 100 : 4. — 4. In nearly all apocryphal works these disturbances are signs of the last times; cf. Drummond, pp. 209–221. The author here evidently confines himself to the period of the sword, 90 : 19; 91 : 8–11, 12. — 5. Even the family ties, so firm among the Israelites, will be horribly broken. — 6, 7. A successful picture of the vain attempts of the sinners to secure aid. *Demons*, 19 : 1; Sibyl. *Prooem.* i. 20 sqq. Tertullian quotes: "Et rursus juro, peccatores, quod in diem sanguinis perditionis justitia parata est. Qui servitis lapidibus, et qui imagines facitis aureas et argenteas et ligneas et lapideas et fictiles, et servitis phantasmatibus et daemoniis et spiritibus infamibus, et omnibus erroribus non secundum scientiam, nullum ab iis invenietis auxilium." — 8. This evil condition will only increase; cf. Wisd. xiv. 12, 27; Rom. i. 21. *Will become impious*, literally will become forgetful or ignorant, i.e. of God's laws, and hence impious; cf. 93 : 8. — 9. *In an instant*, cf. 94 : 1. — 10. But entirely different will be the condition of those who receive the true words of wisdom. They are the wise, 98 : 1. — 11. *Killed*, 22 : 13. *Hell*, the original has *Sheol*, but here he evidently refers to the place of *everlasting* torture, and not to the temporary abode of the wicked dead; cf. also 63 : 10. — 12. *Make a foundation*, cf. 94 : 6. — 13. Cf. 94 : 7; 97 : 8. — 14. *Measure and inheritance of the fathers*, i.e. the old faith and fidelity; cf. e.g. Jer. xiii. 25; 1 Macc. i. 52. — 15. *To the day*, etc. modifies directly the *Woe to those*. *Great judgment*, 16 : 1; 19 : 1; 91 : 7; 94 : 9; 98 : 10.

CHAP. 100. The author expands on the idea of 99 : 6. *Stream of blood*, cf. Isa. xxxiv. 3, 7 ; Ps. lxxix. 3 (Ps. lviii. 10 ; Zeph. i. 17). — 2. On this internecine slaughter, cf. 56 : 7 ; 99 : 5 ; Judg. vii. 22 ; 1 Sam. xiv. 20 ; 2 Chron. xx. 23 ; Zech. xiv. 13 ; Ezek. xxxviii. 21 ; Hag. ii. 22. — 4. All those sinners who escape this slaughter will be searched out by the angels, and will, at least, not be able to escape the final judgment. It may, however, be understood that only the real open sinners shall be slain in the period of blood ; while those that abetted them, escaping, indeed, this punishment, as their crime was not so great, shall, however, be punished at the last day. The distinction between sinners and those that aided and applauded them is observed throughout this adhortative part. — 5. But the just will be protected by these angels that punish the wicked. *Apple of an eye*, cf. Deut. xxxii. 10 ; Ps. xvii. 8. Even if the just do sleep the sleep of death, there need be no fear, for they will rise again ; cf. note on 22 : 12, 13. — 6. In view of this, those who are still capable of learning wisdom (Hos. xiv. 10) will accept the warning given by the book of Enoch. *Riches will not save*, Zeph. i. 18. *Fall*, having the picture of a building in his mind, 94 : 6 ; 99 : 12. — 7. *On the day*, modifies directly *Woe to you* ; cf. 99 : 15. *Trouble*, i.e. persecute on account of their fidelity. *Burn* ; it is known that under Antiochus Epiphanes this took place ; cf. 2 Macc. vi. 18–vii. 24. The story there recorded is, however, considered unhistorical by many critics. — 8. *Watch*, cf. Isa. xxix. 20. — 9. The great crime of the sinners consists in the persecution of the just and in reviling God. These two crimes are almost constantly named together, 5 : 4 ; 81 : 8 ; 91 : 7, 11 ; 94 : 9 ; 96 : 7 ; 97 : 6 ; 98 : 10 ; 99 : 1. — 10. The author's epexegesis on 98 : 6-8 ; cf. 97 : 7 ; 104 : 8. — 11. All nature will testify against you, because they have witnessed your deeds, and will be kept back on your account ; cf. 80 : 2 sqq. ; Jer. iii. 3, 5, 24, 25. Shall not those who could not perform their functions on your account remember you ? — 12. Ironically ; use **your** wealth that these powers of nature may be appeased, and they again descend. — 13. Even the smaller punishments of the elements ye cannot avoid or hinder, how much less the great final punishment!

Chap. 101. Connects closely with the preceding. The perception of these phenomena of nature should produce fear of God, and, in consequence, avoidance of evil. *Children of heaven*, i.e. the faithful, for it would be fruitless to ask the sinners to do so. They are called so, because they do not, like the sinners, concentrate their faith and hope on the things of the earth, but await the blessings of the Messianic kindom from heaven. — 2, 3. Especially should they fear because these powers are means of punishment in the hands of God. The address changes into one to the sinners. *Proudly and boldly*, 5 : 4; 27 : 2, etc.; and examples 98 : 4–8; 102 : 6. — 4. Not to fear in view of these things is entirely unnatural, as is exemplified in various ways, e.g. by the merchant on the sea. References to navigation are found Sir. xxxiii. 2; xliii. 24; Sap. v. 10; xiv. 1 sqq. *Kings*; Dillmann says *owners of the ships*, but better *pilots*, as those that govern the vessel's course. — 5. Even these, although they know how to manage a vessel, fear on account of the treasures entrusted to them, and for their own lives. — 6. But all this is *God's* doings, his whom the sinners despise. *Sealed*, i.e. given it firm laws. — 7. This powerful sea, which ye fear, and is more powerful than ye are, must nevertheless obey and fear God. How much more should ye do so! Cf. on the whole picture Jer. v. 22, 23 (Job xxxviii. 8–11; Ps. lxxxix. 9; civ. 9; Prov. viii. 29); Isa. l. 2 (Nah. i. 4; Ps. cvi. 9). —8. Yes, God has made not only this ocean, but all the heavens and the earth — an ascending climax. He, too, has given more, instinct to animals and reason to man. — 9. The conclusion; cf. on the sentiment the Sibyl. *Prooem.* i. 25 sqq.

Chap. 102. The result of such hard-heartedness and unbelief is destruction by the fire of hell, 99 : 11. *Word*, i.e. sentence of judgment. — 2. The effect of this terrible judgment on the luminaries. — 3. The angels, though they carry out this judgment, 100 : 4, 5, nevertheless, would desire to flee, as it is so terrible. This is involuntary pity, as is shown by Michael, above. *Great in glory*, 14 : 20. — 4. Now his words are almost exclusively addressed to the just. *Hope*, 96 : 1. The day of death is not to be terrible for the just, but is an entrance to a better life, 103 : 3, 4. — 5. The persecutions, indeed, they must bear. He is to wrestle with a problem that had probably often occasioned doubt in the minds of the faithful, Why is it that the just suffer, and suffer even to the end of their lives? How was this to be reconciled with the doctrine of retribution taught in the Old Testament? The end of this verse must be somewhat corrupted. — 6. They must even endure the haughty ridicule of the sinners, that their faithfulness had been in vain ; cf. Sap. ii. 1–5 ; iii. 2–4 ; v. 3, 4 ; Eccl. ii. 14–16 ; iii. 19–21 ; ix. 3–6 ; x. — 7. *In anxiety and darkness*, from the well-known idea of Sheol entertained by the Jews ; cf. notes on chap. 22. — 8. Cf. Ps. xlix. 19. — 9. Answer to these arguments by the author. Sinners are satisfied with what this earth affords, but never look to the time of death, or to that beyond the grave ; therefore, *they* can speak in this manner. — 10. Otherwise, the just who have thought of the future. Their death proves already a difference between them and the unjust. *They* die in peace with a clear conscience, but how different it is with the sinners, for whom death is only the door to future punishment! cf. Wisd. iii. 3, 4, 7 and Isa. lvii. 2. — 11. An objection raised by the author himself, but in reality from the opinions of the exulting sinners. The objection is not that death is annihilation (cf. Job iii. 16 ; Sap. ii. 2), but only that there is no retribution after death.

CHAP. 103. Answer of the author to this self-raised objection. Being about to convey a most momentous fact, his oath is more emphatic than 98 : 1, 4, 6 ; 99 : 6 ; 104 : 1. — 2. He does not lie in this matter, for he has his information from the best of sources, from the tablets of heaven and the book of the holy ones; cf. notes on 81 : 1. *Holy ones,* i.e. holy men, as the last clause shows. Not only the records of the past, but the events of the future are recorded on these tablets; cf. 106 : 19; also, *Test. Levi,* v.; Book of the Jubilees, chap. 24. He is probably opposing the germs that were developed by the Sadducees in their doctrine of the death of the soul with the body; cf. Joseph. *Antiqq.* xviii. 1, 4; *Bel. Jud.* ii. 8, 14; Lightfoot, *Hor. Heb. et Talm.* on Matt. xxii. 23 sqq. Cf. on the expression 108 : 3 and Ps. lxix. 28. — 3, 4. These persecuted just shall be rewarded after death, is the important fact he wishes to inculcate. Of course he means, not an immediate happiness after death, for the just, too, are in Sheol, chap. 22., but the blessings in store for them in the Messianic kingdom. For these just shall rise (cf. note on 22 : 13, 14), and partake of the glories of this reign, 91 : 10; 92 : 3; 100 : 5; 104 : 4, 6; compared with 39 : 1, 4–6. The change of persons is no surprise, as it is frequently found in this part. *Do not fear their shame,* i.e. their ridicule, 94 : 11. — 5, 6. A different fate awaits the sinners, recurring to the idea of 102 : 4. They are, indeed, blessed in their death by those like them and those that disregard the future, because they have enjoyed the benefits of the earth and were not punished during life. — 7. For these there is an especial apartment in Sheol, 22 : 10. — 8. And after that, in the final punishment, they will be given over to an everlasting fire, strictly as represented in 22 : 11. *No peace,* Isa. xlviii. 22; lvii. 21; En. 5 : 4; 94 : 6; 98 : 11, 15; 99 : 13; 102 : 3. — 9. Words spoken by the dead just, as is conclusively shown by the context, to the living just. *Spirits become small,* i.e. were humble. — 10. Cf. Deut. xxviii. 29. — 11. Cf. Deut. xxviii. 13, 30, 31, 44. — 12. Instead of possessing the land, as the Old Testament predictions promised, they became the subjects of their haters. — 14. Cf. chap. 89 and 90. With these rulers they did not find justice, even when they complained. — 15. These rulers even assisted in the persecution, and, instead of bringing it to light, they even kept it secret.

CHAP. 104. Answer to these complaints, which are without foundation. Even if there is no deliverance on earth, they are remembered before God's throne by the angels, 40:5–7; 47:2; 89:76. — 2. Therefore, even in spite of such persecutions, they shall hope, 96:1. *Shine like*, etc., 43:4; Dan. xii. 3, and therefore *will be seen. Portals of heaven will be opened*, not in the sense of entering heaven, but only that from heaven the blessings ye failed to receive on earth will more than abundantly be given to you. — 3. *Continue* the cry uttered, 103:14, 15; cf., also, 97:3, 5; 99:3, 16. — 4. Your hope shall not come to shame, for ye will be even like the angels, explained in verse 6 as being *companions* of the angels. The Parables teach the same; cf. chap. 39. — 5. Therefore, being certain of a happy future, it is unnecessary to hide on the day of judgment, as the sinners try to do, 100:4. — 6. Avoid the association even of the sinners, 94:1–3; 91:3, 4. — 7. *Ye cannot*, etc., i.e. the just cannot fathom the mysteries of the future, for the sins are *not* written down. *They will write*, i.e. the angels, 97:6. — 8. Cf. 97:7; 100:10. — 9. All the false statements of the sinners are based upon falsifying the words of truth as they have been revealed in the Old Testament; cf. 94:59; 98:14–99:2. *Idols*, 99:7–9, 14. — 10. Their statements being nothing but lies, it is necessary to reiterate the truth. This is the object the author had in writing his work; cf., also, Dan. viii. 26; xii. 4, 9, 10. *Books*, 98:15. — 11. We must remember here that the author pretends to write from the time of Enoch, hence his books had to be copied and re-copied for preservation. It was a long period from the time of Enoch to the beginning of the Messianic rule. *In their languages*, presupposing that his work was to be translated, as it was not intended for Israel alone. The idea he probably got from the fact that translations were frequently made in his days. — 12. These other books are probably the different parts of this Book of Enoch. The comfort the just should receive from the Book of Enoch could be called a *mystery*. Both Dillmann and Hoffmann regard this verse as a self-recommendation of Enoch.

CHAP. 105. With the instruction thus gained, the just shall testify over the sons of the earth, and spread this wisdom. — 2. God will be joined with the just, 1 : 8, and in the Parables, 38 : 4, 6 ; and it is also stated that the Messiah will dwell with them (45 : 4, 5), 90 : 37 ; cf. especially 62 : 14. If God can call the chosen his *children*, Deut. xiv. 1, and often, it is not strange that he calls the Messiah his son, and this, therefore, does not indicate a Christian origin, and can easily be understood from an Old Testament basis, Ps. ii. Cf. on the whole chapter what is said in the Introduction, and Ewald, Geschichte des Volkes Israel, Vol. v. p. 94 (Zweite Ausgabe).

SECTION XX.

CHAP. 106. — And after *some* days, my son Methuselah took a wife for his son Lamech, and she became pregnant by him, and gave birth to a son. 2. His body was white as snow and red as the bloom of a rose, and the hair of his head was white as wool, and his eyes beautiful ; and when he opened his eyes, they illuminated the whole house like the sun, and the whole house became exceedingly light. 3. And as he was taken from the hand of the midwife, he opened his mouth, and conversed with the Lord of justice. 4. And his father Lamech was afraid of him, and fled, and came to his father Methuselah. 5. And he said to him : " I have begotten a singular son, unlike a man, but similar to the children of the angels of heaven, and his creation is different, and not like ours, and his eyes are like the feet [i.e. rays] of the sun, his face glorious.   6. And it seems to me he is not from me, but from the angels; and I fear that wonderful things will happen in his days over the earth.   7. And now, my father, I am here petitioning and asking of thee that thou shouldst go to Enoch, our father, and hear of him the truth, for he has his dwelling-place with the angels."   8. And when Methuselah had heard the words of his son, he came to me, at the ends of the earth, for he had heard that I was there, and cried aloud, and I heard his voice and came to him.   And I said to him: " Behold, here I am, my son, because thou hast come to me."   9. And he answered and said to me: " I have come to thee concerning a great thing, and concerning a disturbing vision it is that I have approached.   10. And now, my father, hear me, for there has been born to my son Lamech a son, whose similarity and kind is not like the kind of men; his color is whiter than snow, and redder than the bloom of a rose, and the hair of his head is whiter than white wool, and his eyes like the feet [i.e. rays] of the sun; and he opened his eyes, and they illuminated the whole house.   11. And when he was taken from the hands of the midwife, he opened his mouth, and blessed the Lord of heaven.   12. And his father Lamech was afraid, and fled to me, and did not believe that he was from him, but that his similarity was from the angels of heaven; and behold I have come to thee that thou shouldst teach me justice [i.e. the truth]."   13. And I, Enoch, answered, and said to him: " The Lord will make new things on the earth, and this I know, and have seen in a vision, and I announce it to thee that in the generations of my father Jared some from the heights of heaven departed from the word of the Lord.   14. And behold, they committed sin, and departed from the law, and united themselves with women, and committed sin with them, and married *some* of them, and begat children from them. 15. And great destruction will be over all the earth, and there will be the water of a deluge, and a great destruction will be for one year. 16. This son who is born to thee will be left on the earth, and his three children will be saved with him; when all men who are on the earth shall die, he and his children will be saved. 17. [They beget on earth giants, not according to the spirit, but according to the flesh, and there will be great punishment on the earth, and the earth will be washed of all of its uncleanness.] 18. And now announce to thy son Lamech that he who was born to him is in truth his son, and call his name Noah, for he will be a remnant of you; and he and his children will be saved from the destruction which will come over the earth on account of all the sins and all the injustice which will be completed in his days over the earth. 19. And after that, injustice will exceed that which was first committed on the earth; for I know the mysteries of the holy ones, for he, the Lord, has showed me, and has instructed me, and I have read in the tablets of heaven.

CHAP. 107. — And I saw written upon them that generation upon generation will transgress till a generation of justice arises, and transgression will be destroyed, and sin will disappear from the earth, and all good will come over it. 2. And now, my son, go and announce to thy son Lamech, that this son who is born is really his, and that this is not a falsehood." 3. And when Methuselah had heard the words of his father Enoch — for he had showed him everything that was secret — he returned, after his having seen him, and called the name of that son Noah, for he will make glad the earth for all destruction.

CHAP. 108.—Another book that Enoch wrote for his son Methuselah, and for those who come after him, and keep the law in the last days. 2. Ye who kept it, and now wait in those days till those who did evil are completed, and the power of the transgressors has been completed, 3. wait till sin disappears, for their names will be erased from the books of the holy ones, and their seed will be destroyed to eternity, and their spirits will be killed, and they will cry and lament in a void, empty place, and burn in a fire where there is no end. 4. And there I saw something like a cloud which could not be seen, for from its depths I could not look over it; and I saw a flame of fire burning brightly, and there circled *things* like shining mountains, and they shook to and fro. 5. And I asked one of the holy angels who were with me, and said to him: " What is this shining *thing?* for it is not a heaven, but only the flame of a burning fire, and the voice of shouting and crying and lamenting and of great pain." 6. And he said to me: " This place which thou seest — here are brought the souls of the sinners and of the revilers and of those who do evil and change everything that God speaks through the mouth of the prophets concerning things to take place. 7. For some of these have been written down, and noted above in heaven, that the angels may read and know what will happen to the sinners and to the spirits of the humble who have chastised their bodies, and *for that* receive their reward from God, and of those who are reviled by wicked men ; 8. who loved God, and did not love gold or silver or all the riches of the world, but gave over their bodies to torture ; 9. and who, since they existed, did not long for terrestrial food, but considered themselves a breath that passes away, and lived accordingly, and were often tried by God, and their spirits were found in cleanness to praise his name. 10. All the blessings they received I have marked down in the books; and he has destined for them their wages, because they have been shown as those who loved the everlasting heaven more than their life, and while they were trodden down by wicked men, and heard abuse and reviling from them, praised me." 11. And now I will call to the spirits of the good, from the generation of light, and change those who were born in darkness, who have not been rewarded in their bodies with honor, as was meet for their fidelity. 12. And I will lead out in a shining light those who love my holy name, and will set each one on the throne of honor, of his honor. 13. And they will glitter in times without number, for justice is the judgment of God, for he will give fidelity to the faithful in the dwellings of the paths of rectitude. 14. And they will see how those who were born in darkness will be cast into darkness, while the just will glitter. 15. And the sinners will cry, and see them as they shine; and they will go there where days and times are written for them.

CHAP. 106. The rest of the book is a later addition. This and the following probably belong to the Noachic fragmentist; while chap. 108 is an independent and foreign production; cf. Introd. — 2. *Like wool*, 46 : 2. The two colors are chosen to show the beauty of the child, while the white hair and the power of his eyes exhibit it as a wonder. — 3. *Lord of justice*, 22 : 14; 90 : 40, in this connection very suitable, as this attribute of God was especially shown in Noah's life. — 5. *Children of the angels*, 69 : 4, 5; 71 : 1. — 7. Cf. 65 : 2; 66 : 3. — 13. *New things*, i.e. things that never happened before. *Jared*, cf.

24

note on 6 : 6. — 14. *Law,* i.e. the commands and ordinances given them by God. — 15. Cf. Gen. vii. 11 ; viii. 14. — 17. Is a strange interpolation of the abruptest kind. It could possibly have stood after vs. 14, but Dillmann's conjecture that it is a *gloss* is probably true. — 18. The meaning of the word Noah, from נוח, is different from those given in Gen. v. 29 and En. 107 : 3. Both can, however, be derived from the one Hebrew root, and hence it is no proof that chap. 106 and 107 are from different writers. The interpretation of the name in this verse seems to be accepted, also, in Sir. xliv. 17. — 19. Cf. 93 : 4 ; 91 : 6. *Holy ones,* undoubtedly, the saints, 103 : 2. *Tablets,* cf. 81 : 1.

CHAP. 107. The period from the deluge to the Messianic era. — 3. Cf. 106 : 18.

CHAP. 108. Characterizes itself as a new, foreign addition ; cf. Introd. — 2. The object is to admonish those waiting for the glorious times not to lose their hope. — 3. Cf. Ps. lxix. 28. *Killed,* cf. notes on 22 : 13 ; 98 : 3 ; 99 : 11. — 4. Description of this fiery place ; cf. 18 : 11 ; 21 : 3. — 5. *Voice,* 18 : 13. *Revilers,* 91 : 7, 11 ; 99 : 12. *Change,* 104 : 10. *Prophets* are nowhere expressly mentioned in the other parts of the book. According to chap. 1–37 and 72–105, the Israelites are punished in Gehenna. — 7. *Written,* 81 : 1 sqq. — 9. Job vii. 7. — 10. Enoch speaks. — 11. Words of God. *Light and darkness,* cf. notes on 61 : 12. *In their bodies,* 102 : 5. — 13. It is doubtful who speaks here, God or Enoch. *Without number,* 58 : 6 ; 91 : 17 ; etc. This all is a reward for fidelity, which God will also show by keeping his promises. — 14. *Cast into darkness,* 103 : 8. Cf. on the whole Dan. xii. 2, 3.

Date Due

6258144

377-7665

3744616

7887770

FEB

MAY 2

JAN 15 '80

MAR 15 72

CPSIA information can be obtained at www.ICGtesting.com
226707LV00003B/25/P